THE WAR ON PSYCHOTHERAPY

When Sexual Politics, Gender Ideology, and Mental Health Collide

Christopher Doyle, MA, LPC, LCPC

Blessings,
Christopher Doyle

The war on psychotherapy: When sexual politics, gender ideology, and mental health collide / by Christopher Doyle, MA, LPC, LCPC; preface by Michelle Cretella, M.D.; foreword by Michael L. Brown, Ph.D.

Manassas, Virginia: Institute for Healthy Families, [2019]
Includes bibliographical references and index.

Identifiers: LCCN 2019005199 (print) | LCCN 2019007970 (e-book)
ISBN 9780998043517 (e-book) | ISBN 9780998043500 (paperback: alk. paper)

Subjects: LCSH: Homosexuality--Psychological aspects. | Homosexuality--Genetic aspects. | Sexual reorientation programs--United States. | Gay rights--United States. | Psychotherapy--Religious aspects--Christianity.

Classification: LCC HQ76.25 (e-book) | LCC HQ76.25.D69 2019 (print) | DDC 155.3/44--dc23

LC record available at https://lccn.loc.gov/2019005199

ISBN 978-0-9980435-0-0 (PAPERBACK)

ISBN 978-0-9980435-1-7 (ELECTRONIC)

Cover design by Carol Frye for Canner Street Consulting

Institute for Healthy Families
P.O. Box 3223
Manassas, VA, 20108
IHFINFO@InstituteforHealthyFamilies.org

Institute for
HEALTHY
Families

Printed in the United States of America

THE WAR ON PSYCHOTHERAPY

When Sexual Politics, Gender Ideology, and Mental Health Collide

Christopher Doyle, MA, LPC, LCPC

Preface by Michelle Cretella, M.D.

Foreword by Michael L. Brown, Ph.D

CONTENTS

FIGURES

ACKNOWLEDGEMENTS

℘

Over the past 15 years, I have come to know hundreds, and heard the testimonies of thousands of individuals, clients, and colleagues who refused to accept what the so-called "mainstream" medical and mental health professional communities told them about who and what they are. Instead, they chose to follow their faith and conscience, to fulfill their hopes and realize their dreams of marriage, family, authenticity, and health.

This book would not be possible without these courageous men and women who have struggled to overcome unwanted same-sex attractions and gender identity conflicts. Like myself, these individuals refused to believe the "born gay" myth and forged ahead to fulfill their hearts' desires. Your stories have inspired me to defend the healing you have fought so hard to realize. Of course, without God, our lives would not be possible. Thank you to my Lord and Savior Jesus Christ—from whom all healing and blessings flow!

I would also like to recognize Dennis and Mary Tippmann and the Charlie Tippmann Foundation Charitable Trust. Thank you for your generous financial assistance, part of which underwrote the publication of this book. I am so grateful for your continued support of the healing and educational work of the Institute for Healthy Families!

I am also very grateful for Dr. Michael Brown and Dr. Michelle Cretella for contributing their expertise to this book, as well as my colleagues who reviewed and provided many suggestions to improve the text, including: Dr. A. Lee Beckstead, Rev. Stephen Black, Dr. Michael Davidson, Arthur Goldberg, Sue Halvorson, Dr. Julie Hamilton, Linda Harvey, Jeff Johnston, Dr. Robert Oscar Lopez, Dr. James Phelan, Dr. Christopher Rosik, Peter Sprigg, Jason

Acknowledgments

Thompson, Dr. Andre Van Mol, Dr. Keith Vennum, and Rich Wyler.

I would also like to thank Christina Huth for her superb editing and consulting with this manuscript. You are a true professional, and your work to bring this book to completion was invaluable. Thank you for your passion and courage to take on this important project!

I would be remiss if I didn't thank my many colleagues at the National Task Force for Therapy Equality, specifically, Robin Goodspeed, Dr. Laura Haynes, and David Pickup who have tirelessly dedicated themselves to defending the right of self-determination for our clients. I would also like to recognize my allies at Voice of the Voiceless, especially Daren Mehl and Chuck Peters, as well as all of my colleagues at the Alliance for Therapeutic Choice and Scientific Integrity.

Finally, I owe my wife Sherry a great deal of gratitude. You have been there with me, by my side, encouraging and praying for me as this war has been waged. Thank you for your great wisdom and for your courage to stand with me during these battles, and for all of your support. I love you.

PREFACE: THE WAR ON REALITY

"Look at [the history of] homosexuality. The same thing will happen to gender identity disorder."[i]
~ Michele Forcier, M.D. Brown University 2010

"[S]ome people think ... if you have a penis you're a boy and if you have a vagina or a vulva you're a girl, but actually it's not like that. It's not like that at all."[ii]
~ Barbara Erhensaft, Ph.D. University of California San Francisco 2016

"It is counter to medical science to use chromosomes, hormones, internal reproductive organs, external genitalia, or secondary sex characteristics to override gender identity for purposes of classifying someone as male or female."[iii]
~ Deanna Adkins, M.D. Duke University 2017

ೞ

Ultimately, the war on therapy for atypical sexual attractions is part of a larger war on reality and its Creator. The reality is that purpose is found throughout nature. Our human bodies—and minds—are no exception. Prior to the removal of homosexuality from the *Diagnostic and Statistical Manual of Mental Disorders (DSM)*, normalcy was understood as "that which functions according to its design."[iv]

Applying this definition to human sexuality would work something like this. In nature, reproduction is the rule. Human beings reproduce sexually. Therefore, normal sexual attractions are those ordered toward procreation.

3

Homosexual attractions are not ordered toward reproduction; they are inherently disordered and therefore abnormal.

This definition could be applied more broadly to mental health as a whole. One of the functions of the brain is to perceive physical reality. Thoughts that are in line with reality are normal. Thoughts that do not match reality are abnormal. This obvious definition was generally accepted by professionals and lay persons alike prior to the explosion of the transgender movement. Now we have nationally recognized psychologists and physicians proclaiming that some people are born into the wrong body, and that chromosomes, hormones, and body parts have nothing to do with a person's sex. Children as young as three are being taught that some girls have penises and some boys have vaginas.[v]

Transgender politics has taken Americans by surprise and caught most of us off guard. Only a few short years ago, who would have envisioned three- to six-year-old's being mesmerized by drag queens sharing picture books and stories about "gender fluidity" at public libraries across the nation?[vi]

Most of us did not anticipate the increasing success of campaigns to invite transwomen and trans-girls (biological males) into female restrooms, locker rooms, domestic abuse shelters, prisons, and sports.[vii,viii,ix]

For example, two biological males went from having competed on their boys' high school track team as underclassmen, to literally running away with all-state honors (first and second place) in the State of Connecticut's girls track competition, as upperclassmen.[x] On the world stage, Rachel McKinnon, a biological man, stole first place in the 2018 UCI Masters Track Cycling World Championships in Los Angeles.[xi]

Fewer still could have imagined that a five-year-old girl would be sexually assaulted by a fellow kindergarten student, a biological male but trans-identified classmate, in the elementary school's girls' bathroom. What remains nearly unimaginable is the fact that the victimized girl and her mother were the ones reported to child protective services by school administration.[xii]

Clearly, transgender ideology has intruded into the lives of the most innocent among us—children—and with the apparent growing support of the professional medical community.

The American Academy of Pediatrics (AAP) recently released a policy statement declaring that all children, regardless of age, should be immediately affirmed in accordance with their self-proclaimed gender identity.[xiii] The AAP policy gives the impression that the safety and efficacy of transition affirmation for all children is a matter of settled science. This is categorically false.

In an independent analysis, Dr. James Cantor, a gay-identified psychologist and sexual behavior scientist, demonstrates that this AAP policy of affirming sexual transition for all children is not evidence-based.[xiv]

Dr. Cantor found that the AAP ignored a significant body of research that contradicts its "solely affirm sexual transition" directive. Furthermore, once Dr. Cantor proofed the document's references, he found that much of the research the AAP did cite actually substantiates the consensus-based approach of "watchful waiting," which is dismissed as "outdated" in its policy.[xv] Unfortunately, Dr. Cantor's analysis is not likely to see publication in any mainstream medical or mental health journals.

As explained in my 2016 peer-reviewed article, "Gender Dysphoria in Children and Suppression of Debate," and validated by others, professionals who dare to question the unscientific party line of supporting gender transition therapy will find themselves mercilessly harassed, maligned, and out of a job.[xvi]

How Did This Happen?

I speak as someone intimately familiar with the pediatric and behavioral health communities and their practices. I am a mother of four who served 17 years as a board-certified general pediatrician with a focus in child behavioral and sexual health, prior to leaving clinical practice in 2012.

For the last 14 years, I have been a board member and researcher for the American College of Pediatricians, served two terms as its president, and was recently hired as its executive director.

I also sat on the board of directors for the Alliance for Therapeutic Choice and Scientific Integrity from 2010 to 2015, and continue to serve in an ex officio advisory capacity. This organization of mental health professionals and physicians defends the right of patients to receive psychotherapy for sexual identity conflicts that is in line with their deeply held values based upon science and medical ethics.

I have witnessed an upending of the medical consensus on the nature of gender identity akin to what was witnessed regarding the nature of homosexuality. What doctors once treated as a mental illness, the medical community now largely affirms and even promotes as normal.

Technically, some controversy surrounded gender identity disorder in children (GIDC) right at its debut in the fourth edition of the *Diagnostic and Statistical Manual (DSM-IV)* in 1980. Among children with GIDC, over 80% would come to accept their biological sex by late adolescence, and roughly 60% of these children would declare a homosexual identity. Consequently, over the next 25 years, some clinicians and many activists persistently challenged the GIDC diagnosis as an attempt to identify pre-homosexual children and prevent adult homosexuality.[xvii]

This debate within professional circles, however, paled in comparison to the machinations of adult male to female (MtF) transsexual activists who were increasingly convincing the public that they were in reality just what they felt: women trapped in men's bodies. Brain differences between small numbers of transsexual and non-transsexual men had been identified, and although researchers noted that it was likely those differences were caused by sex change hormones taken by the transsexual men, that was not promoted in the media or understood by the general public. So, like the LGB activists before them, transsexual activists combined ethos with flawed science, to solidify the belief that they were "born that way." They were so successful, that by the mid-2000s, this "feminine essence" born in the wrong body narrative was the predominant cultural understanding. Some psychologists who treated this population spoke out against it. Dr. Michael Bailey, for example, lamented in 2007 that

> This understanding has little scientific basis ... there are two distinct subtypes of MtF transsexuals. Members of one subtype, homosexual transsexuals, are best understood as a type of homosexual male. The other subtype, autogynephilic transsexuals, are motivated by the erotic desire to become women. The persistence of the [feminine essence] understanding is damaging to science and to many transsexuals.[xviii]

In the years that followed, neuroscientists documented conclusively that relationships, behavior and even how we think (for example, meditation), changes the structure and function of the human brain.[xix,xx,xxi] So it is entirely possible that dysfunctional early relationships, subsequent thinking and behavior of people who come to trans-identify shapes their brain and its function.

7

Consequently, although some non-replicated transsexual brain studies have since identified possible differences that are not caused by sex change hormones, it is more likely, given modern neuroscience, that these differences may be the result of early relationships and identifying as transsexual, not the cause of transsexual identification. But, once again, real science does not rule the day even in academe or mainstream health guilds like both APAs and the AAP; political correctness does.

When it came time to reevaluate the DSM for publication of the fifth edition, the clinicians assigned to GID were first and foremost concerned with providing a diagnosis that would both ease social stigma and justify insurance payment for sex-change hormones and sex reassignment surgery.[xxii] The end result was a name change to "gender dysphoria" (GD). Not only was the term "disorder" dropped, but there was also a shift in diagnosis from focusing on a discrepant identity, to a focus solely on emotional distress. In other words, if a person feels and believes that they are not their biological sex but is happy, then they do not, by definition, have a mental illness according to DSM-5.

That the next version of the DSM will drop gender dysphoria altogether is likely because the World Health Organization (WHO) has already done so in its upcoming 11th edition of the *International Classification of Diseases (ICD-11)*.[xxiii]

The ICD provides a common language that allows health professionals to share health information on an international scale. It is also used by health insurers to determine reimbursements, national health program managers, and data collection specialists. With publication of ICD-11, the term gender incongruence is used rather than gender dysphoria, and the term transsexual is eliminated. While gender incongruence is still a bona fide diagnosis it is not classified as a mental disorder. Instead, it has been relocated to a newly invented category of diagnoses dubbed "conditions related to sexual health." This category also includes sexual dysfunctions and sexual pain disorders. The WHO authors explained that the intent is to "destigmatize gender incongruence and highlight it as a strictly medical, rather than psychological, issue."[xxiv] However, declassification as a mental disorder is not the end goal; normalization is. At the heart of transgender activism is a core of individuals committed to queer theory whose goal from the 1970s forward has been to completely de-medicalize transsexualism by framing their "right to transition" (with or without medical interventions) as a basic human right rooted in a "right to self-determination."[xxv]

For the sake of our children, we must not let this happen. We must fight to re-tether psychology and medicine to an authentic definition of normalcy: That which functions according to its design is normal.

A review of how transgender ideology has already harmed children demonstrates the urgency with which we must act.

The New Normal

Pediatric "gender clinics" are considered elite centers for affirming children who are distressed by their biological sex. In 2014, there were 24 of these gender clinics, clustered chiefly along the East Coast and in California. One year later, there were 40 across the nation. With 215 pediatric residency programs now training future pediatricians in a transition-affirming protocol and treating gender-dysphoric children accordingly, the number of gender clinics is bound to grow.

Yet, during the summer of 2016, under the pro-transgender Obama administration, the federal government stated that it would not require Medicare and Medicaid to cover transition-affirming procedures for children or adults because medical experts at the Department of Health and

Human Services found the risks were often too high, and the benefits too unclear.[xxvi]

Undeterred by these findings, the World Professional Association for Transgender Health has pressed ahead, claiming—without any evidence—that these procedures are "safe."

Two leading pediatric associations—the American Academy of Pediatrics and the Endocrine Society—have followed in lockstep, endorsing the transition-affirmation approach even as the latter organization concedes within its own guidelines that the transition-affirming protocol is based on low evidence.

They even admit that the only strong evidence regarding this approach is its potential health risks to children.[xxvii]

The transition-affirming view holds that children who "consistently and persistently insist" that they do not identify with their biological sex are innately transgender. The fact that in normal life and in psychiatry, anyone who "consistently and persistently insists" on anything else contrary to physical reality is considered either confused, emotionally disturbed, or delusional is conveniently ignored.

The transition-affirming protocol tells parents to treat their children as the gender they desire, and to place them on puberty blockers as young as age 9 if they are gender dysphoric.

Between the ages of 9 and 16, these children are then "offered the choice" of cross-sex hormones, and biological girls may obtain a double mastectomy. Recently, girls as young as 13 have received double mastectomies as "treatment" for their gender dysphoria.[xxviii]

So-called "bottom surgeries," or genital reassignment surgeries, are not recommended before age 18, though some surgeons and pediatricians increasingly argue against this restriction.[xxix]

The transition-affirming approach has been embraced by public institutions in media, education, and our legal system, and is now recommended by most national medical and psychological organizations.

There are exceptions to this movement, however, in addition to the American College of Pediatricians[xxx] and the Alliance for Therapeutic Choice and Scientific Integrity.[xxxi] These include the Association of American Physicians and Surgeons[xxxii,] the Christian Medical & Dental Associations[xxxiii], the Catholic Medical Association[xxxiv] and an international professional online community called the gender dysphoria working group.[xxxv]

What the Scientific Research Says

The transgender movement has gained legs in the medical community and in our culture by offering a deeply flawed narrative. The scientific research and facts tell a different story.

Here are some of those basic facts.

1. **Twin studies prove no one's "trapped in the body of the wrong sex."**

Virtually everything about human beings is influenced by our DNA, but very few traits are hardwired at birth. All human behavior—including our personalities, how we think and feel—arise from varying degrees of nature and nurture.

Researchers routinely conduct twin studies to discern which factors (genetic or environmental) contribute more to the expression of a particular trait. The best designed twin studies are those with the greatest number of subjects.

Identical twins are conceived with 100% of the same DNA from conception. As a result, traits that are determined by DNA alone, like skin color, are found in both identical twins virtually 100% of the time. So, if genes contribute significantly to transgenderism, we should expect both twins to identify as transgender close to 100% of the time.

But in the largest study of twin transgender adults, published by Dr. Milton Diamond in 2013, only 28% of the identical twins both identified as transgender. Seventy-two percent of the time, they differed. (Diamond's study reported 20% percent identifying as transgender, but calculations based on his actual data demonstrate a 28% figure).[xxxvi]

That only 28% (a far cry from 100%) of identical twins both identified as transgender suggests that the majority of factors contributing to transgender identification (72%) occur post-birth and are not genetic. Yes, the 28% figure is evidence for a genetic predisposition, but predisposition is not predetermination. Predisposition means that a trait, in this case transgenderism, will not manifest itself without additional non-genetic factors also impacting the individual during his or her lifetime.

2. **Brain appearance and function are not hardwired at birth; there is no evidence for a transgender brain.**

Many transgender activist physicians claim that studies prove that altered brain structure causes transgenderism because several small non-replicated studies have identified differences between those who identify as transgender and those who do not.[xxxvii] These studies, however, do not prove causation, because in scientific terms they are not prospective, serial, longitudinal, randomly sampled and population-based studies of a fixed set of individuals from infancy forward. These are the qualities of rigorous scientific study necessary to demonstrate causation.[xxxviii, xxxix]

The claim that brain differences can prove the existence of a transgender brain must also be dismissed due to neuroplasticity. Neuroplasticity is the process whereby brain appearance, wiring, and function is shaped and altered by interpersonal relationships, behavior, and thinking beginning with the maternal-infant gaze at birth.[xl, xli, xlii]

So, every single brain cell has a genetic sex determined by the presence or absence of the male Y chromosome—a sex established at conception, evident in the womb, and recognized at birth that does not and cannot be changed across a person's lifespan. However, the appearance and function of the brain are not hardwired; they are plastic—open to change based on an individual's environment and lived experiences at least from birth forward.

This means that even if we had rigorous scientific studies demonstrating brain differences, those differences would more likely be the result of transgenderism, not the cause of transgenderism.

3. Gender identity is malleable, especially in young children.

Even the American Psychological Association's *Handbook of Sexuality and Psychology* admits that prior to the widespread promotion of transition affirmation, 75 to 95% of pre-pubertal children who were distressed by their biological sex eventually outgrew that distress. The majority came to accept their biological sex by late adolescence after passing naturally through puberty.[xliii]

But with transition affirmation now increasing in western society, the number of children claiming distress over their gender—and their persistence over time—has dramatically increased. For example, the Tavistock Clinic—the only gender clinic in the United Kingdom—has seen a 4,400% increase in girls alone presenting for sex reassignment in less than ten years.[xliv,xlv]

4. Puberty blockers for gender dysphoria have not been proven safe.

Puberty blockers have been studied and found safe for the treatment of a medical disorder in children called precocious puberty (caused by the abnormal and unhealthy early secretion of a child's pubertal hormones).

However, as a groundbreaking paper in *The New Atlantis* points out, we cannot infer from these studies whether or not these blockers are safe in physiologically normal children with gender dysphoria. The authors note that there is some evidence for decreased bone mineralization, meaning an increased risk of bone fractures as young adults, potential increased risk of obesity and testicular cancer in boys, and an unknown impact upon psychological and cognitive development.[xlvi]

With regard to the latter, while we currently don't have any extensive, long-term studies of children placed on blockers for gender dysphoria, studies conducted on adults from the past decade give cause for concern. For example, in 2006 and 2007, the journal *Psychoneuroendocrinology* reported brain abnormalities in the area of memory and executive functioning among adult women who received blockers for gynecologic reasons. [xlvii, xlviii] Similarly, many studies of men treated for prostate cancer with blockers also suggest the possibility of significant cognitive decline.[xlix]

5. There are no cases in the scientific literature of gender-dysphoric children discontinuing blockers.

Most, if not all, children on puberty blockers go on to take cross-sex hormones (estrogen for biological boys, testosterone for biological girls). The only study to date to have followed pre-pubertal children who were socially affirmed and placed on blockers at a young age found that

100% of them claimed a transgender identity and chose cross-sex hormones.[l]

This suggests that the medical protocol itself may lead children to identify as transgender. There is an obvious self-fulfilling effect in helping children impersonate the opposite sex both chemically and socially. This is far from benign, since taking puberty blockers at age 12 or younger, followed by cross-sex hormones, permanently sterilizes a child.[li]

6. Cross-sex hormones are associated with dangerous health risks.

From studies of adults we know that the risks of cross-sex hormones include, but are not limited to, cardiac disease, high blood pressure, blood clots, strokes, diabetes, and cancers.[lii]

7. Neuroscience shows that adolescents lack the adult capacity needed for risk assessment.

Scientific data show that people under the age of 21 have less capacity to assess risks.[liii] There is a serious ethical problem in allowing irreversible, life-changing procedures to be performed on minors who are too young themselves to give valid consent.

8. There is no proof that affirmation prevents suicide in children.

Advocates of the transition-affirming protocol allege that suicide is the direct and inevitable consequence of withholding social affirmation and biological alterations from a gender-dysphoric child. In other words, those who do not endorse the transition-affirming protocol are essentially condemning gender-dysphoric children to suicide.

Yet as noted earlier, prior to the widespread promotion of transition affirmation, 75 to 95% of gender-dysphoric youth ended up happy with their biological sex after simply passing through puberty.

In addition, contrary to the claim of activists, there is no evidence that harassment and discrimination, let alone lack of affirmation, are the primary cause of suicide among any minority group. In fact, at least one study from 2008 found perceived discrimination by LGBT-identified individuals not to be causative.[liv]

Over 90% of people who commit suicide have a diagnosed mental disorder.[lv] There is no evidence that gender-dysphoric children who commit suicide are any different. Many gender dysphoric children simply need therapy to get to the root of their depression, which very well may be the same problem triggering the gender dysphoria.

9. Transition-affirming protocol has not solved the problem of transgender suicide.

Adults who undergo sex reassignment—even in Sweden, which is among the most LGBT-affirming countries—have a suicide rate 19 times greater than that of the general population.[lvi] Clearly, sex reassignment is not the solution to gender dysphoria.

Bottom Line: Transition-Affirming Protocol Is Child Abuse

The crux of the matter is that while the transition-affirming movement purports to help children, it is inflicting a grave injustice on them and their non-dysphoric peers.

These professionals are using the myth that people are born transgender to justify engaging in massive, uncontrolled, and unconsented experimentation on children who have a psychological condition that would otherwise resolve after puberty in the majority of cases.

Today's institutions that promote transition affirmation are pushing children to impersonate the opposite sex, sending many of them down the path of puberty blockers, sterilization, the removal of healthy body parts, and untold psychological damage.

These harms constitute nothing less than institutionalized child abuse. Sound ethics demand an immediate end to the use of pubertal suppression, cross-sex hormones, and sex reassignment surgeries in children and adolescents, as well as an end to promoting gender ideology via school curricula and legislative policies.

The war on reality must end. Now.

~ Michelle A. Cretella, M.D.
Executive Director, American College of Pediatricians

FOREWORD

☙

Make no mistake about it. We are in the midst of an all-out war. It is an ideological war. A societal war. A spiritual war. It is war of ethics and morality and sexuality. It is a war we cannot avoid.

Our children and grandchildren are entrenched in this war. Our courts and college campuses are caught up in it. Even our churches are engaged in the thick of this battle, as the question comes pressing on each and every one of us: What will you do about LGBT activism? How far will this movement go in terms of redefining marriage, family, and human identity? To what extent will it rewrite the Bible? To what extent will it rewrite our laws? To what extent will it silence those who refuse to fall in line with its radical goals?

And what about those who want to offer a compassionate alternative to the homosexual, bisexual, and transgender identity? What about those who believe change is possible? What about the counselors, therapists, psychologists, psychiatrists, and ministers who want to help those who struggle with unwanted same-sex attractions and gender confusion? Will their efforts be banned? Will those who came out of the closet succeed in putting them in the closet?

Christopher Doyle is a man uniquely qualified to answer these questions. First, he is a former same-sex attracted man, now happily married to his wife and a devoted father to his five children. When he speaks about change, he speaks from firsthand experience. Second, and as such, he has counseled hundreds of people who have struggled with sexual and gender identity conflicts. Here too he knows that of which he speaks. Third, he is a man of faith, recognizing that the God who created us and the God who sent Jesus to redeem us is the God who has the power to change us. That

19

spirit of faith permeates this book, which is also filled with wonderful testimonies of lives that have been dramatically changed.

In the pages that follow, Christopher takes you on a journey, starting with the outrageous situation in which we find ourselves today, then reviewing the recent historical roots of this crisis, dating back especially to 1969, then focusing on the major arenas of warfare, from the world of mental health to the media, from the courts to the classrooms, and from overseas to our own hearts. Christopher then closes with practical guidelines for action, followed by a picture of political incorrectness. And it's clear he has done his homework, offering ample documentation and an abundance of salient quotes.

I encourage you to read this carefully and then share it with a friend. This is a war that can be won. And by winning this war, many will be set free, delivered, and healed. The hour is terribly urgent, but it is not too late. Love, truth, perseverance, and compassion can prevail!

~ Michael L. Brown, Ph.D.
Author of *A Queer Thing Happened to America* and
Can You Be Gay and Christian?

INTRODUCTION

We are in a period now of psychological stupidity.

~ Camille Paglia

 beta

Sexual and gender identity is the most politically incorrect subject to speak openly about, with an array of carnage waiting for anyone who dares to approach the topic. This Catch-22, damned-if-you-do, damned-if-you-don't issue, has become so volatile it has ushered in a period in which scholars and commoners alike have lost the ability to think critically on the subject.

A few years ago, radio talk show host Dennis Prager interviewed Camille Paglia, a lesbian, feminist university professor at the University of the Arts in Philadelphia, Pennsylvania. During the interview, Paglia discussed the current inability to question the prevailing "born that way" view of homosexuality:

> Every single gay person I know has some sort of drama going on, back in childhood. Something was happening that we're not allowed to ask about anymore ... I can see patterns that are similar in my background to that of other women I know who are lesbians, but the biggest patterns are in gay men. Every single gay man I know had a particular pattern where for whatever reason, he was closer to his mother than to his father, and there was some sort of distance between the mother and the father, so that she looked to her son as her real equal or friend, as the real companion of her soul. Sometimes these women were discreet and dignified. Other times, they were very theatrical and in a sense they drafted

21

their son into their own drama. But now, you are not allowed to ask any questions about the childhood of gay people anymore. It's called "homophobic"! The entire psychology establishment has shut itself down, politically ... and also, Freud was kicked out by early feminism in the late 60s and early 70s. So is all the sophistication of analysis that I knew in my college years when I went to the State University of New York—there was a group of radical young Jewish students from the New York area, they were so psychologically sophisticated in being able to analyze the family background. It's all gone, that entire discourse is gone. Everything is political now. Families are bankrupting themselves, sending their kids to the elite schools to learn a political style of analysis (that says) "every single thing in the human person has been formed by some external force upon us, we are oppressed, it's being inscribed on us." It's really sick. It's a sick and stupid way of looking at human psychology ... we are in a period now of psychological stupidity.[lvii]

If you copy the hyperlink found in the citation you can also listen to the entire 35-minute interview (the section featured above begins at 5:35), and I encourage you to do so. What Paglia so profoundly remarks is the simple, but frightening statement: "You are not allowed to ask any questions about the childhood of gay people anymore. It's called 'homophobic'!" Unfortunately, we have now entered a period of what Paglia calls "psychological stupidity," because we are afraid to ask each other the difficult questions, and if we cannot ask these questions, we cannot learn. If we cannot learn, we lose our ability to think critically.

Introduction

Imagine that for just a moment, a life where we are not allowed to ask questions about our origins. These are important questions! In fact, many people spend considerable amounts of time and resources to determine where they came from in order to understand how they have come to be, who, and what they are. It's tremendously important for individuals to ask these questions of themselves, and, I would argue that it's even *more* important for trained mental health professionals to ask these questions of their clients. But as Paglia said: "It's all gone. The entire discourse is all gone. Everything is political now."

After experiencing a shift in my sexual attractions nearly 15 years ago, I became engaged in the politics of sexual orientation and gender ideology in the mental health field. I have learned a lot working in the mental and behavioral health field over the years, and one thing I know for certain is this: sexual and gender identity is complex. The older I become, the more I question my assumptions from one, five, and ten years ago. As a licensed psychotherapist, I have dedicated my life's work to helping individuals and families come to terms with their sexual and gender identity and be able to understand how they can make choices in their sexual behavior without compromising their personal and spiritual values.

As I write this book, lesbian, gay, bisexual, and transgender (LGBT) activists have successfully convinced over a dozen liberal states, over 45 counties or cities, and the District of Columbia, to ban sexual orientation change effort (SOCE) therapy for minors. Currently, there are campaigns in very liberal parts of the country to restrict therapy for adults as well. Abroad, several countries have banned the practice altogether, with the United Kingdom currently debating the very question: Should it be legal for licensed medical professionals to help clients and patients alter their sexual orientation? Should clinicians even be able to talk about this and present options for those who experience distress? It's an unprecedented assault on personal freedom and religious liberty, and it has happened, in large part, because too many well-meaning politicians have not asked the important questions; and when we fail to ask the most important questions, the facts no longer matter.

As I finished writing this book, the state of Maryland became the 14th state to ban licensed therapy for clients under the age of 18 who wish to reduce or eliminate unwanted same-sex attractions or gender identity conflicts. Because I am a licensed clinical professional counselor in Maryland, and directly affected, I have partnered with Liberty Counsel, a non-profit religious liberty law firm, to challenge the ban as unconstitutional. Below is the beginning of the complaint, which summarizes perfectly the injustice of these laws to ban so-called "conversion therapy":

> Since time immemorial, the relationship between clients and their mental health professionals has represented a sacred trust. In this vital relationship, licensed mental health professionals ("LMHPs") are tasked with providing essential care to their clients and forming critical therapeutic alliances that represent the unique relationship between professional and client. This therapeutic alliance is designed to facilitate the foundational principle of all mental health counseling: the client's fundamental right to self-determination. Throughout the history of this learned profession, clients have provided mental health professionals with their goals, and objectives that conform to their sincerely held desires and concepts of self, and mental health professionals have provided counseling that aligns with the clients' fundamental right to self-determination. That unique relationship has, until now, been protected, revered, and respected as

sacrosanct and inviolable. Now, Defendants have seen fit to storm the office doors of mental health professionals, thrust themselves into the therapeutic alliance, violate the sacred trust between client and counselor, and run roughshod over the fundamental right of client self-determination and the counselors' cherished First Amendment liberties. Defendants' purported justifications for such unconscionable actions: they do not like the goals, objectives, or desires of certain clients when it comes to one type of counseling. The First Amendment demands more, and Defendants' actions have caused, are causing, and will continue to cause irreparable injury to Plaintiff's fundamental and cherished liberties.[lviii]

As you read this book, I hope you can put aside your pre-conceived notions and biases about sexuality, sexual orientation, gender identity, and therapeutic efforts to assist those who struggle. The facts I present will lay a case for why therapy for sexual and gender identity conflicts should be available and legal for all who seek it; however, I will not try to convince you that all efforts to reduce, change, or manage unwanted attractions, desires, or behaviors are effective or safe.

In reality, some well-meaning mental health clinicians, religious counselors, and life coaches are offering ineffective, ill-advised, and/or unsafe counseling. The majority of these individuals are doing so, not out of malicious intent, but rather, ignorance, lack of professional training, or poor technique.

Please do not confuse these individuals with the professionals I will write about that are being smeared by LGBT activists, the mainstream media, and biased mental and medical health trade associations.

Introduction

The stories I share in this book will highlight some of the more egregious tales, both fact and fiction, that are permeating our culture about professional therapy and transformational ministry for sexual and gender identity conflicts. The majority of the "horror stories" documented in this book have been sensationalized by the media, and in many cases, downright fabricated in order to advance a false political narrative. In other cases, biased and ill-informed professionals, whom I believe are sincere, but sincerely wrong, are advancing an agenda that is not only incorrect, but also potentially harmful to unsuspecting consumers, politicians, and the general public.

I will conclude this book with meaningful solutions on how licensed mental health professionals, informed legislators, and responsible citizens can work together to identify and correct fraudulent testimony, end truly harmful therapeutic practices, and ensure safe and effective help for those who are sincerely struggling and seeking help for sexual and gender identity conflicts.

But first, let's consider a day in the life of a politically correct psychotherapy office.

CHAPTER 1
A DAY IN THE LIFE OF A
POLITICALLY CORRECT (P.C.) PSYCHOTHERAPY
OFFICE

KATHERINE: I'm bulimic. I stick my fingers down my throat.
DR. SWITZER: Stop it! Are you a nut of some kind? Don't do that.
KATHERINE: But I'm compelled to. My mom used to call—
DR. SWITZER: No, no. We don't go there.

~ Bob Newhart, *Stop It!* (MAD TV)

ℭℜ

October 1, 2012

(Telephone rings…)

Receptionist: "Good morning, how can I help you?"

Client: "Uh, yes. I would like to make an appointment with Dr. P.C."

Receptionist: "Absolutely, will you be using your health insurance benefits for psychotherapy?"

Client: "Yes, I would very much like to use those benefits. I didn't realize the doctor took health insurance. That's great news!"

A Day in the Life of a Politically Correct (P.C.) Psychotherapy Office

Receptionist: "Yes it is, but I must warn you, certain emotional and mental disorders are not covered by health insurance companies, so if the doctor diagnoses you with one of these issues, your health insurance won't cover the visit and you'll be forced to pay for his services out-of-pocket."

Client: "Oh, I see. Well, what are those conditions?"

Receptionist: "I'm sorry, but I am not authorized to disclose that information. But what I can tell you is that if you refuse to answer any questions the doctor asks you, he probably won't have enough information to diagnose you with one of those problematic conditions, and you'll be covered."

Client: "I see. But if I don't answer any questions, wouldn't that affect my treatment outcome? How am I supposed to get well if the doctor cannot ask questions and really understand my condition?"

Receptionist: "Yes, that is the kicker, isn't it? If you tell the truth, your mental health may improve, but the insurance company won't pay for services if you're truthful. If you play the game and withhold the truth, your insurance company will most likely cover the eight sessions."

Client: "Eight sessions? Is that *all* I get?"

A Day in the Life of a Politically Correct (P.C.) Psychotherapy Office

Receptionist: "Oh yes, I'm sorry. I shouldn't have told you that. Most insurance companies only reimburse for eight sessions. So whatever diagnosis the doctor gives you will have to be cured in eight sessions or you'll have to pay for the rest out-of-pocket."

Client: "This doesn't sound promising. It took a great deal of courage for me to make this call. I was feeling very discouraged this morning. Now that I've talked with you, I feel even more discouraged."

Receptionist: "Oh, I'm sure the doctor can help you with your discouragement! He's really good at that."

Client: "Well my discouragement is not really the problem. You see, I've been struggling with certain unwanted sexual attractions for quite some time now. It's hard for me to even speak about them, but I think it's important I see someone to help me work through this problem."

(Long silence…)

Client: "Hello? Is anyone there?"

Receptionist: "I'm sorry sir, I think we should end this conversation."

Client: "Why, did I say something wrong?"

Receptionist: "It's just that I am not allowed to ask potential clients *any* questions about their sexuality. The doctor has given me strict instructions not to ask these questions. In fact, I'm not even allowed to tell him that you brought this issue up!"

Client: "Really, why?"

Receptionist: "It's complicated. The doctor can explain this to you when you see him."

Client: "I see. Well how do I know if my psychotherapy sessions will be covered by insurance if I can't discuss this information before I see the doctor?"

Receptionist: "You won't know. That's a risk you have to be willing to take. But remember, if you don't tell the truth, the insurance company will cover your eight sessions."

Client: "Oh right, of course. I'll make sure *not* to tell the truth."

Receptionist: "Good boy. Now, when would you like to schedule an introductory session?"

Client: "Well, how long will it take?"

Receptionist: "The doctor suggests 75 minutes for an effective introductory session, but insurance will only cover 45 minutes. It's up to you."

Client: "Well I guess I'll go with the 45-minute session since insurance will only cover that."

A Day in the Life of a Politically Correct (P.C.) Psychotherapy Office

Receptionist: "Ok, but remember 45 minutes will *not* be effective...and make sure *not* to tell the truth."

Client: "Something seems wrong about this whole process."

Receptionist: "Tell me about it...oh wait, *don't* tell me about it!"

One week later...

Doctor P.C.: "Hello, I'm Doctor P.C. ...it's nice to meet you."

Client: "Soooo...is it Peter, Paul, maybe Patrick?"

Doctor P.C.: "Oh no, we don't use real names here. The health insurance companies now require that we take all personal experience, opinions, values, and even our names, out of psychotherapy. They give us a number and ask us to identify ourselves to our clients by two letters. So I chose P.C."

Client: (chuckles) "I see...*Politically Correct.*"

Doctor P.C.: (Looking away) "I'm sorry, I'm not familiar with that term."

Client: (awkward silence) "Ok then, well, shall we get started?"

Doctor P.C.: "Certainly. But before we begin, let me explain to you my treatment protocol. I have two forms of treatment. The first treatment involves lots of questions, assessments, and analysis, followed by a lengthy dialogue between you and I where we'll discuss certain aspects of your feelings, behavior, and goals, and then come to an understanding between the two of us as to how I can best treat your problem. We might not agree on everything, and there could be some occasional conflict or frustration, but we'll always discuss any problems that come up during treatment so that your best interests are at heart and your goals are respected."

Client: "That sounds great!"

Doctor P.C.: "There's only one problem."

Client: "What's that?"

Doctor P.C.: "Insurance will not reimburse for this treatment approach."

Client: "I see...well, how about the other treatment approach?"

Doctor P.C.: "Sure, well, this approach is rather simple. You have eight sessions to tell me about your problem. During each 45-minute session, I will nod my head and enthusiastically agree with everything you say, no matter if it's true or not. I will never ask any questions, and I will not provide you with any analysis based on my years of mental health training."

Client: "I see. Well, what if I need your advice on an important issue related to ethics or values?

A Day in the Life of a Politically Correct (P.C.) Psychotherapy Office

What if I can't solve the problem by simply talking the whole session? What if I get stuck?"

Doctor P.C.: "Well, usually that is not a problem."

Client: "Why?

Doctor P.C.: "Our state licensing board instructs us not to impose our ethical values on the client, so you are free to discuss your values, but I won't be discussing any of mine during our sessions. Nor will I agree or disagree with yours."

Client: "But what if I experience a conflict with my values? I mean, the whole reason I'm here is because my sexual attractions are at odds with my religious values!"

Doctor P.C.: "I already told you; I will enthusiastically nod my head and agree with you. No Matter What!"

Client: "But what if I don't want you to simply agree with me? What if I want you to challenge me, or provide me information that I do not have access to? I mean, isn't that your job, to have a thorough understanding of issues related to emotional and mental health so you can guide me?"

Doctor P.C.: "No, the health insurance company pays me, and my state board licenses me, to affirm everything you feel, think, or believe, regardless of the truth or any information I possess that you may not have access to."

A Day in the Life of a Politically Correct (P.C.) Psychotherapy Office

Client: "Well...what if I don't want that...?"

Doctor P.C.: "Shhhhhhh...!"

Client: "Excuse me?"

Doctor P.C.: "Shut your mouth..."

Client: "But..."

Doctor P.C.: "Shhhhhhh...they're listening."

Client: "Who's they?"

Doctor P.C.: "The government."

Client: "What? I thought our discussion was confidential and privileged?"

Doctor P.C.: "Well, it is. I mean, if you have *certain* goals for your therapy. But other goals, well, those are not allowed anymore."

Client: "I thought we were all equal in this country."

Doctor P.C.: "Well yes, but some people are *more* equal than others..."

Client: "More equal? When did that happen?"

Doctor P.C.: "Well, it all started in the year 1969. But before we proceed, I have to warn you. Any conversation we have from here on out will *not* be covered by insurance. In fact, I could lose my

A Day in the Life of a Politically Correct (P.C.) Psychotherapy Office

license if I go any further. So, from this point on, we will not call this 'therapy'…is that clear?"

Client: "So what is this called?"

Doctor P.C.: "Politically Incorrect!"

Client: "So should I call you Doctor P.I. now?

Doctor P.C.: "Good one…"

CHAPTER 2
THE WAR IN CALIFORNIA: BANNED

Pay your surgeon very well
To break the spell of aging
Celebrity skin is this your chin
Or is that war you're waging

~ Red Hot Chili Peppers, *Californication*

ভ

In 2012, LGBT activists began working with politicians in the state of California to pass legislation to prohibit licensed mental health practitioners from helping minors who experience unwanted same-sex attractions, or wished to change their sexual orientation. I remember the day in late spring that year, when politicians in the California Senate were voting on the bill. As the roll call made its way through and the "yeas" outnumbered the "nays," I sat in my office and stared in disbelief at the computer screen. "This is the end of freedom," I said out loud to myself.

"Could this actually be happening?" We asked ourselves. We, being a small number of mental health practitioners numbering less than 1,000 affiliated with the National Association for Research and Therapy of Homosexuality (NARTH), were in utter shock. LGBT activists successfully convinced gay-identified California Senator Ted Lieu (Lieu is now a United States Congressman from California) to sponsor SB 1172, the first bill of its kind to ban *any* therapeutic goal for psychotherapy with a licensed mental health therapist.

On September 30, 2012, Governor Jerry Brown signed into law SB 1172, which essentially outlawed the practice of sexual orientation change effort (SOCE) therapy for clients under the age of 18 in the state of California. In a press release from the governor's office, Brown said the following of SOCE therapy: "These practices have no basis in science or medicine, and they will now be relegated to the dustbin of quackery."

As justification for the law, SB 1172 said the following in Section 1(b)):

> The American Psychological Association convened a Task Force on Appropriate Therapeutic Responses to Sexual Orientation. The task force conducted a systematic review of peer-reviewed journal literature on sexual orientation change efforts, and issued a report in 2009. The task force concluded that sexual orientation change efforts pose critical health risks to lesbian, gay, and bisexual people, including confusion, depression, guilt, helplessness, hopelessness, shame, social withdrawal, suicidality, substance abuse, stress, disappointment, self-blame, decreased self-esteem and authenticity to others, increased self-hatred, hostility and blame toward parents, feelings of anger and betrayal, loss of friends and potential romantic partners, problems in sexual and emotional intimacy, sexual dysfunction, high-risk sexual behaviors, a feeling of being dehumanized and untrue to self, a loss of faith, and a sense of having wasted time and resources.[lix]

Despite the claims of harm cited in SB 1172, the American Psychological Association task force did not actually provide evidence to back up the 28 health risks listed above. In fact, none of these health risks have been documented in the scientific peer-reviewed literature outside of a few published and unpublished anecdotal reports from adults.[lx] Additionally, there is not one single outcome-based study in the scientific literature of minors undergoing SOCE therapy to back up these claims.[1]

In the Land of Fruits and Nuts, It Is Illegal to Be a Vegetable

It's not surprising that California was the trailblazer to make SOCE therapy illegal. The Golden State has a long history of liberal activism, and recently, has taken some very radical stances when it comes to sexuality and religious liberty. For example, a 2015 article in the *Los Angeles Times* reported that according to prison medical data, California has nearly 400 transgender prison inmates receiving hormonal treatment, and while the State argued (in a recent federal lawsuit) that sexual reassignment surgery was a not a "medical necessity" for inmates suffering from gender dysphoria, they decided to settle with prison inmate Shiloh Quine (originally Rodney) instead of continue defending against the federal lawsuit. After the settlement was announced, the corrections department released the following statement:

> Every medical doctor and mental health clinician who has reviewed this case, including two independent mental health experts, determined that this surgery is medically necessary for Quine.[lxi] "Medically necessary" was the term these so-called "experts" provided as the answer to relieve the inmate's suffering. That's right, just take these hormone pills, cut off your genitals,

---

[1] A few months before the publishing of this book, a study was published in the *Journal of Homosexuality* on the perceived outcomes of LGBT adolescents whose parents initiated SOCE therapy. Several research reviews have also looked at the multitude of outcome-based studies on SOCE therapy for adults in the last 100 years. I will discuss these reviews and the adolescent study in Chapter 4.

insert new ones, and all your pain and suffering will be gone. Keep in mind; this treatment costs, at a minimum, $15,000. For those who wish to reconstruct their face to make it appear more feminine or masculine, the total cost can be upwards of $50,000![lxii] Then one has to consider, how effective is sexual reassignment surgery for long-term mental health, and why are so-called "experts" pushing for these "treatments" for young people, rather than pursuing safer, evidence-based interventions?

Dr. Paul McHugh, former chairman of the Department of Psychiatry at Johns Hopkins University Hospital, wrote about this in a 2015 article published by The Witherspoon Institute:

> The most thorough follow-up of sex reassigned people—extending over thirty years and conducted in Sweden, where the culture is strongly supportive of the transgendered—documents their lifelong mental unrest. Ten to fifteen years after surgical reassignment, the suicide rate of those who had undergone sex-reassignment surgery rose to 20 times that of comparable peers ... There are several reasons for this absence of coherence in our mental health system. Important among them is the fact that both the state and federal governments are actively seeking to block any treatments that can be construed as challenging the assumptions and choices of transgendered youngsters. "As part of our dedication to protecting America's youth, this administration supports efforts to ban the use of conversion therapy for minors," said Valerie Jarrett, a senior advisor to President Obama. In

two states, a doctor who would look into the psychological history of a transgendered boy or girl in search of a resolvable conflict could lose his or her license to practice medicine. By contrast, such a physician would not be penalized if he or she started such a patient on hormones that would block puberty and might stunt growth.[lxiii]

While liberal politicians on the state and federal levels are dead set against psychotherapy for minors who do not wish to accept a gay, lesbian, or transgender identity, they are now going out of their way to enshrine rights for gender-confused youth in all of their public schools under the guise of "protection."

In fact, not long after Governor Brown banned so-called "conversion therapy" for minors, he signed AB 1266 into law, which afforded protections for transgender youth to use the bathroom of their choice and play for their preferred sports team, based entirely on the students' "self-perception" and "regardless of their birth gender."[lxiv]

So, if you wish to change your sexual orientation in California and you're under 18, you are homophobic and repressed. But if you want to change your biological sex, you're celebrated as a hero.

So much for tolerance! In fact, while California affords choice, free expression, and special rights to pretty much anyone who is non-heterosexual or gender-non-conforming, they have recently made efforts to crack down on higher education religious institutions that have morality codes on sexual expression.

Your Funding or Your Faith: Choose One Only

That was the message the California Senate sent to religious colleges and their students when it passed SB 1146 on May 26, 2016. Had it passed in its original form, SB 1146 would have banned Christian colleges from receiving funding from the state if they "discriminated" on the basis of sexual orientation or gender identity.[lxv] The term "discriminated" in this case means that if a religious college holds a set of standards on sexual behavior, whatever those standards might be, and refuses to allow students to engage in sexual behavior against those standards, they are guilty of discrimination. Let's examine the insanity of this proposition.

Suppose "Christian College A" had a rule prohibiting any sexual activity outside man/woman Biblical marriage. If that rule were broken, say, by a heterosexual student who had sex outside of Biblical marriage and was caught by administration, he/she would not have the right to sue the college if he/she were expelled from the school. Now let's take another example. What if a bisexual-identified female college student was engaging in sex with both men and women at the college? The man she is having sex with is heterosexual-identified, while the woman she is having sex with is lesbian-identified. Under this law, punishment for the two women involved would allow the women to sue the school for discrimination, but the straight guy would be subject to discipline with no ability to challenge the school. Yet, he was engaging in the same unbiblical sexual behavior as the two women! What sense does that make?

Thankfully, after intense opposition from a coalition that was formed by the Christian colleges, the author of this bill amended the language by dropping a provision that would have allowed LGBT students to sue the college if they were disciplined for violating the school's religious rules on sexuality. Instead, the bill would require these private Christian universities to "disclose if they have an exemption for the anti-discrimination law and report to the state when students are expelled for violating morality codes."[lxvi]

But don't think this issue is going away anytime soon. With the 2015 Supreme Court decision legalizing gay marriage in all 50 states, Christian higher education institutions now have to reexamine their policies on sexuality and benefits to married students. For example, in a 2015 article published in *The Atlantic*, author David R. Wheeler writes:

> At the moment, there is no federal non-discrimination law that prevents schools from enforcing these policies. Fifteen states plus the District of Columbia offer protections to gay and lesbian students, but they usually grant exemptions to religious institutions. The first serious challenge to such policies came last summer, when the New England Association of Schools and Colleges asked Gordon College, a Christian school in Massachusetts, to review its ban on "homosexual practice" and determine whether it violated the association's accreditation standards. Gordon announced in March that it had completed the review and decided to keep the ban in place.[lxvii]

What's at stake for these schools are millions of dollars of federal grants and loans that make it possible for students to attend. If the government decides to enact policies that forbid religious schools to have morality standards, those dollars can quickly go away, making it nearly impossible for some students to attend. That's why only a handful of Christian colleges in the United States have refused to accept any federal funding, fearing that someday the government will try to force their brand of morality on the school while dangling a carrot of federal funding in front of them. For example, my undergraduate alma mater, Grove City College in Pennsylvania, is one of these schools.

Similarly, Patrick Henry College in Virginia (where I am employed as a mental health counselor) states on its website: "In order to safeguard our distinctly Christian worldview, we do not accept or participate in government funding. We believe such financial independence to be a critical component of a Patrick Henry College education."[lxviii] While forgoing these funds often has a dramatic effect on the college's enrollment (for example, Patrick Henry College has fewer than 500 students, while Grove City College boasts just under 3,000), their administration and educators believe that keeping Christian standards will prove to be, in the long run, an asset to the students and educational community.

Big Brother Is Watching You

What would happen in a society where the government favors one form of speech over another, less politically correct, form of communication? Look no further than George Orwell's classic *1984*. In his well-known 1949 novel, Orwell describes a totalitarian state where its rulers dominate its inhabitants with constant surveillance, known as "Big Brother." Throughout the course of the novel, the phrase "Big Brother is watching you" is repeated to warn the citizens of their constant surveillance from the overpowering government.

But surely, no reasonable court of law would uphold such a violation of free speech like California's SB 1172. Yet, that's exactly what the Ninth Circuit Court of Appeals did when it was challenged in federal court. In 2013, *Pickup v. Brown* argued that the law banning therapy for minors violated three statutes:

1) Mental health providers' First Amendment right to free speech;
2) Mental health providers' freedom of association rights;
3) Parents' fundamental right to make important medical decisions for their children.[lxix]

It also argued that the law is void for vagueness or overbreadth.

In its infinite wisdom, the Ninth Circuit ruled against all four arguments of the plaintiff and upheld the law. How did they do it, you ask? According to a *Washington Post* article: "In his dissenting opinion, Judge O'Scannlain wrote that the appeals court had undercut the First Amendment by relabeling professional speech as 'conduct' unprotected by the Constitution."[lxx] What was even more disturbing about the court's decision was that it did not actually examine the scientific evidence to determine whether the law was doing what it intended to do—which was to protect LGBT youth from a harmful practice; and since there have been no outcome studies that have followed youth in SOCE therapy, that would have been impossible.

The court got around this by affording the law only a "rational basis review" in its decision that "SB 1172 is not an abridgement of free speech rights ... wherein it will be upheld if the law has a rational relationship to a legitimate state interest."[lxxi] In other words, the court said it doesn't need to actually determine if the law did what it says it did because it deemed therapy to be primarily medical conduct (and deemed that SB 1172 would have only an "incidental effect" on speech); and if it's *primarily* medical conduct, the state can rationally ban something deemed harmful, regardless of the evidence.

In a legal analysis of the California law, University of Michigan law student, Wyatt Fore, summarized the issue of rational basis review as such:

> The Ninth Circuit found, under rational basis scrutiny, that the legislature rationally could have determined that SOCE for minors was a public health risk because it relied on qualified scientific determinations, such as the American Psychological Association's task force on

Appropriate Therapeutic Responses to Sexual Orientation and a wide variety of professional groups of mental health providers. and counselors.[lxxii]

Note, however, in Fore's analysis, that he relies on a statement that was used in court proceedings from the American Psychological Association's *Report of the Task Force on Appropriate Therapeutic Responses to Sexual Orientation*, that concluded that "[s]exual orientation change efforts (SOCE) pose critical health risks to lesbian, gay, and bisexual people." Yet, nowhere in his analysis is it stated, nor is there a mention in court proceedings, that this task force report failed to survey any outcome research for youth undergoing SOCE therapy.

The reason there is no mention, of course, is because the research simply does not exist! To date, there have been no outcome-based studies on SOCE therapy for minors. Yet, legislation continues to pass in liberal states to ban the therapy, and federal court rulings ignore the inconvenient fact that they are upholding a ban on a therapy that has not been studied at all in the psychological literature.[lxxiii] However, the Third Circuit Court of Appeals disagreed slightly with the notion that SOCE therapy contains speech when it reviewed New Jersey's ban for minors, and this conflict between the Third Circuit Court and Ninth Circuit Court may actually result in these "conversion therapy" bans being overturned.

In *King v. Christie*, the court examined whether the law was intending to regulate medical conduct or speech to determine if it was a violation of the First Amendment:

While *Pickup* acknowledged that Senate Bill 1172 *may* have at least an "incidental effect" on speech and subjected the statute to rational basis review, here the District Court went one step further when it concluded that SOCE counseling is pure, non-expressive conduct that falls wholly outside the protection of the First Amendment. The District Court's primary rationale for this conclusion was that "the *core characteristic* of counseling is not that it may be carried out through talking, but rather that the counselor applies methods and procedures in a therapeutic manner" (emphasis added). The District Court derived this reasoning in part from *Pickup,* in which the 9th Circuit observed that the "key component of psychoanalysis is the treatment of emotional suffering and depression, *not* speech." On this basis, the District Court concluded that "the line of demarcation between conduct and speech is whether the counselor is attempting to communicate information or a particular viewpoint to the client or whether the counselor is attempting to apply methods, practices, and procedures to bring about a change in the client—the former is speech and the latter is conduct."[lxxiv]

An analysis in the *Michigan Journal of Gender & Law* compared and contrasted the New Jersey and California "conversion therapy" bans when it discussed the medical conduct vs. speech issue, and how the courts may determine what is and is not constitutional:

> As a result, the tension lies in whether the legislature is banning SOCE as expressive conduct (more like speech), or if it is a more mainstream scientific regulation of public health. Here, the court concluded that the purpose of the legislation was the latter. However, if legislatures veered closer to the regulation of expressive conduct of mental health therapists by, for

example, forbidding them from discussing SOCE, these laws would become more problematic. Indeed, courts have struck down analogous restrictions of the doctor-patient relationship in medicinal marijuana, abortion, and physician-assisted suicide cases.[lxxv]

While the differences in these rulings are subtle, it's important to distinguish the Third Circuit from the Ninth Circuit's decision. In *Pickup v. Brown*, the Ninth Circuit concluded that banning SOCE therapy would have an effect on speech (albeit incidental), while in the *King v. Christie* case, the Third Circuit said the law was only intended to curtail medical conduct within SOCE therapy that could be deemed harmful, not the speech, or viewpoint expressed, in the counseling relationship.

For example, a client and therapist theoretically should be allowed, under the Third Circuit's decision, to discuss how the client experiences his/her same-sex attractions or gender identity conflicts; why the client feels these conflicts (whether they are religious objections or otherwise, the source of distress, and/or the possible underlying causes for the attractions, etc.); and how the client would like to respond to the feelings. This is all speech based on one's viewpoint. But, as a practical matter, it is impossible under the law for either a counselor or enforcement official to distinguish protected speech from prohibited conduct because speech *is* the treatment for clients who desire to change, resolve, or alter their attractions or feelings, and therefore this speech would be deemed prohibited medical conduct.[2]

---

[2] In Chapter 7, I will discuss how a 2018 (*NIFLA v. Becerra*) decision at the Supreme Court of the United States will likely settle the "medical conduct" speech issue in favor of therapy equality.

If you are an advocate for therapy equality, as I am, you might be thinking: "Okay, sure, but how does that help the cause of therapy equality for minor clients that are distressed by unwanted same-sex attractions or gender identity conflicts?" The reason to be hopeful is that it produces a conflict between the Third and Ninth Circuit Courts; and when such conflicts exist, the Supreme Court of the United States (SCOTUS) usually decides them. In fact, in January 2017, Pacific Justice Institute launched another appeal to the SCOTUS to overturn California's law.[3, lxxvi]

Overly Broad and Ill-Defined
As it currently stands, one of the main problems with "conversion therapy" ban laws are the overly broad definition of SOCE therapy and what is actually considered medical conduct. Most of the laws written to ban SOCE therapy are ill-defined; typically, they read something like this, and I paraphrase: "Therapeutic efforts to change sexual orientation or gender identity and/or reduce same- sex attractions and/or gender identity expression, are prohibited under this law." Exactly what in the talk therapy is considered "medical conduct" and not merely "speech" isn't clearly defined in these laws, and such a distinction is likely too artificial to be defined in a practical or constitutionally permissible way.

How does a counselor know what may or may not have an effect on a client's sexual or gender identity? For example, it is very possible that a therapist's interpretation of why a client may experience certain same-sex attractions

---

[3] Note, however, that the appeal on SB1172 was not based on the court's inconsistency, but rather, a new legal argument that California's law was enacted to suppress the free exercise of religious persons to pursue psychotherapy that helps them align their sexuality with their faith. The plaintiffs in this appeal argue that the California law's underpinnings are inherently anti-religious, and thus, against the Constitution. The Supreme Court declined to hear this case.

or engage in specific sexual behaviors may alter the client's understanding of themselves and their sexuality, thereby producing a cognitive restructuring which, in turn, could lead to a change in sexual desires, behaviors, or feelings. Would this be considered "speech" or "medical conduct"?

The reality is that no matter how carefully practitioners describe their practices to avoid scrutiny from officials that may accuse them of violating the law; or how carefully they work to inform clients of the nature of their counseling methods, and the corresponding benefits and risks that entail; these therapists remain subject to discipline in any jurisdiction where such a ban is on the books. The consequence of this scrutiny—even if therapists are somehow able to successfully navigate through the complexities of what may or may not be against the law—is that it has a chilling effect on counselor autonomy and client self-determination, so much so, that a therapist may refuse to work with a client that seeks to work through sexual and gender identity conflicts simply to avoid the possibility of violating the law.

Because of the overly broad and ill-defined nature of "conversion therapy" ban laws, the LGBT-identified client sincerely seeking "conversion" to heterosexuality is, ironically, a victim of discrimination by the very laws that purpose to protect them from harm. While disguised as "protection," the laws could essentially be a strategy by activists to keep unhappy LGBT-identified persons locked into an unwanted identity for life. It sort of reminds me of a line from the Eagles' song *Hotel California*—"you can check out anytime you like, but you can never leave!"

Ironically, these bans will actually hurt the very people the LGBT activists intend to protect: themselves. Consequently, if an LGBT-identified person walks into a counselor's office, unhappy with his or her sexual orientation or identity, and sincerely seeks help to leave that lifestyle behind, the counselor would have to tell the client:

"I'm sorry, but it is impossible, unethical, and quite illegal, for me to help you with that problem. Besides, you're born that way, so why even try?" Don't believe me? Read the story of Robin, a former lesbian, who was told for years, from counselor after counselor, that she was "born gay" and could not leave the homosexual lifestyle.

Robin's Story

I am a grateful Christian ex-homosexual, ex-queer. I was born in the 1950s and I lived most of my adult life as a lesbian. In 2009, in my fifties, by the grace of God and the power of Jesus Christ. I was freed from the horrible homosexual life I lived

I was not born homosexual. I was not "born that way."

I was sexually abused in a life-threatening way at the age of two by a female pedophile babysitter without the knowledge of my family. I was born and raised in the midwest and came from a middle-class family with a working, agnostic father and a stay-at-home, Christian mother. I was the oldest of three siblings. I went to school and attended church. However, as a result of being sexually abused, I began to eat compulsively and had bouts of uncontrollable anger. I suffered an undiagnosed nervous breakdown at the age of 13, lapsed into untreated clinical depression, and began a life-long battle with depression, addiction, and suicide. I developed crushes on female teachers and coaches. I went from being a happy, active "A" student to an angry, depressed "D" student. I knew I needed help so I went to my church youth group. My youth pastor, instead of helping me, offered me marijuana and wanted to be "friends" and "smoke grass" with the kids. I knew this was not help and refused. I turned away from the church and from God and became an angry atheist. I needed help desperately but my parents could not afford and did not believe in therapy. They lived through the depression and

World War II and to them therapy was weakness. I limped through junior high and high school in a fog and began making choices that led to a life of homosexuality.

I had my first lesbian sexual experience in college after getting drunk and waking up in bed with my best female friend. In spite of my depression, eating disorder, alcohol addiction, and suicidal thinking, I was deeply ashamed of my first lesbian encounter. In my heart of hearts I knew it was wrong. My sexual abuse driven self-loathing was so deeply rooted that I refused to speak to school counselors. I stopped going to class and purposely flunked out of that school, trying to leave my lesbian partner and lesbian desires behind.

This began another dysfunctional, life-long pattern of geographical cures, but it also forced my parents to admit that I needed help and the next year I saw my first therapist, an M.D. psychiatrist, while I went to junior college in my home town. However, I never talked about my lesbian experiences and lesbian desires. I only talked about my depression and compulsive overeating with no real relief from either one. I had no conscious memories of sexual abuse, only unexplainable consuming anger and fear. The next year I went to my home state university and the shame I felt about my lesbian attractions lessened as my addictive eating, alcoholic drinking, and suicidal obsession increased. I developed compulsive attractions to female students and finally began a secret, closeted lesbian relationship with one of my sorority sisters. My alcoholic drinking and suicidal obsession escalated and many nights I would get drunk, get behind the wheel of my car with the intent of killing myself, and wake up the next morning suffering from a blackout and not remembering how I got home. I know now that it was the grace of God that kept me from killing myself and/or anyone else.

I finally managed to graduate from college, but my lesbian partner left me and I struck out for another city in the

Midwest and became an "out", angry, atheist lesbian. My depression, addiction, and suicidal obsession never left me and I sought counseling help and was told for the first time that I was "born homosexual." This was by a lesbian therapist at the state university in that city who also tried to seduce me. Even in the sick, suicidal state I was in, there was still enough desire for health that I refused.

I sought out 12-Step groups, which have been called "poor man's therapy," because due to my dysfunctional life and dysfunctional work life, I did not have the money or insurance coverage to seek out more professional therapy. I found the same "born homosexual" belief there and that fit well with my atheist belief system. My atheist beliefs worshipped at the altar of science and if a "professional" or the growing atheist culture told me that I was "born homosexual," then it was my DNA or my genes that were responsible for my life and my choices, not me. I also embraced the Higher Power concept of the 12-Step programs. As an atheist, I was the center of my own universe and the 12-Step programs taught me that I could make my Higher Power anything I wanted. That was code for my Higher Power being me. In spite of never finding healing or peace, I did keep from killing myself, learn to manage my misery better, and become a little more functional and productive.

I went to seven different counselors for depression, addiction, and suicide during the 1970s, 80s, and 90s and, beginning with the lesbian counselor, every one of them told me what I have come to know as the blatant, bold faced lie of being "born homosexual." On my 40th birthday, facing another suicidal crisis brought about by my emerging memories of life-threatening sexual abuse, I was finally able to see a therapist who helped me face what had happened to me as a small child.

Every morning for six months, I woke up in a pool of sweat screaming from night terrors. The memories slowly came back in a fuzzy small child way, but the suicidal obsession and compulsion began to heal. But even then, this therapist who was a Masters' level psychologist working on her Ph.D., and helping me recover memories of sexual abuse, told me: "You're a homosexual. That's who you are." Never once did she mention the possibility that it was my homosexual choices and behavior that were contributing to my anger, depression, and addiction. My suicidal risk was lessening, but I was still on antidepressants. She was the last therapist I went to and I have come to call her approach the "born queer, be happy, take a pill" therapy. Again, a "professional" perpetrated the lie and I embraced the lie because, as a homosexual, I was never held accountable for my choices or the damage that I did to myself and others. As I began to feel better I dove into another lesbian relationship, did another geographical cure this time to the west coast, and plunged into the most complete lesbian world I could create for myself.

I embraced the homosexual life and lived for most of 35 years as an "out" lesbian. I brought my lesbian partners to work and all work functions in the corporate world where I worked in various administrative assistant positions. I participated in homosexual rights political groups like Human Rights Campaign (HRC) as a volunteer. I was an in-your-face, dyke-on-a-bike, and rode my motorcycle in black leather with my lesbian partner in gay pride parades. I helped manage a lesbian club committed to supporting the lesbian community where I lived and facilitated "hook-ups" for "late-blooming" lesbians. I vacationed at homosexual resorts like Provincetown, MA. But eventual long-term sobriety and multiple lesbian relationships did not bring peace or remove my deep-seated shame. I never even considered confronting the lie that I was "born that way." I became a permanent, angry, atheist homosexual victim constitutionally incapable of being honest with myself.

In 2007, three life-changing events occurred: the breakup of another lesbian relationship, the loss of another but more lucrative job, and the death of my father. Suffering shame, guilt, and grief and with the help of another 12-Step program, Adult Children of Alcoholics, for the first time I began to honestly question whether I was "born queer." The only person in my life who had never surrendered to that lie was my mother, a devout Christian. She never stopped praying for my healing, and in my heart of hearts, I knew that she was right and that I was wrong. God allowed these events, that I considered crises at the time, in order to reach me and I came to admit, eventually and then emphatically, that I was not "born homosexual."

I went back to church. At first, I attended the denomination of my childhood at a large downtown cathedral in the west coast city where I was living. It embraced homosexuality and all of the men in the large choir, including the choir master and his partner, the main soloist, were homosexual. I began to realize that I had made choices that led to my life of homosexuality and that I and I alone, was responsible for those choices. As a permanent homosexual victim, I had made everyone and everything else responsible for my desperate unhappiness.

I understand now that victims of sexual abuse sometimes are angrier with those who did not protect them from the abuse than they are at the abuser. This was true of me. As irrational as it was, my small child mind had blamed my father for a lifetime of not keeping me safe. With his death, I had no one left to blame.

The last obstacles to my healing were the mountain of shame that I lived under and the paralyzing fear that I was too bad, too sinful for God to forgive me. I knew that I was going to hell because I had been living in my own hell on earth for a lifetime. I began searching for a Bible- believing church and finally, in 2009, God led me to witness the filmed testimony of a man freed from alcoholism, drug addiction, and suicide through the power of Jesus Christ. I knew instantly that Jesus Christ could heal me of homosexuality. With tears streaming down my face, I fell to my knees in a dark, empty theater and I asked Jesus to come into my heart and forgive me, and He did. I was freed immediately from all desire to continue in the homosexual life and filled with an amazing and powerful peace.

I spent the next several years extricating myself from the lesbian prison that I had created for myself. God led me to a supportive Christian evangelical Bible-preaching church and Christian singles group where I was free to talk about my conversion experience, talk about leaving homosexuality, and share my ex-homosexual testimony.

I adopted a very simple litmus test for any Christian church that I wanted to attend. If a Christian pastor or minister refused to state that homosexuality is a sin from the pulpit or any of the congregation refused to state that homosexuality is a sin in public, then that was not a church that I wanted to be a part of. As an active atheist homosexual, I was a committed unrepentant sinner. As a Christian ex-homosexual, I knew that I was not born that way and that homosexuality is a choice, a behavior, and a sin.

There is no such thing as an unrepentant, committed, active homosexual Christian. The two are mutually exclusive. For my continued healing, I left the lesbian groups, friends, and small business that I had been a part of. Through God's grace, I was able to eventually move from the west coast to the mountain west to be closer to my mother who had become ill. God facilitated a profound healing in me and a heartfelt reconciliation between me and my mother. My mother went to her heavenly reward in 2012, but she lived to see me accept Jesus Christ as my Lord and Savior, leave the heathen homosexual life that I had chosen, and begin to speak the truth about the choice, behavior, and sin of homosexuality.

I did not choose to be sexually abused as a child, but I did choose homosexuality. I was not "born homosexual." And through the grace of God and the power of Jesus Christ, today I am one of thousands of ex-homosexuals who have left homosexuality. There are now excellent licensed professional therapists, doing reparative therapy, that help children, adults, and families heal from sexual abuse and unwanted same-sex attraction. All children, families, and adults deserve the choice to heal.

CHAPTER 3
THE WAR THAT STARTED AT STONEWALL

For better or for worse, mental health professionals exert influence that greatly exceeds the actual wisdom we demonstrate.

~ Dr. Jeffrey Satinover
Homosexuality and the Politics of Truth

ୠ

The politics surrounding gay rights is both fascinating and disheartening. No matter your viewpoint on this issue, one has to appreciate the absolute power the gay rights movement has achieved in the last 50 years. To understand this powerful force, and its influence in the mental health field, we need to revisit a historic event that occurred on June 28, 1969. On the coattails of the civil rights movement, the modern gay rights movement began in a bar in Greenwich Village, New York called the Stonewall Inn.

For years, police officers would regularly raid the homosexual-friendly bar and abuse its patrons, who were among the most outcast members of society at the time. But one night, the homosexual men and women had had enough. They began to resist. Fighting back against police brutality, the patrons rioted for several nights against the police, who quickly lost control of the residents in the neighborhood. What resulted was six nights of protests, which later led to various activist groups within the community organizing to help gays and lesbians feel safer to share their sexual identity.

Within several months, official organizations and several newspapers were established in New York City to support the gay and lesbian community, and the following year, on June 28, 1970, the first gay pride marches took place in New York, Chicago, Los Angeles, and San Francisco to commemorate what later became known as the "Stonewall Riots."[lxxvii] The Stonewall Inn, which was designated a national landmark by President Barack Obama in 2016, is considered the birthplace of actions which lit the fire of the modern gay rights movement. As a part of his designation, President Obama said the following:

> Raids like his were nothing new, but this time the patrons had had enough, so they stood up and spoke out ... The riots become protests, and the protests became a movement, and the movement ultimately became an integral part of America.[lxxviii]

A Birthplace Marked by Exploitation

In his book, *Stonewall: The Riots That Sparked The Gay Revolution*, historian David Carter documents the early years of the homophile movement in New York City, specifically that of the Mattachine Society of New York.[4] The Mattachine Society was an exclusive fraternity of gay men, and in its early years, activists within its ranks spearheaded campaigns to fight against societal oppression of homosexuals, specifically police harassment and mafia exploitation. It is interesting to note that founding members of the society were long-time Communist Party USA cadre, including Harry Hay. Hay was a founder of NAMBLA—the infamous North American Man/Boy Love Association—and

---

[4] It should be noted that some mid-20th century homophile (gay) activist groups (such as the Mattachine Society of New York) accepted psychiatry's illness model as an alternative to societal condemnation of homosexuality's "immorality" and were willing to work with professionals who sought to "treat" and "cure" homosexuality. For more information, see: Drescher, J. (2015). Out of DSM: Depathologizing Homosexuality, *Behavioral Science. 2015, 5,* 570.

the Radical Faeries, a loosely affiliated gay spiritual movement. He left the party to concentrate his efforts on gay militancy and to prevent questions about the connections between the Communist Party and the homosexual rights movement in Western society.[lxxix]

These connections are well documented in *The Naked Communist*, anti-communist historian Cleon Skousen's 1958 exposé of the Communist Party USA's campaign to encourage open homosexuality to weaken the West. On Skousen's famous list of goals adopted by the Communist Party to undermine the social and moral fabric of the West, number 26 reads: "Present homosexuality, degeneracy and promiscuity as 'normal, natural and healthy'." [lxxx]

When Stonewall happened, it was far more than a spontaneous eruption of frustration from within the homosexual community in response to police brutality. The battering of the American family and attempts to tear down the sexual norms of the nation by the architects of the gay movement had been going on behind the scenes for decades. There remains much to be learned and documented about how the tipping point into mass resistance was reached in 1969.

As usual, the foot soldiers of the movement were on the front lines, legally and physically. They were targets of opportunity not only for corrupt law enforcement, but organized crime.

Perhaps the most troubling issue facing homosexual men in the 1960s was police oppression. Because of the anti-sodomy laws in dozens of states, consensual homosexual sex could be punished at the discretion of a particular judge's political or personal leaning. In most cases, those caught in the act would suffer the penalty of a light fine, a slap on the wrist, if you will. But in other cases, homosexual activity could result in years of prison time or forced incarceration in mental institutions that administered shock therapy, castration, and lobotomies. While the 1960s conjure up images of free love and sexual liberation, "the irony is that for almost the entirety of that decade, homosexual men and women, far from experiencing a great burst of freedom, found themselves in the worst legal position they had been in since the republic's birth."[lxxxi]

Legally speaking, no other problem was more threatening for homosexuals than entrapment. Because most homosexuals were not able to publicly acknowledge their sexual preferences, the door was open for police to exploit vulnerable men that had a lot to lose by being outed, or even worse, prosecuted for their illegal sexual activities. Depending on the political party in charge, or around election time (in New York City), police would ramp up their efforts via the mayor's directives to "clean the streets" of homosexuals.[5] But according to Dick Leitsch, a prominent activist and officer in the Mattachine Society (who would field dozens of calls at the society's headquarters from desperate men trying to avoid having their reputations ruined), the common belief that gay men were being arrested for "prowling the city making unsolicited advances was patently false." [lxxxii]

> The entrapped men had been arrested by police officers in plain clothes who had gone into gay bars and cruising areas dressing and acting as though they were interested in sex. When the gay men had responded in kind, the cops arrested them. Gay men also noticed that the policemen who did this kind of work tended to be very attractive men who dressed provocatively for the occasion ... other patterns emerged as well. For example, it was not uncommon for the police to

---

[5] David Carter also documents a massive effort by Mayor Robert F. Wagner, Jr. to crack down on homosexuals cruising for sex in advance of the 1964 World's Fair in New York City.

suggest the names of certain attorneys who might be able to defend the men arrested for solicitation and/or loitering. When those charged consulted the attorneys, they were asked to pay exorbitant fees, far beyond the normal charge for such an infraction ... entrapped gay men commonly concluded that one reason for the high fees charged by the lawyers the police steered them to was to grease the wheels of 'justice.'[lxxxiii]

Because of their vulnerable position, the exploitation of homosexuals was a profitable business, so much so that it attracted the mafia to open up establishments uniquely positioned to cater to the gay community. They did so with the cooperation of New York City law enforcement, which regularly received kickbacks from the exploitation of homosexual-friendly businesses in Greenwich Village, the Bohemian-style neighborhood that attracted the most unconventional and non-conformist citizens of New York. The Village was most prominently known as a homosexual hangout, a community of *avant garde*, free-thinking hippies. Many of the Village's inhabitants were comprised of young gay adults (mostly men) who had left their families as soon as they were old enough to make it on their own.

In the 1960s, most of the country's communities were an unsafe place for homosexuals—prejudice and discrimination were not only common and acceptable, but also legalized. Not only was homosexual behavior a crime in most states, but one could also be fired from employment and have his reputation ruined simply because he was discovered to be a homosexual. All of this created a climate of hostility and oppression for homosexual youth growing up in this era, so much so, that when word began to spread of Greenwich Village's large queer community, it attracted these youth, some of whom were looking for liberation from their unaccepting families, while others simply wanted to find people like themselves in the effort to fit into a segment of population that welcomed and celebrated their existence. According to Karen Ocamb, author of *Stonewall Remembered*:

> The Stonewall Inn had a diverse gay-male dominated crowd. Some more politically minded gays such as Craig Rodwell and yippie Jim Fouratt considered Stonewall "a real dive" and a haven for "chicken hawks."[6] Others, however, considered it an oasis, including tony East Siders, some hippies, street queens, Latinos, blacks, some under-aged teens (the drinking age was 18) and gays who just wanted to dance, since Stonewall was the only gay bar where dancing was permitted.[lxxxiv]

It mattered not that Greenwich Village represented the very fringe of society—for it was a place these youth could be open and honest about their sexuality, perhaps for the very first time in their lives. Other gay youth found a haven for their homosexuality by attending university or finding employment in New York City's thriving art and music scene while simultaneously becoming involved in the city's emerging homosexual activist community. Whatever the reason or means by which these young people arrived in Greenwich Village, the sexual nonconformist neighborhood became their home, and Christopher Street, where the Stonewall Inn was located, was their stomping ground. In fact:

---

[6] Chicken hawk is another name for pedophilic men who are sexually interested in younger men and boys. For more information, see: http://articles.latimes.com/1994-08-14/entertainment/ca-27046_1_chicken-hawk

Christopher Street became so gay in the 1970s that some gay men wrongly assumed that Gay Street had been named in their honor.[7] Still, from a turn-of-the-century perspective, this confused knot of streets could certainly be termed, however anachronistically, a queer geography. It was in the midst of this tangle of irregular streets and triangular open spaces that the largest gay club of the 1960s opened.[lxxxv]

Operating a club for primarily gay-identified patrons in New York City was no easy task in the 1960s. Because of the New York's State Liquor Authority's (SLA) interpretation of post-prohibition laws categorizing homosexuals as "lewd and dissolute," any bar known to openly serve gays and lesbians would be considered "disorderly" and be put out of business. "Making it illegal for bars to serve homosexuals created a situation that could only attract organized crime. The Mafia occupied the vacuum to run gay bars, which in turn set up a scenario for police corruption and the exploitation of the bars' customers."[lxxxvi] The Stonewall Inn catered mostly to gays in their late teens to early 30s, and was operated by three Mafia friends from Little Italy:

> 'Mario' (Stonewall's manager), 'Zucchi,' and 'Fat Tony' Lauria, the meth-addicted controlling partner who lived with openly gay Chuck Shaheen, though (sources) say their relationship "was secretarial, not erotic." The Mob partners made regular payoffs to the district and local Mafioso and the NYPD's infamously corrupt Sixth Precinct ... reports (suggest) that the police

---

[7] Ironically named, Gay Street, which could not "keep itself straight," only comprised one block and intersected with Christopher Street.

received $2,000 each week. This bought
"protection" since Stonewall did not have a
liquor license and functioned as a private "bottle
club," and "good-will," such as tip-offs before
the monthly police raids and relatively quick
release of arrested employees."[lxxxvii]

Exploitation by the Mafia and corruption within the
police became the norm in Greenwich Village's premier gay
club in the 1960s. While the owners made a concerted effort
to shield their illegal activities from the police by running
the Stonewall Inn as a private club, thereby tightly
controlling who could enter by designating its patrons as
"private members," the Mafia-controlled establishment still
provided monthly financial kickbacks to the chief of police,
who then carefully orchestrated raids on the homosexual
establishment early in the evening on weekdays, where few
patrons would be present, thus minimizing the
establishment's financial loss.

While the few patrons inside the club would suffer
the consequences, including harassment and occasional
arrests, the club owners would have had advance warning of
the raid from the police, who provided enough lead time for
the owners to rid the bars of alcohol and empty the cash
registers, well before the arrival of authorities, who would
shut down the club for several hours, only to see it reopened
later in the evening when most of the club's private members
would arrive for a night of entertainment.

Despite the regular police harassment and Mafia
exploitation, the Stonewall Inn's patrons were willing to deal
with the watered-down drinks, deplorable bathroom
conditions, and accompanying risks that came along with
frequenting the bar. After all, there really wasn't anywhere
else for them to drink, dance, and meet other romantic
partners—unless of course, one was willing to have casual,
anonymous sex in the park or at the docks by the river, where

homosexual men regularly gathered to hook up. But one Friday night in late June 1969, all of the usual routines of police raids that the regular patrons of the Stonewall Inn had come to expect, were broken.

Unlike the usual police busts, Friday night, June 28 was a weekend night, and it was past midnight (1:00 a.m.), when the police conducted the raid. Whereas previous crackdowns may have affected dozens of patrons, this night it would be hundreds —and the way the police behaved that night was especially demeaning and brutalizing, particularly toward some of the patrons that didn't appreciate their evening being disrupted, and by vocalizing their disapproval, became targets of physical abuse, and were, eventually, taken into custody.

But the police could not have predicted that their break in routine would have backfired on them like it did. The patrons who were already expelled began to fight back. Not only had this been the second raid in one week (highly unusual), the crackdown happened during the "peak" of the night. Unlike previous raids, in which only a dozen or so patrons were present, this crackdown occurred during a very busy period. Hundreds of customers were affected, and were agitated. In other words, the bee's nest was disturbed, and now the bees were ready to sting. As Carter documents:

> The police had chosen to raid the bar at peak time—1:00 a.m. on a summer Saturday morning—so that with a large number of customers in the club when it was raided, there were enough people present to form a crowd. Also, the larger the crowd, the more patrons there were who might be there with friends, hence the larger number who might be inclined to wait and see if their friends were arrested or beaten. However, a rarely noted contemporary account attributes the eruption of anger that night to the

previous raid on the Stonewall Inn, noting that customers had already complained about the earlier raid (on Tuesday night of the same week).[lxxxviii]

Thus, not only were the riots sparked because of the raids occurring during peak time, but also, the patrons were sick and tired of being harassed and exploited by the police's political games. According to a *New York Times* article that marked the death of the Deputy Seymour Pine, the police officer who led the raid in 1969:

> About 200 people were inside. When the officers ordered them to line up and show identification, some refused. Several cross-dressers refused to submit to anatomical inspections. Word of the raid filtered into the street, and soon hundreds of protesters gathered outside, shouting "gay power" and calling the police "pigs." The turning point came when a lesbian fought with officers as she was pushed into a patrol car. The crowd rushed the officers, who retreated into the club. Several people ripped out a parking meter and used it as a battering ram; others tried to set fire to the club. It took police reinforcements an hour and a half to clear the street.[lxxxix]

Five more nights of gathering, picketing, and rioting on Christopher Street and the surrounding parks and areas in Greenwich Village followed. Each night, police had to use force to disperse the crowds, which sometimes numbered in the thousands.

In the Aftermath of Stonewall
After the riots at the Stonewall Inn, the Gay Liberation Front (GLF) formed as a militant movement to

attain rights for all gays and lesbians. While the GLF eventually disbanded, it was a trailblazer for what commonly became known as the Gay Liberation Movement.

Out of this movement grew organizations such as the Gay Activists Alliance, which eventually led to the modern gay rights movement, producing groups such as the Human Rights Fund (which eventually became the Human Rights Campaign in 1995), National Gay Task Force, Lambda Legal, and the Gay and Lesbian Alliance Against Defamation (GLAAD), among many others.

One of the most notable results of the coalescing of the formal Gay Liberation Movement was the successful infiltration of LGBT activism into three key fields, including the psychiatric mental health field. Notable LGBT activist Barbara Gittings, who was the first head of the American Library Association's gay task force, said the following about the necessity of going after the psychiatric field's mental disorder classification as a means to gain credibility:

> Psychiatrists were one of the three major groups that had their hands on us. They had a kind of control over our fate, in the eyes of the public, for a long time. Religion and law were the other two groups that had their hands on us. So, besides being sick, we were sinful and criminal. But the sickness label infected everything that we said and made it difficult for us to gain any credibility for anything we said ourselves. The sickness issue was paramount.[xc]

Most in the Gay Liberation Movement believed that homosexuality would first need to be declassified as an illness in need of curing before the other two fields would soften their condemnation and discrimination of gays. After all, if secular society could say that homosexual behavior is normal, per se, stigmatization would then decrease, and the logical outcome would be that "normal" non-heterosexual persons should not be incarcerated or discriminated against in the legal system. It would only be a matter of time until gay marriage would be legal, with major religious denominations blessing homosexual unions.

In his book, *Homosexuality and the Politics of Truth*, Dr. Jeffrey Satinover describes the process of how much of this occurred from a strategic standpoint:

> In the early years of gay liberation, this reality was used for the fledgling gay activists' advantage. They anticipated that if the influential American Psychiatric Association (APA) could be convinced to redefine homosexuality, the other guilds would follow shortly thereafter and then would the rest of society. Their plan was implemented with swift and near-total success.[xci]

So how did it happen so swiftly? As key strategists within the gay rights movement observed early on, in order to change hearts and minds that homosexuality was not a mental illness in need of a cure, the younger generation must be won over, and in order to do this, gays must be portrayed as victims. According to Marshall Kirk and Hunter Madsen, authors of *After the Ball: How America Will Conquer Its Fear and Hatred of Gays in the 90's,* the central role to be played by gay victimhood in the homosexual revolution was that gay strategists must push the theory that homosexuals are "born that way"—in other words, that their sexual orientation is determined at birth, whether or not there existed any scientific basis for such a claim.

Thus, LGBT activists should instruct their followers that they should portray themselves as victims of circumstances who "no more chose their sexual orientation than they did, say, their height, skin color, talents, or limitations." Interestingly, gay individuals such as Kirk and

Madsen stressed the need for homosexuals to stand behind the "born that way" theory, even though the authors themselves recognized the argument's invalidity:

> For all practical purposes, gays should be considered to have been born gay—even though sexual orientation, for most humans, seems to be the product of a complex interaction between innate predispositions and environmental factors during childhood and early adolescence.[xcii]

Accordingly, LGBT activists in the 1960s and 70s knew they did not have the scientific evidence to prove that people are born gay (and they still don't have it today, by the way), but that didn't stop them from using political activism to lobby the APA to remove homosexuality from the *Diagnostic and Statistical Manual of Mental Disorders (DSM)*.

According to Dr. Jack Drescher, a gay-identified psychiatrist (and one of the current, leading critics of "conversion therapy" within the American Psychiatric Association) who documented the events leading up to the 1973 APA landmark decision to remove homosexuality from the *DSM*, while there was "an emerging generational changing of the guard within APA comprised of younger leaders urging the organization to greater social consciousness...the most significant catalyst for diagnostic change was gay activism," not scientific evidence. In the years following the 1969 Stonewall Riots:

> Gay activist protests succeeded in getting APA's attention and led to unprecedented educational panels at the group's next two annual meetings. A 1971 panel, entitled "Gay is Good," featured gay activists Frank Kameny and Barbara Gittings explaining to psychiatrists, many who were

hearing this for the first time, the stigma caused by the "homosexuality" diagnosis. Kameny and Gittings returned to speak at the 1972 meeting, this time joined by John Fryer, M.D. Fryer appeared as Dr. H Anonymous, a 'homosexual psychiatrist' who, given the realistic fear of adverse professional consequences for coming out at that time, disguised his true identity from the audience and spoke of the discrimination gay psychiatrists faced in their own profession ... [W]hile protests and panels took place, APA engaged in an internal deliberative process of considering the question of whether homosexuality should remain a psychiatric diagnosis. This included a symposium at the 1973 APA annual meeting in which participants favoring and opposing removal debated the question, 'Should Homosexuality be in the APA Nomenclature?'[xciii]

Leading up to the APA vote, and behind the scenes, a committed group of activists called the National Gay Task Force (NGTF)[8] was engaging in an aggressive, yet deceptive, letter writing campaign to urge the APA membership at large to vote to retain the nomenclature change that was to remove homosexuality from the *DSM*.[xciv] No doubt, they were aided by top officials at the APA that had their minds set on a diagnostic change, as they were able to make timely appeals to the APA membership (without the membership even knowing it was a group of activists, not scientists, writing the appeal). According to Dr. Jeffrey Satinover:

---

[8] Lesbian was later added to their name, and for many years, the organization was called the "National Gay and Lesbian Task Force" until very recently. Its current name is "National LGBTQ Task Force."

When the committee met formally to consider the issue in 1973 the outcome had already been arranged behind closed doors. No new data was introduced, and objectors were given only fifteen minutes to present a rebuttal that summarized seventy years of psychiatric and psychoanalytic opinion. When the committee voted as planned [to remove homosexuality from the current nomenclature as a mental illness] a few voices formally appealed to the membership at large, which can overrule committee decisions even on "scientific" matters.[xcv]

But the NGTF quickly responded by writing a letter to the APA membership at large. Somehow, they were able to obtain the APA member addresses and write letters to over 30,000 members without ever identifying itself as an organization. As Dr. Ronald Bayer documents:

A decision was made not to indicate on the letter that it was written, at least in part, by the Gay Task Force, nor to reveal that its distribution was funded by contributions the task force had raised. Indeed, the letter gave every indication of having been conceived and mailed by those [psychiatrists] who [originally] signed it ... Though each signer publicly denied any role in the dissimulation, at least one signer had warned privately that to acknowledge the organizational role of the gay community would have been the "kiss of death." There is no question however about the extent to which the officers of the APA were aware of both the letter's origins and the mechanics of its distribution. They, as well as the National Gay Task Force, understood the letter as performing a vital role in the effort to turn back the challenge.[xcvi]

But this was just one of the subtler forms of intimidation waged by LGBT activists. As will be discussed in the next chapter, during the years leading up to the APA's removal of homosexuality, activists routinely disrupted APA meetings throughout the country, sometimes using violent tactics, all for the cause of decreasing the stigma that was brought about by classifying homosexuality as a mental disorder. This stigma black- balled homosexuals from living their lives openly, making it very difficult for them to hold public office or rise to the top of their professional fields. In fact, being outed as a homosexual was such a liability that J. Edgar Hoover, head of the FBI in the 1930s and 40s, who was rumored to be gay, had the publishing company of a major "tell all" book about famous closeted celebrities and VIPs remove his name from the contents so his reputation wouldn't be tarnished.[xcvii]

Religion: The Final Frontier

Now that the LGBT community enjoys considerable protections in the mental health and legal systems, their next natural target, and perhaps their greatest historical foe, is organized religion.

After all, what greater stigma could exist than the notion that God—the creator of the universe and the judge of all mankind is against your sexual behavior? If one buys into the discredited "born gay" myth, it is especially punishing. If God is against my sexual attractions, then why did He create me this way? If He didn't create me this way, then why do my prayers for Him to change me go unanswered?

So distressing are these questions that it has prompted entire movements, organizations, and thought-provoking books to be written on the subject. Gay-affirming

Christian communities such as the Gay Christian Network and Revoice; spiritual organizations such as Soul Force and Dignity; and many gay-identified "religious" writers have sought to reinterpret the Bible and traditional Christianity in order to justify and celebrate their homosexuality—all because of the stigma that has accompanied their inability to reconcile their sexuality with their faith.

But if it were only stigma that was causing all of this distress, wouldn't that be resolved by simply changing the laws and/or normalizing homosexual behavior in the mental health field?

Looking back, perhaps the reduction of stigma is a good thing, at least from a mental health and legal perspective. After all, a fair, secular, and egalitarian society finds it hard to discriminate against consenting adults who freely choose to engage with one another sexually, and consequently, accept the benefits and consequences that come with such relationships. To add on additional societal discrimination and/or religious condemnation for feelings not consciously chosen, seems cruel and unfair.

But if homosexual-oriented persons experience distress because of their own unwanted attractions or feelings (or the consequences that result from such actions), is it a bad thing for them to seek assistance from those who provide counseling or ministry and can help them resolve their distress, perhaps even heal the underlying causes of their undesired impulses? Should those homosexually oriented men, women, and children suffer further stigma and discrimination for choosing a different path than their LGBT-identified brothers and sisters?

Thus, it stands to reason that reducing stigma for simply experiencing homosexual or gender identity conflicts may be good, but only provided that there are effective solutions and equal opportunities for those who experience the internal distress for having these conflicts and do not wish to act out on them.

If not, only half the problem is being treated, and in the process, we are alienating and creating a separate underclass of sexual minorities out of ignorance and political correctness. In a truly diverse society, we should all be able to co-exist in our own value systems, yet as a loving, tolerant community, respect each other's unique experiences while maintaining our differences.

But one of the biggest problems plaguing this ideal today is that organizations like the American Psychological Association (APA) and other medical and mental health associations have morphed from professional guilds to political bodies that compromise facts for political correctness.

They no longer consider all of the evidence in their deliberations and in their formation of policy statements, and thus, have alienated an entire sexual minority (those who experience unwanted sexual/gender identity conflicts and do not identity as LGBT) and thus, have failed the sexual minority community (including those who are LGBT) at large.

The results are devastating: record levels of substance abuse; disproportionately high rates of sexually transmitted infections (especially among men); higher-than-average proportions of intimate partner abuse; and continuing escalating suicide rates, especially among post-operative transgender persons.[xcviii]

This list of disparities goes on and on, and it's only getting worse.

Former APA President, Dr. Nicholas Cummings, describes this collision of mental health and politics well in his book *Destructive Trends in Mental Health*:

> In 1973, American Psychological Association (APA) President Leona Tyler enunciated the principle which we would advocate in the name of psychology and when we would do so as

concerned citizens. This principle became APA policy. In speaking as psychologists, our advocacy should be based on scientific data and demonstrable professional experience. Absent such validation, psychologists are free to speak as any concerned citizen, either as individuals or collectively through dedicated advocacy organizations. This separation is necessary if society is to ascribe credibility to advocacy when psychologists are speaking authoritatively as psychologists. Violation of this principle erodes the credibility of the science and profession to represent fact and evidence, and we become another opinionated voice shouting to be heard in the vast arena. Since enunciation of this principle, advocacy for scientific professional concerns has been usurped by an agenda-driven ideology that shows little regard for either scientific validation or professional efficacy. Although I am in agreement with many of APA's stances, I am opposed to the process that has diminished its credibility. It is no longer perceived as an authority that presents scientific evidence and professional facts. The APA has chosen ideology over science, and this has diminished its influence on the decision makers in our society.[xcix]

CHAPTER 4
THE WAR IN THE "MAINSTREAM" MEDICAL AND MENTAL HEALTH COMMUNITY

I gather from your letter that your son is a homosexual. Homosexuality is assuredly no advantage but it is nothing to be ashamed of. No vice, no degradation. It cannot be classified as an illness. We consider it to be a variation of the sexual function produced by a certain arrest of sexual development.

~ Dr. Sigmund Freud

There is no question in my mind: Every male homosexual goes through an initial stage of heterosexual development, and in all homosexuals, there has been a disturbance of normal heterosexual development, as a result of fears which produce anxieties and inhibitions of sexual function. His sexual adaptation is a substitutive adaptation.

~ Dr. Irving Bieber, former clinical professor of psychiatry at the New York Medical College and chairman of the research committee on male homosexuality

☙

On December 23, 1973, the *New York Times* published a special article titled: "The APA Ruling on Homosexuality: The Issue Is Subtle, The Debate Still On."[c] In the article, a lively discussion on the nomenclature of the American Psychiatric Association's recent declassification (which occurred one week prior to publishing of the article) of homosexuality in its *Diagnostic and Statistical Manual of Mental Disorders* was facilitated between two prominent psychiatrists at the time: Dr. Robert Spitzer of Columbia

University and Dr. Irving Bieber of the New York Medical College.

What was remarkable about this discussion was the free-flowing exchange of ideas and information, absent political correctness. These were two highly respected mental health experts who agreed on quite a bit, yet came to an impasse on one very important aspect of how to classify a mental illness: Subjective distress. What follows is just part of the conversation. I encourage you to read the entire manuscript, which is available to access freely online.

> **Dr. Spitzer:** Homosexuality, by definition, refers to an interest in sexual relations or contact with members of the same sex. Now, when we come to the question of whether or not homosexuality is a psychiatric illness, we have to have some criteria for what a psychiatric illness or disorder is. The criteria I propose applies to almost psychiatric disorders: The condition must either regularly cause subjective distress or regularly be associated with some generalized impairment in social effectiveness or functioning. Clearly homosexuality *per se* does not meet these requirements: Many homosexuals are satisfied with their sexual orientation and demonstrate no generalized impairment. If homosexuality does not meet the criteria for psychiatric disorder, what is it? Descriptively, we can say that it is one form of sexual behavior. However, in no longer considering it a psychiatric disorder, we are not saying that it is normal, or that it is as valuable as heterosexuality. We must recognize that for those homosexuals who are troubled, or dissatisfied with their homosexual feelings, that we are then

dealing with a psychiatric disorder because we
then have subjective distress.

Dr. Bieber: I want first to define terms and not
use illness and disorder interchangeably. The
popular connotation of mental illness is
psychotic illness. Now I don't believe
homosexuality is a mental illness in that
connotation. As far as civil rights go, I am in
complete favor of all civil rights for
homosexuals: No matter how a particular sexual
adaptation is arrived at in an adult, sexual
behavior between consenting adults is a private
matter. The central question is: Is homosexuality
a normal sexual variant, that develops like left-
handedness does in some people, or does it
represent some kind of disturbance in sexual
development? There is no question in my mind:
Every male homosexual goes through an initial
stage of heterosexual development, and in all
homosexuals, there has been a disturbance of
normal heterosexual development, as a result of
fears which produce anxieties and inhibitions of
sexual function. His sexual adaptation is a
substitutive adaptation. I'd like to give you an
analogy. In polio, you get a range of reactions of
injuries. Some kids are totally paralyzed. Their
walking function is gone. Others are able to walk
with braces, others have enough muscle left so
that they can be rehabilitated and can actually get
to walk by themselves. The analogy falls down
only in that the injury of polio is irreversible. But
what you have in a homosexual adult is a person
whose heterosexual function is crippled like the
legs of a polio victim. What are we going to call
this? Are you going to say this is normal? That a

81

person who has legs that have been actually paralyzed by polio is a normal person even though the polio is no longer active? The fears that have created the homosexuality, and the psychological inhibitions, belong in some kind of psychiatric representation.

Dr. Spitzer: It now appears that although Dr. Bieber doesn't believe homosexuality is a mental illness, he would like to categorize it some place in between. If that is the case, why is he upset about the recent decision? It doesn't say homosexuality is normal. It only says it doesn't meet the criteria for psychiatric illness or disorder.

Dr. Bieber: I didn't say homosexuality was a mental illness. And the *Diagnostic and Statistical Manual of Psychiatric Disorder (DSM)* contains other conditions [that do not satisfy Dr. Spitzer's definition] that I don't consider mental disorders either, such as voyeurism and fetishism.

Dr. Spitzer: I haven't given as much thought [as Dr. Bieber] to the problems of voyeurism and fetishism, and perhaps that's because the voyeurs and fetishists have not yet organized themselves and forced us to do that [remove the conditions from the DSM]. But it is true that there probably are some other conditions, and perhaps they include voyeurism and fetishism, which do not meet the criteria [of mental disorders]. I would be for reviewing those conditions as well. I would like to ask you: Would you be in favor of adding the condition of asexuality, or celibacy, to the *DSM*?

Dr. Bieber: In individuals who have no operational sexuality, apart from those in certain professions, like the clergy, where it is demanded? Yes, I would.

Dr. Spitzer: Well, you see, that exactly illustrates our difficulty here. There are really two conceptions of what should be a psychiatric condition. There are those who, with me, believe there should be a limited conception, which is close to a medical model, and there are those who believe that all psychological behavior which does not meet some general standard of optimal behavior, such as fanaticism, racism, male chauvinism, vegetarianism, asexuality should be added to the nomenclature. By removing homosexuality from the nomenclature we are not saying it is abnormal but we are not saying it is normal. And I also believe that normal and abnormal are, strictly speaking, not psychiatric terms.

Later in the article, Dr. Spitzer went on to say: "I would agree with Freud that something has happened in the development of the sexual instinct that leads one to be incapable of or not interested in heterosexual functioning." His main problem, however, was the categorization of homosexuality as a mental disorder, because according to his experience, many (or most) homosexuals were not subjectively distressed by their sexual attractions. What is fascinating is one key point in his argument: When he discusses other psychiatric conditions not considered mental disorders that still exist in the *DSM*. His justification for why they still exist was: "Perhaps that's because the voyeurs and fetishists have not yet organized themselves and forced us to do that (remove the conditions from the *DSM*)."

Think about that statement for a moment. What Spitzer was essentially saying is that psychiatry as a profession is so fragile, that if a group of individuals who exhibit a classified mental illness organize themselves, they could "force" the APA to reclassify their condition; and that is exactly what the LGBT activists did.

In his book *Homosexuality and American Psychiatry*, Dr. Ronald Bayer, former professor at Columbia University, documented this series of events at the APA:

> Instead of being engaged in a sober consideration of data, psychiatrists were swept up in a political controversy. The APA had fallen victim to the disorder of a tumultuous year [1973], when disruptive conflicts threatened to politicize every aspect of American social life...The result was not a conclusion based on an approximation of the scientific truth as dictated by reason, but was instead an action demanded by the ideological temper of the time.[ci]

Following the narrow vote to remove homosexuality from the *DSM* in 1973, newspapers worldwide reported: "Doctors Declare Homosexuality Normal," even though psychiatrists did not say this. Essentially, two of the APA's most prominent experts admitted, as demonstrated in the dialogue above, that there was no objective way to classify a mental disorder except to ask the person experiencing the mental disorder if they were "subjectively distressed" by the condition. While this isn't unusual in the medical community, it is troubling how homosexuality was removed from the DSM. For example, many conditions exist in the body that are not "normal" or even painful, yet still merit the "disorder" label.

The War in the "Mainstream" Medical and Mental Health Community

I have a rare condition called *Alopecia universalis* that caused me to lose all of the hair on my body. I lost all of my hair when I was a young man, in my late twenties, due to a variety of genetic and environmental factors. This condition causes me no pain, and other than the emotional discomfort I experienced when my hair rapidly fell out in two weeks, I have experienced little subjective distress. Does this mean I am normal? That my condition is simply a variant of the majority of people who have a full head of hair? That no problem exists? No, that statement is utter nonsense!

Had I the choice, I would much prefer to have a full head of hair! But up to this time, treatments for *Alopecia* have been under-researched, and outside of a few rare cases, individuals that have undergone medicinal trials have not had successful results. If one uses the same declassification protocol for *Alopecia* as for homosexuality, it would be removed not for scientific reasons, but for politics. I cannot imagine, however, that a group of bald guys would get together and storm the American Medical Association's annual conference, demanding their condition be de-stigmatized and normalized due to a lack of effective treatment.

But that is exactly what happened at the APA. For a few years leading up to the 1973 decision, LGBT activists disguising themselves as scientists would scream and shout when a clinician presented research on the treatment of homosexuality at the annual APA Convention. "You're killing us," they would yell at the top of their lungs while jumping on tables and disrupting the presentation.

In 1970, LGBT activists were successful in shutting down dialogue at several APA meetings, including the national conference in San Francisco, California, where militants took over the speaker's podium and microphone during a presentation on the treatment of homosexuality. Activists intent on mocking and disrupting any discourse went as far as to have Konstantin Berlandt, a prominent member of the Gay Liberation Front (and student at the University of California, Berkeley) "parade through the hall in a bright red dress" as "paper airplanes sailed down from the balcony. With two papers still unread, the chairman announced adjournment." Later that year, speakers at APA meetings in Chicago and again in California were shouted down by activists, who again took over the microphone and podium during their disruption and shut down discourse.[cii]

After a number of years of this, coinciding with a successful lobbying and letter writing campaign by the National Gay and Lesbian Task Force (NGLTF), the LGBT activists could smell change. It was the beginning of the end for classifying homosexuality as anything but a normal variant of heterosexuality. In fact, it was fairly evident that the NGLTF must have been aided by key activist members at the top of the APA, some who made open statements and spearheaded resolutions leading up to the 1973 decision.

Looking back to that era, *Psychiatric News* wrote the following in 1999:

> In the APA elections of 1972 and 1973 concern over social issues brought in a number of individuals as members of the Board of Trustees who were committed to change, including removal of homosexuality *per se* from the official APA nomenclature. As a matter of fact, at the meeting of the newly elected Board in Hawaii in May 1973, the late Dr. Jack Weinberg made a motion to make the change in *DSM-II*, but while it was evident that the motion might pass, it was felt by the Board that input from the Assembly and other components of APA as well as a recommendation from the task force on Nomenclature was necessary. However, major credit must be attributed to Dr. Robert Spitzer for

the action of the Board. Dr. Spitzer was a member of the task force on Nomenclature, chaired by Dr. Henry Brill. Dr. Spitzer had been in contact with LGBT activists who appeared at meetings in New York. He organized a symposium at the APA annual meeting in Hawaii with representatives from all sides including gays and lesbians. Dr. Spitzer concluded from this meeting that action was necessary. He brought the issue to the attention of Dr. Brill who then assigned Dr. Spitzer the task of preparing a resolution and a memo ensuring that the document to be presented was scientifically sound and persuasive.[ciii]

But how could this declassification really be scientifically sound? There was no additional research to justify this removal. No scientific method or unbiased panel of researchers was convened to carefully study all of the evidence or make recommendations for further study. Following the 1973 vote, homosexuality as a mental disorder was not defined differently; but rather, it was relabeled altogether in the *DSM II.* According to Dr. Jack Drescher, a prominent gay-identified psychiatrist and member of the APA:

> ... in "homosexuality's" place, the *DSM-II* contained a new diagnosis: Sexual Orientation Disturbance (SOD). SOD regarded homosexuality as an illness if an individual with same-sex attractions found them distressing and wanted to change ... SOD was later replaced in the *DSM-III* by a new category called "Ego Dystonic Homosexuality" (EDH). However, it was obvious to psychiatrists more than a decade later that the inclusion first of SOD, and later

EDH, was the result of earlier political compromises and that neither diagnosis met the definition of a disorder in the new nosology. Otherwise, all kinds of identity disturbances could be considered psychiatric disorders. "Should people of color unhappy about their race be considered mentally ill?" critics asked. What about short people unhappy about their height? Why not ego-dystonic masturbation? As a result, ego-dystonic homosexuality was removed from the next revision, *DSM-III-R*, in 1987. In so doing, the APA implicitly accepted a normal variant view of homosexuality in a way that had not been possible fourteen years earlier.[civ]

But wait! What happened to the patient's right to label his mental illness only if it caused him to experience subjective distress? As predicted by many, the argument of removing homosexuality from the *DSM* due to subjective distress was only the slippery slope LGBT activists needed at the time.

Once they had accomplished that, the politics within the APA would eventually decide that a patient's subjective distress was subservient to the objective idea that homosexuality *in any form* was not a condition to be treated.

We're Here! We're Subjectively Distressed! And We're Not Going Anywhere!

Despite the APA's 1973 decision and subsequent removal of the word "homosexuality" from the *DSM*, many homosexually-oriented individuals did not identify themselves as "gay" or "lesbian" and were still distressed by their attractions, so much so, that they continued to seek out psychotherapy to help reduce or eliminate the attractions. In 1999, after a run-in outside the annual APA Convention with a group of "ex-gay activists" who asserted that therapy reversed their condition (these ex-gays said that therapy helped reduce their unwanted same-sex attractions and become more opposite-sex attracted), Dr. Robert Spitzer agreed to author a new study about their experiences.[cv] Ironically, Dr. Spitzer, the same prominent psychiatrist who spearheaded the removal of homosexuality in 1973, was now fascinated by the "ex-gay" phenomenon and wished to study it! And so he did!

In 2003, Spitzer published a landmark study in the respected *Archives of Sexual Behavior* scientific journal, titled: "Can Some Gay Men and Lesbians Change Their Sexual Orientation? 200 Participants Reporting a Change from Homosexual to Heterosexual Orientation."[9] Almost immediately after the study was published, activists, gay-identified scientists, and LGBT advocates attacked Spitzer as a traitor! After the name-calling ceased and these folks actually read the study, the next charge was that the 200 participants were lying or exaggerating the results. Fortunately, Spitzer had predicted this would happen, and addressed these very concerns in the paper. In fact, he even went out of his way in the study's abstract (and in the discussion section) to address the possibility that the subjects were, in fact, lying.

However, the data itself provides compelling evidence against the chance of exaggerating, and Spitzer addressed this in the discussion section:

> 1) If the subjects were lying, "one might expect that many participants would report complete or near complete change in all sexual orientation measures" at post-test (one year after therapy).

---

[9] While gay activists have heavily criticized this study, including labeling the subjects as 'liars,' I personally know several men who were included in this research who are happily married and continue to experience normal heterosexual functioning.

But only 11% of the males and 37% of the females reported this categorical change.

2) Another inconvenient fact was that most participants, on average, did not experience any sexual orientation change until they were in treatment for two years. If the subjects were lying, one would have expected them to experience a more "rapid onset of change in sexual feelings after starting therapy;" they did not, according to the study.

3) If the subjects wanted to hide their homosexual attractions, the 24% of males and 4% of females wouldn't have acknowledged in the post-survey that they had used gay pornography.

4) The study also found gender differences in pre- and post-test. For example, females in the study showed scores closer to the heterosexual spectrum before and after treatment, which was consistent with previous research that indicates "greater female plasticity in sexual orientation."

5) Married participants would have reported a much greater level of marital adjustment after therapy had they been biased; however, while the results showed an improvement in functioning, it was not higher than the norm.

6) Finally, many of the participants used common strategies to help facilitate their change. Had they been lying, the methods of change may have been much more diverse than reported.[cvi]

The War in the "Mainstream" Medical and Mental Health Community

In the years that followed Spitzer's paper, many efforts were made to discredit and invalidate the study's results. In fact, because the topic was highly controversial and politicized, even before it was published, *Archives of Sexual Behavior* editor Kenneth Zucker told Spitzer he would only publish the article if it passed peer-review and that commentaries, both positive and negative, were published alongside the research. In fact, 26 commentaries were included with the 2003 article. But ten years after the article's appearance in the journal, something odd happened. Spitzer contacted Zucker, saying he wished to retract the study. According to a 2012 article in *Psychology Today*, Zucker said the following:

> A few months ago ... Spitzer had called Zucker wanting to talk about the latest *DSM* revision. During that call ... Spitzer made some reference to regretting having done or publishing the study, and he said he wanted to retract it. My recollection of the conversation was something like this: I said, 'I'm not sure what you want to retract, Bob. You didn't falsify the data. You didn't commit egregious statistical errors in analyzing the data. You didn't make up the data. There were various commentaries on your paper, some positive, some negative, some in between. So the only thing that you seem to want to retract is your interpretation of the data, and lots of people have already criticized you for interpretation, methodological issues, etc. ...' "If Spitzer wants to submit a letter that says he no longer believes his interpretation of his own data, that's fine. I'll publish it. But a retraction? Well, the problem with that is that Spitzer's change of heart about the interpretation of his data is not normally the kind of thing that causes an editor

to expunge the scientific record …You can retract data incorrectly analyzed; to do that, you publish an erratum. You can retract an article if the data were falsified—or the journal retracts it if the editor knows of it. As I understand it, he's just saying ten years later that he wants to retract his interpretation of the data. Well, we'd probably have to retract hundreds of scientific papers with regard to re-interpretation, and we don't do that."[cvii]

What Have You Done for Me Lately?

So what happened? Why the change of heart? According to a 2015 article in the *Washington Post*, in 2012, Spitzer had a change of heart after meeting with a gay journalist who described his own "painful debacle" of "reparative counseling."[cviii] Not long after, he published an apology to the gay community:

Several months ago I told you that because of my revised view of my 2001 study of reparative therapy changing sexual orientation, I was considering writing something that would acknowledge that I now judged the major critiques of the study as largely correct. After discussing my revised view of the study with Gabriel Arana, a reporter for *American Prospect*, and with Malcolm Ritter, an Associated Press science writer, I decided that I had to make public my current thinking about the study. Here it is.

Basic Research Question. From the beginning it was: "Can some version of reparative therapy enable individuals to change their sexual orientation from homosexual to heterosexual?" Realizing that the study design made it impossible to

92

answer this question, I suggested that the study could be viewed as answering the question, "how do individuals undergoing reparative therapy describe changes in sexual orientation?"—a not very interesting question.

The Fatal Flaw in the Study. There was no way to judge the credibility of subject reports of change in sexual orientation. I offered several (unconvincing) reasons why it was reasonable to assume that the subject's reports of change were credible and not self-deception or outright lying. But the simple fact is that there was no way to determine if the subject's accounts of change were valid.

I believe I owe the gay community an apology for my study making unproven claims of the efficacy of reparative therapy. I also apologize to any gay person who wasted time and energy undergoing some form of reparative therapy because they believed that I had proven that reparative therapy works with some "highly motivated" individuals.

[Signed]

Robert Spitzer, M.D.
Emeritus Professor of Psychiatry
Columbia University

So that's it! There you have it! Ten years after the study was published, Spitzer was convinced by one meeting with a gay reporter, who disassembled all of his arguments as to why the study was legitimate. I'm sorry, but it's hard to believe that a mind like Spitzer's didn't analyze and reanalyze the study's results for years before this meeting. So what set this meeting apart from others critiques and commentaries? Two words: Parkinson's disease.

According to the same *New York Times* article that proudly rumored Spitzer's coming apology, the writer wrote the following of Spitzer's condition.

> He pushed himself up and staggered into the dark. His desk seemed impossibly far away; Dr. Spitzer, who turns 80 next week, suffers from Parkinson's disease and has trouble walking, sitting, even holding his head upright. The word he sometimes uses to describe these limitations—pathetic—is the same one that for decades he wielded like an ax to strike down dumb ideas, empty theorizing and junk studies.[cix]

The article didn't tell the reader about the intense vitriol from militant gay activists that Spitzer received for many years after the publishing of the article. The harassment, coupled with his declining health due to Parkinson's disease, may have caused Spitzer to decide to issue the apology. According to a May 31, 2012 interview of Dr. Gerard van den Aardweg, a colleague, Spitzer was emotionally broken from years of harassment from the gay activist community:

> Sometime after his 2003 article I had a conversation with him on the telephone. I asked him if he would continue his research, or even if he would try to guide a few people with homosexual problems and who sought "alternative" professional help, that is, help and support to change as much as possible from homosexual to heterosexual interests. In his interviews with people who had walked along

that path, he certainly had learned a lot, among other things, the great need among many homosexually inclined persons for this kind of help. I felt that Dr. Spitzer was the kind of psychiatrist who could do much good for some of these persons. So why not give it a try? His reply was adamant. No, he would never touch the whole subject ever again. He had nearly broken down emotionally after terrible personal attacks from militant gays and their supporters. There was an outpouring of hatred. A man can indeed be broken by such a traumatizing experience. At the time, I thought that his stance was perhaps not the most courageous one, but it was certainly understandable. After all, his cautious recognition of the reality of changes in some people with a homosexual orientation already represented an enormous about-face. He had been one of the leading figures of the lobby which in 1973 succeeded in normalizing the definition of homosexuality in the *Diagnostic Manual* of the American Psychiatric Association. Now the hero of the gay movement was marked as a Judas.[cx]

It just goes to show you how flippant gay activists are with their use of mental health and scientific data: They use it to achieve political purposes, but if it contradicts their goals, then they must kill the messenger. This "what have you done for me lately" attitude was, sadly, lost in the sensationalism of Spitzer's apology. Yet, to this day, the results of Spitzer's study still remain valid in the *Archives of Sexual Behavior*. While critics can point to Spitzer's apology, they cannot erase the data. The data speaks for itself.

The War in the "Mainstream" Medical and Mental Health
Community

A Task Force for This, a Task Force for That

It seems that if anyone wants to get something done
these days, the emperor must appoint a "task force" to do the
job. Apparently, Spitzer's study had created so much rank
and file hysteria at the APA, there needed to be a task force
to thoroughly study the problem of reparative therapy. After
all, we can't have these gays and lesbians going around
"changing" and such. That's not good for business! So, in
2007, the APA appointed a six-member task force—each
member of which was gay-identified, a gay advocate, or had
previously made position statements against "change
therapy."

At the outset of the task force, proponents of "change
therapy" were alarmed by the obvious bias and one-sided
ideological presence. For example, consider that the
following candidates applied to the APA to participate, but
were rejected:

- Dean Byrd, Ph.D., M.P.H., M.B.A., past
  president of the National Association for
  Research and Therapy of Homosexuality
  (NARTH) and distinguished professor at the
  University of Utah School of Medicine.
- George Rekers, Ph.D., professor of neuropsychiatry
  and behavioral science at the University of South
  Carolina and a National Institutes of Mental Health
  grant recipient.
- Stanton Jones, Ph.D., provost and dean of the
  graduate school and professor of Psychology at
  Wheaton College, Illinois, the coauthor of
  *Homosexuality: The Use of Scientific Research in
  the Church's Moral Debate.*
- Joseph Nicolosi, Ph.D. a founder of NARTH, (late)
  practitioner of reparative therapy for 25 years, and
  author of *Reparative Therapy of Male*

The War in the "Mainstream" Medical and Mental Health Community

Homosexuality and the 2009 book, *Shame and Attachment Loss.*

- Mark A. Yarhouse, Ph.D., professor of psychology, doctoral program in Clinical Psychology at Regent University in Virginia Beach, Virginia and coauthor of *Homosexuality: The Use of Scientific Research in the Church's Moral Debate.*

Instead, APA President Dr. Brehm appointed the following individuals, who again, were either gay-identified, advocates of gay-affirming therapy, or had previously made position statements against "conversion therapy":

- Judith M. Glassgold, Psy.D., chair of the task force. Board member of the *Journal of Gay and Lesbian Psychotherapy,* and past president of APA's Gay and Lesbian Division 44.
- Jack Drescher, M.D., a well-known gay-identified psychiatrist, editorial board member of the *Journal of Gay and Lesbian Psychotherapy,* and a vocal opponent of "conversion therapy."
- A. Lee Beckstead, Ph.D., psychologist who counsels LGBT-oriented clients. He is also a staff associate at the University of Utah's Counseling Center and although he believes reorientation therapy can sometimes be helpful, he has expressed strong skepticism, and has urged the Mormon Church to revise its policy on homosexuality and instead, affirm church members who believe homosexuality reflects their true identity.
- Beverly Greene, Ph.D., ABPP, founding co-editor of the APA Division 44 (gay and lesbian division) series, *Psychological Perspectives on Lesbian, Gay, and Bisexual Issues.*
- Robin Lin Miller, Ph.D., a community psychologist and associate professor at Michigan State

University. From 1990-1995, she worked for the
Gay Men's Health Crisis in New York City and has
written for gay publications.

- Roger L. Worthington, Ph.D., is the interim chief
diversity officer at the University of Missouri-
Columbia. In 2001 he was awarded the "2001
Catalyst Award" from the LGBT Resource Center,
University of Missouri, Columbia, for "speaking up
and out and often regarding LGBT issues."[cxi]

But surely, their sexual identities and biases would
not get in the way of their ability to report the science, right?
Unfortunately, the scales were tipped so far to the left, it was
nearly impossible for a fair outcome to be presented in this
report. In 2009, the long-awaited document was finally
published under the title *Report of the task force on
Appropriate Therapeutic Responses to Sexual Orientation.*[cxii] There were numerous problems. I coauthored a
commentary of the report in the *Journal of Human
Sexuality.*[cxiii] The summary listed many concerns:

- A failure to review and report all of the evidence.
For example, 34 psychoanalytic reports, involving
more than 500 patients who had undergone change
therapy, were dismissed as inadequate;

- Inconsistent application of standards for research.
For example, the task force used one standard to
criticize the research for change therapy studies, and
in some cases, cited other studies with the very
same (or similar) research limitations to make their
case for gay-affirming therapy;

- Different standards for gay affirmative approaches
than for change therapy. For example, the task force
did not demand a comparable standard for the
outcomes of gay affirmative psychotherapy as they

demanded for change therapy, yet reported gay-
affirming therapy the best form of treatment for
clients with sexual conflicts; and

- Inaccurate conclusions on harm. For example, the
authors stated that they found no study that
systematically evaluated potential harm. Yet, they
claimed that change therapy "can produce harm,"
which is anecdotal, not scientific. But since they
accepted anecdotal claims of harm for change
therapy, they should have also accepted anecdotal
claims of success of change therapy, which of
course, they did not.

What is abundantly clear about this report, and its
authors, was that objectivity was abandoned in favor of
political correctness. Had the APA sought a truly objective
outcome, it would have appointed a diverse panel of
scientists and clinicians with different ideological views and
perspectives.

But as is so often witnessed, "diversity" often has a
self-serving goal—to serve the interests of those who are in
the minority in order to further certain political objectives.
For example, as was stated above, one of the task force's
principal rationales for the creation of its report was that
advocates who opposed change therapy and those who
promoted change therapy asked for such a report. However,
when it came to assembling the task force, advocates who
were pre-opposed to change therapy were actually chosen to
be members of the task force, while no proponents of change
therapy were chosen.[cxiv]

Ramifications of the APA Task Force

The APA task force report, although nuanced to
some degree in its findings that sexual orientation is unlikely
to change and that there is insufficient evidence to conclude
that change therapy is safe or effective, nonetheless provided

a rubber stamp for gay activists and liberal elites to run wild with their own conclusions. Almost immediately after the APA Governing Board accepted its conclusions, the *Los Angeles Times* headlined: "Psychologists say sexual orientation *can't* [emphasis added] be changed through therapy."[cxv]

This type of embellishment is very common in the liberal media. For example, when Dr. Dean Hamer, a gay-identified scientist, published his famous genetic study on homosexuality in 1993, newspapers were quick to make conclusions. "Report Suggests Homosexuality Is Linked to Genes," said the *New York Times*.[cxvi] In actuality, Hamer commented in the study that he did *not* find a gay gene.

Like the APA task force report, the findings of sexual and gender identity scientific research are often complex and nuanced. But that doesn't sell newspapers, nor does it appeal to politicians, who often believe what their constituents and supporters tell them, regardless of the truth. So when gay activists began touting the APA task force report as definitive proof that change therapy is ineffective and harmful, politicians in far-left states believed them, regardless of the facts. What has resulted, as a consequence, is that 14 states, the District of Columbia, and over 45 major cities have enacted laws prohibiting change therapy (or what they dub "conversion therapy") for minors. In some jurisdictions, including Toledo, OH and New York City, change therapy for adults has also been outlawed in some way.[10]

---

[10] For example, as of late 2017 in New York City, it is now illegal to offer "conversion therapy" to minors and adults for a fee. However, members of the faith community or other non-licensed counselors can provide help for those who seek to change, providing they accept no financial compensation. Similarly, in 2018 the California legislature introduced a bill that would define all efforts to help a client change sexual orientation—whether minor or adult—as consumer fraud, subject to criminal penalty.

The irony is that no qualified licensed counselor has ever, or will ever, call their work "conversion therapy," nor will it ever appear as a diagnostic or CPT code for insurance reimbursement. Thus, "conversion therapy" ban laws have not protected LGBT youth because licensed mental health practitioners do not practice "conversion therapy" — especially the type of aversive and harmful practices that LGBT activists accuse licensed therapists of performing.

It is possible that unlicensed, rogue, religious extremists may do such things, but these "counselors" would not even be affected by "conversion therapy" ban laws because they already operate outside the regulation of state licensing boards. What these misguided laws have accomplished, however, is to prohibit or chill essential dialogue between licensed, ethical practitioners and their clients, to the detriment of both.

It has resulted in very little change of actual therapy practice among qualified, licensed mental health practitioners. In fact, this much has been recognized by those at the APA, including members of the 2009 APA task force. At the end of the book, I'll discuss this more and suggest practical steps that all clinicians can take to avoid confusing the general public, as well as how to properly inform clients about therapy outcomes, values, and how they can make choices regarding their sexual and gender identity. But first, I believe it's important to discuss a very recent study that surveyed the perceived outcomes of adolescents undergoing so-called "conversion therapy."

Parent-Initiated Sexual Orientation Change Efforts with LGBT Adolescents

When LGBT activists began lobbying politicians in 2012 to pass laws banning "conversion therapy" for minors, they had very little scientific evidence to back up their claims of harm and ineffectiveness. Most of their testimony in front of state legislatures was focused on anecdotal stories of "therapy torture" or relied on policy statements from medical and mental health trade associations condemning the practice of "gay-to-straight" therapy. The only peer-reviewed research they could cite was the 2009 APA Task Force (which did not find any outcome-based studies on adolescents undergoing SOCE) and a study published in 2009 on the negative health outcomes of LGB youth who experienced parental and family rejection.

Despite the fact that this 2009 study—published by San Francisco State University researcher Dr. Caitlin Ryan—did not survey therapeutic outcomes of LGBT youth (but rather, found that higher levels of family and parental rejection led to an increased risk of depression, suicidal ideation, illegal drug use, and unprotected sex) LGBT activists nonetheless inaccurately conflated its results with the so-called harms of "conversion therapy," despite the fact that this wasn't even a research variable in the study.

What these activists argued was that parental rejection of LGB youth was a sort of de-facto "conversion therapy," and therefore, the negative outcomes of these youth could be attributed as such. Unfortunately, this same type of logic was used in a 2018 study recently published by the same researcher, Dr. Caitlin Ryan, in her work with the Family Acceptance Project. The study, which reported the retrospective perceptions of adolescents ages 21–25, found that children whose parents tried to change their sexual orientation and/or sent them to therapists or religious leaders for "conversion interventions" had higher associations of depression, suicidal thoughts, suicidal attempts, less educational attainment, and less weekly income, than adolescents whose parents did not try to change them or send them to "conversion interventions."[cxvii]

There are many flaws and limitations in this study that should caution those who seek to come to conclusions on the associations it found:

The War in the "Mainstream" Medical and Mental Health Community

1) The study surveyed 245 self-identified LGBT adolescents, recruiting them from local bars, clubs, and community agencies. The adolescents had to have been open about their LGBT status to at least one parent during adolescence, with the criteria being that the parent(s), not the adolescent, initiate the "conversion intervention."

   - Critique #1: Client motivation, not parental motivation, is a large factor that may affect successful treatment. In this study, the motivation to change sexual orientation was entirely that of the parents, not the adolescent. Thus, negative and/or ineffective outcomes are hardly surprising. The authors actually excluded six participants who reported "conversion efforts" that were not initiated by parents. Therefore, the data does not measure the effectiveness or helpfulness of any intervention or effort by a self-motivated adolescent.

2) Youth in the study were self-identified as LGBT, a different population than adolescents who are questioning their sexual orientation/ gender identity or have unwanted same-sex attractions or gender identity conflicts.

   - Critique #2: The authors do not distinguish between these two populations and admit this in the limitations section of their study (they describe these adolescents as those who were unhappy with their LGBT identity or whose sexual orientation may have been more fluid). Adolescents that self-identify as LGBT may not be as motivated to seek assistance from therapists or even have as many conflicts around

103

their sexual orientation or gender identity as a
young person who is questioning or has
unwanted same-sex attractions or gender
identity conflicts.

3) The authors conflate religious counseling with
licensed therapy. They make no distinction between
counseling by a religious leader to convert or cure a
child and licensed mental health therapy with a
therapist trained in sexual and gender identity
providing ethical interventions.

- Critique #3: The authors made no distinction
between these approaches, nor did they ask
questions about the diverse outcomes of youth
that received religious counseling vs. licensed
ethical therapy vs. parental efforts to change
sexual orientation (the authors suggest these
efforts may include excluding LGBT children
from family events and activities to discourage,
deny, or minimize their identity; or using
religion to prevent or change their sexual
orientation).

4) The authors provided no evidence that the
adolescents actually received an intervention, nor
did they describe or provide a definition of a
"conversion intervention."

- Critique #4: Did the adolescent go to one
religious intervention or counseling session or
multiple mental health therapy sessions?
Perhaps they talked to their pastor or priest once
or twice. Is that "conversion therapy?" If so,
what was the name of the religious counselor or
licensed therapist who administered the

treatment? If the adolescent simply had a parent discourage their LGBT identity, can that really be considered an attempt to change a child's sexual orientation? The sample of adolescents and the vagueness of the treatment they received begs a basic research question: What were the authors actually studying? The nuanced and misuse of the words "conversion therapy" and "sexual orientation change effort therapy" in academia and the general public require a clearer definition of the subject matter being studied.

What is perhaps the most disappointing aspect of this study (as well as Ryan's previous study on family rejection and LGB adolescents), is that countless LGBT activists and LGBT media have incorrectly interpreted Dr. Ryan's research for political purposes. In a recent letter to the editor of the *Journal of Homosexuality*, Dr. Christopher Rosik expresses similar concerns when he states that Ryan et al.'s study "has clear political advocacy aims" and "is likely to be immediately adopted in the legislative efforts to prohibit SOCE" and therefore, the authors should "exercise restraint in order to not overstate the scientific implications of their work." Rosik continues:

Ryan et al. imply their research supports legislative and professional regulatory efforts to prohibit licensed therapists from assisting some religiously devout sexual minority clients in their self-determined goal of exploring sexual attraction and behavior fluidity. This is problematic on a number of fronts. Ryan et al. did not disentangle participants' perceptions of the effects of licensed therapists from that of unregulated and unaccountable religious leaders,

so it is impossible to rule out the common-sense
suspicion that negative effects were an outcome
far more attributable to the practices of the latter
group ... By limiting their sample to LGBT
identified young adults who self-identified in
adolescence and who did not report experiencing
any sexual orientation fluidity, the sample
excludes by definition those sexual minorities
who may have felt some benefit from religious
and professional experiences that could be
viewed as non-affirming. Thus, the nature of the
sample may overestimate harm. There is growing
evidence that constructs and conclusions derived
from LGBT-identified samples may not be easily
transferrable to non-LGBT identified sexual
minorities with primary religious identities.[cxviii]

Finally, while Dr. Ryan and her colleagues are clear
to state the limitations of "associations" vs. "causality" in
retrospective studies such as this, bias against SOCE therapy
is clearly evident throughout the study's discussion. For
example, the authors minimized any positive benefits in the
2003 Spitzer research, labeling the study "controversial,"
and failed to mention any recent SOCE therapy study that
has reported positive benefits, such as the 2007 Jones and
Yarhouse longitudinal study, or the 2018 Santero et al. study
that was published in the peer-reviewed literature months
prior. Clearly, Dr. Ryan and her colleagues were not
interested in discussing any positive reports of SOCE
therapy for adults or adolescents.

Efficacy and Harm of SOCE Therapy

For the purposes of ending this chapter, I think it's
important to recognize the fact that several researchers have
surveyed the efficacy of SOCE therapy, or therapeutic
efforts to help clients that seek healing, change, reduction,

and/or elimination of unwanted sexual and gender identity
conflicts (for adult clients).

While it is outside the scope of this book to include
such exhaustive or comprehensive reviews, it is appropriate
to mention these reviews.

Regarding the efficacy of SOCE, two documents
stand out as especially comprehensive:

Phelan, J., Whitehead, N., & Sutton, P.M. (2009). What
research shows: NARTH's response to the APA claims on
homosexuality: A report of the scientific advisory committee
of the National Association for Research and Therapy of
Homosexuality. *Journal of Human Sexuality, 1: 1−121.*
Available at: https://scinapse.io/papers/2182121567

Phelan, J. (2014). *Successful Outcomes of Sexual
Orientation Change Efforts (SOCE): An Annotated
Bibliography.* Available at:
https://www.amazon.com/Successful-Outcomes-Sexual-
Orientation-Efforts/dp/097797734X

Regarding the harmful outcomes of "conversion
therapy," there is not an exhaustive or comprehensive
bibliography yet published. My thanks to Dr. A. Lee
Beckstead for providing me an extensive bibliography that
can be viewed at Appendix B. Please note, I have included
only published reports in scientific, peer-reviewed literature
or academic books in this bibliography. For more
information on SOCE studies that include measures of harm,
see:

APA task force on Appropriate Therapeutic Responses to
Sexual Orientation. (2009). *Report of the task force on
Appropriate Therapeutic Responses to Sexual Orientation.*
Washington, DC: American Psychological Association.

Additionally, two academic documents were recently published on the fluidity of sexuality, sexual orientation, and gender identity that also discuss the efficacy of efforts to change sexual orientation and/or gender identity:

Tolman, D. & Diamond, L. (2014). *APA Handbook of Sexuality and Psychology,* Washington, DC: American Psychological Association. Available at: https://www.apa.org/pubs/books/4311512.aspx

National task force for Therapy Equality. (5/2/2017). *In Their Own Words—Lies, Deception, and Fraud: The Southern Poverty Law Center, Human Rights Campaign, and National Center for Lesbian Rights' Hate Campaign to Ban Psychotherapy for Individuals with Sexual and Gender Identity Conflicts*. Complaint to the Federal Trade Commission. Available at: http://www.therapyequality.org

CHAPTER 5
THE WAR IN THE MAINSTREAM MEDIA

Truth is not based on fact or reason. It's just what everyone agrees with.

~ *Wicked,* the musical

ॐ

It was a cold winter day in early February 2017 when I got a call from Alex Hosenball, associate editor of American Broadcasting Channel's (ABC) *20/20*. I remember the country's mood in these days very well. Two weeks earlier, Donald Trump had been inaugurated as the 45th President of the United States. The mainstream media was in disbelief over its huge miscalculation of the presidential election outcome. Hillary Clinton had lost, and lost BIGLY, as Trump would say. The American people had elected an outsider to the Oval Office, and reporters across the country were clamoring for any story that would make Trump and conservatives look bad. Brian Epstein, Hosenball's superior and one of *20/20's* main producers, wanted him to call me for background, and eventually, to schedule an interview for him to speak with me and appear on the ABC prime time show. The topic: "Gay conversion therapy" torture camps.[11]

It wasn't long into the conversation with Hosenball that I figured out his game. The story had already been

---

[11]Brian Ross, ABC's "chief investigative reporter" who did the "gay conversion therapy camp" story, is no longer with the network. He left in July 2018 (see https://www.latimes.com/business/hollywood/la-fi-ct-brian-ross-abc-20180702-story.html), a few months after being suspended (in December 2017), for inaccuracies in a report about President Trump's former national security advisor Michael Flynn. See https://www.hollywoodreporter.com/news/abc-news-suspends-brian-ross-four-weeks-michael-flynn-gaffe-1063780 for the full report on this.

written: "WATCH: Gay teen describes traumatizing experiences at gay conversion camps,"[cxix] read the promo video, published on March 6, just four days before the expose would air on ABC. Of course, I didn't know this at the time, but I suspected as much. This wasn't my first rodeo with the "gay conversion therapy camp" narrative. The timing was also curious—early February. Just about the time when most of the country's state legislatures start to convene their annual sessions, which typically only last for a few months. Yes, I had seen this pattern before. It's no accident that these types of stories tend to appear around the same time a couple of dozen of bills were to be introduced in liberal to moderate states across the country. So I humored Alex and went along with the charade.

"Do you practice 'gay conversion therapy'?" Alex asked.

"No, that is a term made up by gay activists to describe a practice to convert 'gay' youth to 'straight' against their will. I don't do that. I do work with clients who experience distress over their sexual or gender identity, but what you are describing is a practice that ethical, licensed therapists simply do not do," I answered back.

"I see…well, ABC's *20/20* has located several Christian 'gay conversion therapy camps' in the south, in an undercover investigation, and we are looking for licensed therapists who practice this to appear on our show." Alex said.

"I can almost guarantee that these 'therapists,' if these places actually exist, are not licensed, and I doubt they are actual therapists," I answered back.

"I can confirm they do, indeed, exist, and the therapists are *not* licensed," said Hosenball.

"Yeah, we've seen these stories before, and they are usually tall tales. If they do exist, they are never trained mental health professionals. And like I said, I don't do this work; it's unethical and wrong," I emphasized again.

Alex: "I see. Well, do you know any licensed therapists that do 'gay conversion therapy' and believe that homosexuality is morally wrong?"

I fired back: "Licensed, ethical mental health counselors don't do that. They don't make moral judgment statements to clients as you are insinuating. We work with clients and help them formulate their own goals, and we never shame them or tell them they are wrong for experiencing sexual attractions of any sort. I don't know any licensed counselors who do that; and if I did, I wouldn't be associated with them."

"Uh huh," said Alex. "Would you be able to speak with my producer, Brian Epstein, over the phone about your work?" Alex questioned.

After that conversation, I exchanged several e-mails with Alex, in one of which I asked for the source of the supposed "gay conversion therapy camps" he referenced. Below is a short back-and-forth exchange, as Alex was trying to arrange a phone call between me and Brian Epstein:

From: cxxxx@instituteforxxxxxxxx.org
Sent: Friday, February 03, 2017 4:15:34 pm

To: Hosenball, Alex R.
Subject: [FWD: Call with ABC News Producer Brian Epstein]

Monday would theoretically work, but I've only got 10-minute time slots all day (at the end of each hour) as I'm back to back with clients from 9-5 p.m. and then 7-9 p.m. at night. If ten minutes works, I could do it. If he needs more time, he could call me at 8:30 a.m. on my way to work and we can chat for about 20 minutes. My cell is: XXX-XXX-XXXX. As a follow-up to our conversation, is this the story of abuse you referred to on our call?

http://www.al.com/news/birmingham/index.ssf/2017/01/three_convicted_for_child_abus.html

Sincerely,
Christopher Doyle, MA, LPC, LCPC

Subject: Re: [FWD: Call with ABC News Producer Brian Epstein]
From: Hosenball, Alex R.
Axxxxxxxxl@abc.com
Sent: Sun, Feb 05, 2017 4:59 pm
To: cxxxx@instituteforxxxxxxx.org

Hi Christopher,

Yes, that is the story I was referring to on the call. Sorry for the delay in reply—would tomorrow at about 12:50 PM or 1:50 PM be alright for you, do you think?

That call from Brian Epstein never did come. In fact, it wasn't until Tuesday, March 7 that I *did* get a call from Epstein. This time, the phone call wasn't for inclusion in *20/20*, but in response to my threat to issue a press release denouncing the ABC producer's unethical reporting in advance of the show on Friday night. The conversation Brian and I had was less than cordial. I called him out on his bias and lack of intellectual honesty in reporting. In the promo video and article posted on the ABC website on Monday, March 6 in advance of *20/20* that Friday night, it read: "Gay conversion therapy advocates heartened by Republican electoral victories."

> Advocates of long-discredited gay conversion therapy programs say they are heartened by the election of Donald Trump and are counting on Vice President Mike Pence and congressional Republicans to help fight off efforts to make such programs illegal ... Conversion therapy has been outlawed for licensed mental health providers in California, Oregon, New Jersey, Vermont, Illinois, and the District of Colombia, according to the Human Rights Campaign, an LGBT advocacy group ... The "20/20" report includes revelations of two programs that conducted conversion therapy in Alabama, including one in which Christian pastors overseeing dozens of teens were convicted of child abuse amid stark allegations of beatings administered to teens who resisted efforts to change their sexual orientation. The camps practicing conversion therapy uncovered by the "20/20" investigation were not operating as licensed mental health facilities and are therefore not covered by laws prohibiting the practice.[cxx]

A look at the second promo video later in the story depicted a harrowing portrayal of a "gay conversion therapy torture" camp, with red lighting to insinuate blood and torture. The photo in the video appears to be something out of haunted house (see Figure 5.1, which though reproduced here in black and white, actually depicts a blood-red set).

Figure 5.1: The Set for *2020*'s Scare Piece on "Conversion Therapy"

What Epstein and ABC were doing in the program was an intentional conflating of an unethical, illegal practice considered by many to be dangerous, with licensed, ethical therapy that abides by state regulations and ethics. It was not only inaccurate, but irresponsible. When I presented this to Epstein, and then asked him why he didn't include a licensed therapist on the program to explain what licensed therapy actually is (and is not), his response was:

> "This program is not about therapy, it's about child abuse."

> "Then, why is ABC conflating the two together?" I asked?

Of course, he couldn't respond because there was no good response, and unfortunately, there is little account-ability for reporters and large, conglomerate news agencies like ABC. "Gay conversion" therapy is one of those issues that liberals take pride in uniting against. On its face, it would seem unlikely for any liberal to oppose the banning of such a practice—after all, why would it be necessary, or desirable, to convert a vulnerable teenager from gay to straight? Why would our egalitarian, tolerant, and compassionate society want to send a message to *any* teen that their sexual orientation is wrong and needs changing? Phrased that way, and when you add in the stories of "electroshock" and other "torturous" therapies that highly educated, licensed therapists are supposedly doing to these youth across the country, it seems like a slam dunk liberal cause. Now we can all join hands, sing *Kumbaya*, and get behind it, right?

The expose did air that Friday night on ABC, to echoes of cheers among liberals in their snowflake echo chambers. It prompted me to write an opinion editorial the following week in *The Christian Post*:

> In the first minute (of the broadcast), the commentator mentioned that five states have banned licensed counselors from engaging in "gay conversion therapy" with another 20 considering legislation this year. The show then quickly jumps to several sensational stories of desperate parents who send their children, some of whom are gay and lesbian identified, to reform schools that work with a variety of youth who display oppositional behaviors. But none of these schools were "gay conversion therapy" camps with licensed therapists. The scenes at these schools were horrific. Experiences were

115

described where "pastors" intimidated gay youth with the "Bible or the belt" and in some cases, locked them up in small, isolated rooms for hours or days at a time as punishment for non-conformity. Let's be very clear: this is not acceptable; this is not justifiable in any circumstance; and this is *not* therapy. The fact that *20/20* did not even show or discuss professional therapy by licensed therapists, which is about healing and emotional change, is irresponsible journalism. It's fake news! ABC is playing a sick, bait and switch game with the public. They report a story of abuse by unlicensed, untrained "counselors" abusing gay youth, and then subtly mention it alongside licensed therapy without clearly distinguishing between the two practices. This is a psychological technique called "jamming." The media compares something legal, like licensed, ethical therapy, to something illegal or unethical such as unlicensed abuse in rogue camps, and then ties them together without clearly distinguishing between the two. The problem is that what was shown on *20/20* was not therapy at all. Licensed, ethical therapists do not force or coerce teenagers to change, nor do they manipulate desperate parents to send their kids away to be reformed.[cxxi]

There was one more major problem with the *20/20* story that probably went unnoticed by the average viewer. In their *Tony Perkins' Washington Update,* the Family Research Council described troubling aspects of ABC's reporting. [It]:

. . . focused primarily on two unregulated, unaccredited boarding schools (not "camps") in Alabama, and the personal testimony of one self-identified gay teenager named Lucas who told Ross he had the misfortune of being physically beaten at both of them. (In fact, the hour-long episode depended so much on this single personal testimony that it was titled, "A Boy Named Lucas."). Despite ABC's breathless commentary, this was hardly breaking news. Alabama media have had many reports on these schools, and the three leaders of one facility were recently convicted and sentenced to 20 years in prison for child abuse. However, if you listened very closely, you would have noticed that, even on *20/20*, neither the police investigator, the prosecutor, nor the judge *ever mentioned sexual orientation as being a factor in the abuse.* Nor did half a dozen local news reports, adding up to thousands of words ... ABC presented no evidence that the percentage of the "troubled youth" in these facilities *who identified as "gay"* was any larger than the percentage in the general population who do so. That's why FRC's Peter Sprigg, who gamely attempted to inject some reason and accuracy during his interview with *20/20*, stands by his belief that the idea of a shadowy network of "camps" focused primarily on forced "conversion therapy" for youth is largely a myth.[cxxii]

A Familiar Pattern, a Complicit Media

In the discussion above, I mentioned a familiar pattern I began to notice in 2013-2014. Media stories of "therapy torture" would suddenly begin to appear, in large measure, around January/February/March, right at the height of the political season on the state level. Coincidence? I think not. Not only were the media reporting supposedly true stories of "therapy torture," but they were also beginning to manufacture authentic fictitious accounts in situational dramas on mainstream television. Take for example, the popular television show on CBS called *Criminal Minds.*

The February 20, 2013 episode followed a team of FBI investigators tracking a serial killer who is murdering women and gay men in a series of sex crimes. Titled *Broken*, it quickly became defamatory when investigators discovered that the killer attended a "conversion therapy camp" as a teenager to overcome same-sex attractions. What is even more disturbing is how CBS portrays the motives of the killer.

Due to his Christian upbringing, the Bible's scriptures on homosexuality are the key force behind the killer's violence (according to the FBI investigators). The FBI traces the time of the killings, 6:22 p.m., to a passage in the Old Testament/Torah book: "Thou shalt not lie with mankind, as with womankind: it is abomination" (Leviticus 18:22).

> "He converted 18:22 to 6:22 p.m., like military time ... it wouldn't be the first time someone took the good book and twisted it for his own agenda," says the FBI agent.

The scene then changes to a flashback in which the teenage serial killer is confessing his attraction for another school boy to his father, who is outraged, refusing to accept his son's homosexual feelings. Investigators then comment:

> "This man can't accept his same-sex desires, but he can't fight them either. He's most likely been repressing all sexual urges for quite some time ... but he's trapped in a scenario with an impossible

outcome. He can't force himself to like women, so when he's unable to get aroused he becomes depressed again and lashes out in anger to the people he blames for his impotence. The circular logic dictating his never-ending cycle was not formed overnight, it most likely came about from years of serious abuse, either emotional, physical, or both."

The scene then flashes back to the father, trying to force his son to have sex with a prostitute in order to make him a "real man," presumably to rid the boy of homosexual feelings. The investigators then instruct the other FBI agents searching for the killer:

"The most popular motive for trying to overcome same-sex attraction is the need to be accepted by the parent or loved one who has rejected the individual because of his or her homosexuality. So focus on men who grew up in a broken home, who suffered under the guardianship of a domineering parent as well as those who fell victim to bigotry or bullying."

As the plot unfolds, it appears that a "conversion therapy camp" makes the killer believe that acting on his homosexuality is wrong, which causes him to repress his sexual urges, and ultimately, resort to violently attacking people due to these conflicts. During the episode, CBS portrays therapists and ministries that seek to help persons with unwanted same-sex attractions to be child abusing religious cults, capitalizing on the fears of homophobic parents with gay children. Speaking with the so-called "conversion camp" director, the FBI remarks:

"There doesn't seem to be much room for self-expression," comments the FBI agent.

"We try to keep things as uniform as possible. We're not trying to stifle them; it's just that progressive behavior can unravel their recovery efforts," comments the camp director.

"Such as colors?" Asks the FBI agent.

"Earth tones such as brown or tan are the go-to, navy blue if the color doesn't fade or become too bright," comments the camp director.

"Because light blue would be too feminine…"

"Exactly!" Comments the camp director.

The camp director then explains that the "therapy" has participants partake in masculine activities, such as auto work, to reinforce traditional gender roles. For participants who do not follow the rules, "enhanced therapeutic methods" are used.

Stranger Than Fiction

Criminal Minds wasn't the first, or the last time, that gay activists have presented fiction as real life. Take, for example, a 2017 novel by Nick White called *How to Survive a Summer*, which tells the tale of a homosexual young man sent away to "pray away his malady at gay conversion therapy camp" in the Deep South. White's debut novel was smothered in praise by the *Washington Post*, which revels in telling the long-repressed tale of the main character in the novel:

> "In the summer of 1999, when I was fifteen years old, I spent almost four weeks at a camp that was supposed to cure me of my homosexuality," says Will 'Rooster' Dillard. He's a grudgingly self-accepting gay student at a Midwestern university

who seems to have repressed some of the worst things that happened in that long-ago summer ... Choking under the pressure of recovered memory, Will jumps in his old car and embarks on a going-back-to-face-my-past road trip to end all road trips. What ensues is a plunge into deeper, darker layers of Will's personal history, with the slow revelation of cruelties and perversions.

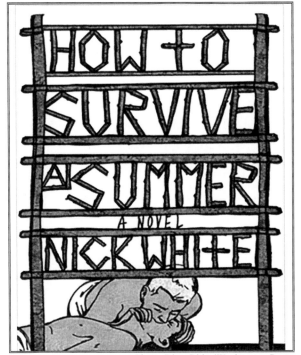

Photo: Blue Rider/*Washington Post*
Figure 5.2: Cover of *How to Survive a Summer*

The *Washington Post* review describes Dillard's religious and repressed family's attempt to discourage his homosexuality through homophobic shame, only to then compare the fictitious account to real, professional psychotherapy, all in the name of art and gay liberation:

All that grit and local color undermines some of the genuine trauma of the gay conversion experience, which in real life has been denounced, discredited and, in some locales, outlawed. But therein lies the novel's savvy: it adheres to a gay aesthetic tradition in which even the darkest subject matter isn't too dark to be played for camp ... But in keeping with another gay literary tradition, there is an abiding sorrow, a ruefulness, underneath the histrionics. We learn that Will has been abandoned by a previous boyfriend seeking "someone more open to something more real." Will tells us, "I knew what he had meant. I'd heard it all before from the men who found themselves in my bed for longer than a night ... They spotted the trouble and sooner or later they were gone." He is still too injured by his past experience to give of himself completely.

So, there you have it. Will's trauma of "gay conversion therapy camp" is the reason why he is unable to successfully attach to, and keep, a boyfriend. You would think with all of that drama playing out in camp over four weeks, that the boys would have found some time to exchange contact information and "experiment" with each other after the camp was over. But I suppose the initial outcome of "turning straight" in four weeks may have had a halo effect for at least some of the "gay conversion" therapy success stories.[cxxiii]

So Tonight I'm Gonna Party Like It's 1999

Do you remember where you were in 1999? How about New Year's Eve, when we all collectively held our breath to see if any of us would spontaneously combust or disappear with all of the craze about Y2K?[12] As it turned out, we did not disappear (thankfully) and civilization continued on as normal. However, it seems the year 1999 was a very bad year for LGBT youth, thousands of whom were apparently sent to "gay conversion therapy camps" all over the country that summer. But no "gay conversion camp" rivals the one that transgender activist Brielle Goldani was sent to just a couple of years earlier:

> "Twice a week I was hooked up to electrodes on my hands," she said. "I, a child, was shocked repeatedly by people who had my parent's permission to torture me." Goldani, now 29, claims that she had no rights when her parents sent her away as a male teenager. She claims that the torture occurred at conversion camp called True Directions. "This is nothing more than legalized child abuse!"

Having attended and testified at the hearing myself, I was shocked and horrified to hear about such abuse. As a former same-sex attracted man, and a licensed psycho-therapist, I had never heard of such inhumane treatment, except from anti-ex-gay activists who often claim that [therapy] employs such barbaric methods. So I tracked down Goldani and talked to her on the phone to get more information. Goldani claimed that an Assemblies of God

---

[12] For those readers too young to understand this reference, Y2K was a hysterical attempt by the media to make the general public believe that because computers were coded to read two-digit years only (i.e., 72 or 85, as in 1972 or 1985), this would somehow cause the world to end at 12:00am on January 1, 2000, since computers would have to be converted to now read four-digit years, a detail overlooked by computer program developers in the late 20th century. By the way, if you didn't get the Y2K reference, you probably also didn't get the "1999" subtitle reference, which comes from a 1982 song by Prince called *1999*.

Church in Columbus, Ohio, ran the True Directions conversion therapy camp:

> There were 12 boys, and 12 girls. The first Sunday I was there, I was forced to sit in their church service, which was nothing but hate speech. Then, on Monday, the heavier therapy began. We were forced to masturbate to hetero-sexual images and soft-core pornography, such as *Sports Illustrated* swimsuit models. Twice a week, my hands were hooked up to electrodes for two hours at a time while we were shown positive images such as a nuclear family, a female with children, a male construction worker and a female receptionist. I was also subjected to forced IV injections twice a week for two hours each while being made to watch negative images of what they didn't approve of ... The injections made me vomit uncontrollably. Every Friday and Saturday evening, we were forced to go on 'flirting dates' where a camp counselor coached us on how to talk to the opposite sex roman-tically... We were also given uniforms to wear, black pants and white shirts for boys, black skirts and white blouses for girls.

Sounds pretty horrible, right? What "Christian" church or therapist would use such barbaric, violent treatments? In a phone interview, the Rev. John Wooton, superintendent of the Ohio Council of Assemblies of God Churches, denied that any such program exists or has ever existed in their church, as Goldani claimed. But if such an abusive camp did exist, surely a participant or parent would have filed ethics complaints long ago. Surely, the Ohio legal authorities would have put an end to this abuse!

But according to the office of the Ohio secretary of state and attorney general, no such camp called True Directions had ever existed. In fact, the only trace of this camp is from a 1999 film called *But I'm a Cheerleader*, starring drag queen RuPaul. In the film, the main character is suspected of being a lesbian by her family, which then proceeds to send her to a "conversion therapy" camp called True Directions.

Throughout the course of the film, two disgruntled gay men encourage the campers to rebel against the program and discover their true identities as gays and lesbians. The final scene of the film shows the main character's parents attending a Parents and Friends of Lesbians and Gays (PFLAG) meeting to accept their daughter's homosexuality.

When asked if such a camp exists, Dr. Elton Moose, a licensed counselor who has been working in Springfield, Ohio, said in a written statement: "I have been in this business for 24 years and have not heard of this camp ... These types of shock-therapy accusations have been around for many years, but I have not actually known a practice that has used this therapy."

Goldani, who worked as a "peer specialist" and "mental health counselor," claimed that the church she attended as a teenager in New Jersey, paid for her to attend the camp, which lasted a month and a half. Goldani also claimed to have been counseled by the pastor of the church on staff at the time, which included talking, reading Bible verses, and listening to statistics about HIV/AIDS. The church's current leader, Pastor Lou LaFauzia, whose church is affiliated with the Reformed Church of America, said in a phone interview: "We love everyone regardless of sexual orientation ... I can say that this would have never happened at this church, and I can't imagine any church members in 1997 who would do this. It's outlandish!"[cxxiv]

What About Police Reports and Ethical Complaints?

The question that immediately comes to mind for a person with any common sense is: Where's the proof? I suppose, however, that ideological politicians beholden to special interests don't really need to consider this in the face of sensational stories of "gay conversion therapy torture" heard in legislature committee hearings across the United States and beyond. Let's just assume that a child was tortured, or harmed, or even worse, murdered, at a "gay conversion therapy camp." Wouldn't there be a police report recorded or an ethics complaint filed with the state licensure board?

In 2016, one of the more shocking tales of "therapy torture" was told by Matthew Shurka, a prominent spokesperson for the National Center for Lesbian Right's (NCLR) *#BornPerfect* campaign. During a late January committee hearing in the Commonwealth of Virginia, Shurka (who allegedly went through "ex-gay therapy" from the ages of 16-21) testified to the following, according to an article in a Richmond-based gay activist newspaper:

> "I was in camp in Charlottesville," he said about a short stint in a conversion therapy camp called Journey Into Manhood located about 50 miles outside of the city. "Not everyone walked out alive." Shurka has been involved in fighting ex-gay therapy since he abandoned the treatment, and he is unafraid to share some of the darker parts of his treatment, including "masturbation therapy" and being kept from his mother and sister for three years to avoid picking up feminine traits. He said folks like himself entered the treatments believing they could change, hoping to please their family and/or their faith, and were emotionally destroyed when they failed. "Every week someone is committing suicide or over-

dosing on drugs because they know they can't succeed."[cxxv]

Perhaps the most disturbing part of Shurka's testimony is that no one, not even the press, asked him why he didn't report the so-called "deaths" that occurred during his experience with Journey Into Manhood. Surely, if a crime, suicide, or homicide had occurred, a police report would have been filed. Yet, these stories continue to be recorded as testimony in front of state legislatures and printed in gay activist media outlets.

Let Us Teach You How to Speak (and Think)

The war in the mainstream media is being fueled, in large part, by the overwhelming influence and power of the gay lobby. Equality and fairness in the media towards the LGBT community has gone from lobbying the major cable TV networks and Hollywood industry for positive portrayals of gay characters in mainstream entertainment to downright indoctrination. It is no longer good enough to portray the LGBT community in a positive light—instead, they must paint all those who oppose the gay lifestyle, including those individuals with unwanted same-sex attractions and gender confusion and the therapists and counselors who assist them—as monsters, fueled by religious extremism, animus, or internalized homophobia.

Organizations such as the Gay and Lesbian Alliance Against Defamation (GLAAD) not only promote the gay agenda, but also seek to silence any person or organization that speaks out against LGBT practice. This includes providing talking points and reference guides for the media when they discuss the subject of therapy for sexual minorities on TV or in the movies.

For example, GLAAD has produced media talking points on their website titled: "GLAAD Media Reference

Guide—In Focus: Conversion Therapy." Some of the highlights include the following:

*Distorting and misquoting research from the
"mainstream" mental and medical health associations:*

> The American Psychiatric Association has condemned the 'treatment' of 'homosexuality,' saying, 'The potential risks of 'reparative therapy' are great, including depression, anxiety and self-destructive behavior, since therapist alignment with societal prejudices against homo-sexuality may reinforce self-hatred already experienced by the patient.'

> In 2009, a task force of the American Psycho-logical Association drafted a landmark report on Appropriate Therapeutic Responses to Sexual Orientation. Following a comprehensive analysis of peer-reviewed research on what the APA labeled 'sexual orientation change efforts (SOCE)' the APA 'concluded that efforts to change sexual orientation are unlikely to be successful and involve some risk of harm, contrary to the claims of SOCE practitioners and advocates.' The APA's governing body adopted the report''s recommendations by an overwhelm-ing 125–4 vote. In addition, the American Medical Association, the National Mental Health Association, and the American Academy of Pediatrics have also spoken out against these attempts to 'cure' lesbian, gay men and bisexual people.

It is important to note that licensed practitioners working with clients distressed over unwanted sexual and

128

gender identity conflicts do not use terms such as "cure" or "treatment" of homosexuality. Typically, counselors work on identifying with clients the underlying causes for their unwanted attractions and seek to help them resolve those issues. However, since GLAAD and other media bullies would have you believe people are born gay, they fail to mention exactly what counselors do, and instead like to paint a picture of ignorant, uneducated bigots using barbaric and outdated practices such as electroshock therapy or spiritual interventions such as prayer or exorcism.

Talking points on appropriate terminology for media hosts:

> In reporting, the terms "conversion therapy" or "reparative therapy" should be placed in quotation marks or avoided altogether, as the terms are most often used to insinuate that people attracted to the same sex, or who are transgender, are "disordered" or "broken" and need to be "repaired." It is usually best simply to describe the actions and motivations of those who seek to change the orientation of people attracted to the same sex and/or someone's gender identity.

What is simply amazing in this paragraph is the assumptions made by GLAAD. How would they presume to know what the motivations of licensed mental health counselors are, and what business is it of theirs? If a client seeks out therapy from a qualified practitioner and appropriate informed consent occurs, the only motivation that matters is the client's motivation, which varies and is certainly not uniform. It's a private matter between client and therapist. Imagine GLAAD's response if one dared to question the motivation of a doctor performing an abortion, or better yet, a gender reassignment surgery. They would label you a narrow-minded, flat-earther who is on the wrong side of history! After all, the patient has a right to his or her own body, right? If they wish to work through sexual or gender identity conflicts, apparently not!

Conversion Therapy Survivors:

> Any story about "conversion therapy" programs should include the perspective of those who survived it. For each "success story" featured by "conversion therapy" activists, there are hundreds who have gone through the programs with no change in orientation or gender identity, but who have suffered trauma, depression, even suicidal thoughts or actions.[cxxvi]

While GLAAD is happy to publish a general guideline to the media on how to portray "conversion therapy," there are additional tactics I have noticed throughout the years that make it nearly impossible for therapists and individuals with unwanted same-sex attractions to get a fair shake in the mainstream media. First, the majority of stories that are written about so-called "conversion therapy" are done by gay journalists, often with an axe to grind. Even if the gay journalist never had an experience in change therapy, they often come to the story with what researchers call "confirmation bias," that is a pre-conceived set of assumptions they have adopted before the story is written.

For example, in my many interviews and dealings with the mainstream media, I have observed that the story had been written even before I was interviewed. The reporter already had reached a conclusion before contacting me. This is especially troubling, because the stories written about "conversion therapy bans" are typically presented as hard news. They are in fact opinion pieces by gay journalists peddled as objective reporting. It is typical for "conversion therapy torture" stories to get a lot of press at the height of the state legislative season—in February or March—when most of the bills are going to be heard in committee. This is an attempt by gay activists to "saturate" the market with indoctrination, hoping this will seep into the committee room and sway the opinions of politicians, most of whom have very little time to actually investigate whether the claims by gay activists are true.

Another tactic, which will be explored in Chapter 6, is called bait and switch. It goes like this:

> Mike Jones was a sensitive, artistic young man when he came out as gay to his religious parents at the age of 13. Alarmed by their son's homosexuality, Mike's parents subjected him to three years of electroshock "gay conversion therapy" with a licensed therapist. The "therapy" traumatized Mike, and when it didn't work, Mike's parents kicked him out of the house for not trying hard enough.

This is common media balderdash. Usually a liberal news outlet such as *The Huffington Post* will feature a story of a gay activist who claims to have been subject to some kind of "gay conversion" torture in a church basement. Yet, when I have contacted the reporter to ask for specific details of the story; for example, the name of the so-called "licensed therapist" and or the location or the church or counseling center, my e-mail has never been answered. What usually follows is the retelling of this "gay conversion torture" story in a state legislative committee hearing by a gay activist— and if a clever legislator asks the activist for specific details of who did what, where, and how, suddenly the activist has temporary amnesia and cannot remember the details of how this happened, to whom, and when.

Then, we see the use of an astonishingly dishonest tactic: the Bait and Switch method. Another witness will follow the sensational story and say: "Even if the counselor is not using aversion torture therapy, conversion talk therapy can be just as harmful… the therapy is based on stereotypes, outdated practices, debunked theories, and harmful ideology. We shouldn't just ban aversion therapy—but all therapy." Notice the bait and switch? Even if the gay activists cannot prove that therapy torture actually occurred, they have just distracted you with a tall tale that is shocking, that may or may not be verified, and sounds almost believable. By the way, the witness testifying often cries or is very theatrical, a further distraction in their questionable testimony.

Another common tactic, similar to the Bait and Switch method is the human-interest story. The typical pattern is this:

> Gay advocates applaud Rep. Bleeding Heart Liberal, who recently introduced a bill that will prohibit harmful "conversion therapy" for gay youth in (insert liberal state or city). Rep. Bleeding Heart Liberal was prompted to introduce the legislation after being contacted by his constituent, token gay activist, who underwent years of torture at the hands of his church counselor, who weekly prayed that the demon of homosexuality would leave his body. Token gay activist says he was so traumatized by the therapy that he cannot remember the name of the counselor, who is also licensed in (insert liberal state), but is sure his parents paid for his weekly "conversion" sessions. Token gay activist is now working with state leaders to outlaw the harmful practice so that others can be saved from such abuse.

This type of story will be released just before the therapy ban gets introduced in whatever body in which it is to come up for consideration. The newspaper will never verify the report. The gay activist will never be challenged. No accountability for the reporter or media outlet will be provided. Large, well-funded gay activist organizations are, no doubt, working behind the scenes to orchestrate these stories while working with sympathetic "journalists" and media outlets that are eager to cooperate with the anti-therapy agenda.

In fact, a February 13, 2018 blog post by Media Matters, a far-left media "watchdog" proves as much. The article, deceptively titled: "How journalists can avoid spreading misinformation about anti-LGBTQ conversion therapy"[cxxvii] discusses a number of ways that media outlets and journalists should and should not frame stories about so-called "conversion therapy." Among the many "tips" in the Media Matters article are the following:

- **Avoid suggesting that the most extreme forms of conversion therapy are the only practices that are harmful.** "There are a range of practices that fall under the umbrella of conversion therapy, from talk therapy to shock and aversion treatments, all of which are considered harmful. In their coverage of conversion therapy, jour-nalists must resist pushing misinformation such as saying that the practice is harmless when it does not involve shock treatment or other blatantly physically harmful practices."

- **Note that major medical associations have found no scientific validity for conversion therapy and that sexuality and gender identity cannot be forcibly changed.** "Reporters cover-ing efforts to protect LGBTQ youth from conversion therapy should always include that the practice has been debunked and rejected by all major medical associations as ineffective, harmful, and unscientific and that sexuality and gender identity cannot be forcibly changed."

- **Include that conversion therapy has a myriad of harmful side effects, including suicidal ideation.** "Journalists have a responsibility to educate the public not just about the ineffectiveness of conversion therapy but also its harmful side effects and universal condemnation from major medical associations. According to HRC, 'every major medical and mental health organization in the United States has issued a statement condemning the use of conversion therapy because 'there is significant anecdotal evidence of harm to LGBTQ people resulting from attempts to change their sexual orientation and gender identity.'"

- **Don't uncritically feature conversion therapy proponents, who often distort facts and spread misinformation.** "Media sometimes fall into the trap of providing a platform for conversion therapy proponents to spread misinformation about the practice, and outlets often fail to contextualize those figures' affiliations and backgrounds. Journalists should resist allowing these proponents to spew misinformation in an attempt to show 'both sides' of the story, particularly as the practice has been opposed by all major medical organizations."

- **Include personal narratives of LGBTQ people and conversion therapy survivors when**

possible to add important context and reinforce medical consensus on the practice's harm. "Survivors should never be forced to relive their traumatic experiences with conversion therapy to a reporter or the public; however, outlets should make space for survivors who are ready and willing to share their experiences or for LGBTQ individuals who understand the risk it poses to their community. For example, AZCentral's report on a recently introduced bill in the states of Arizona featured comments by Sam Brinton, a survivor and advocate who works with the Trevor Project. The report noted that Brinton, who uses the gender-neutral pronoun they, experienced post-traumatic stress disorder after undergoing conversion therapy and quoted them saying that 'we need to be addressing this' problem in order 'to stop LGBT youth from dying by suicide.'"

Far left-advocacy groups and gay activists are so afraid that professional therapists may come across as credible or be given a platform for their work, that they discourage honest questions and honest answers. Instead, they demand to frame the issue only one way: Any type of therapy open to fluidity or change is harmful, and journalists must present it this way or else they are contributing to the torture and abuse of LGBT people. It's interesting that Media Matters fails to mention that aversion techniques such as electroshock therapy haven't been used to treat homosexuality for well over 50 years, yet they put it in the same category of "harm" as talk therapy. They go on to state that sexuality and gender identity cannot be "forcibly changed" yet conveniently forget to mention the many individuals who have voluntarily experienced change, with or without therapy![cxxviii] Finally, Media Matters instructs journalists not to give a platform for therapy proponents, while encouraging them to feature discredited gay activists, such as Sam Brinton! So much for objective reporting!

Coming to a Theater Near You

By the time you read this book, two full-length movies will have been released featuring the experiences of teenagers sent to the Love in Action intensive program for LGBT-identified youth to get "cured."

Love in Action was originally co-founded in northern California by the late Frank Worthen (considered by many to be the father of the ex-gay movement), and later moved its operations to Tennessee. In 2005, the residential program for teens became embroiled in a legal battle with the state over allegations of child abuse.[cxxix] In the aftermath of the investigation, Love in Action sued the state of Tennessee for discrimination. The case was eventually settled out of court with the judgment ordering the state to pay legal fees to the residential program, allowing it to stay open with the condition that it not prescribe, administer, or regulate medication to its clients.[cxxx]

One of the films based on the Love in Action controversial program is historical fiction, while the other is based on a memoir of a former client.

The first movie, released on August 3, 2018, is called *The Miseducation of Cameron Post* and tells the story of 12-year-old Cameron, who begins to feel homosexual feelings in the aftermath of her parents' traumatic death in a car crash. As a result, her grandmother and conservative aunt come to live with her in Montana, and Cameron is subsequently outed to her family after she starts to engage in a lesbian relationship. She is then sent to Love in Action (in the movie, it's called God's Promise) a residential program that conducts "gay to straight" therapy. But Cameron resists, refusing to go along with the camp's teaching of traditional gender roles and Christian sexuality.

The 2017 Sun Dance Film Festival awarded the film its Grand Jury Prize.[cxxxi] *The Atlantic* magazine opined:

> Cameron's hero's journey is that she doesn't need to change—yet [film director] Akhavan still conjures a real sense of growth from her stasis, crafting a narrative about teenage rationality in the face of extremism, and making its pivot point the realization that the grown-ups around Cameron are even less self-assured than her (*sic*). Much of the movie has a warm, surprisingly gentle summer-camp vibe considering the searing subject matter; it's less interested in active rebellion and more in Cameron understanding her own emotional well-being. It's a queer narrative that thrives on its low-key ordinariness, and that casts some of its villains as naive and tragic rather than malevolent.[cxxxii]

The second film based on Love in Action was released on November 2, 2018. The Focus Features production is a "coming-of-age" drama starring Russell Crowe and Nicole Kidman called *Boy Erased.* Based on the memoir of the same title, the film tells the story of the son of a Baptist preacher who is outed to his parents (Crowe and Kidman) at the age of 19 and forced (or pressured) into a two-week "gay conversion" program called Love in Action. Garrard Conley, the protagonist in the film, recounts being told that his sexual attractions were "unfixable" and "disgusting" over and over in the program.[cxxxiii] Needless to say, if Conley's experience with counseling is actually true, this is horrible. Shaming of this nature is not only ineffective, but is also harmful and not a practice any trained therapist would use to help a client overcome any issue, sexual or otherwise.

In 2008, the long-time director of Love in Action, John Smid, stepped down from leadership, and a couple of years later apologized to the teens he "further wounded" that "were already in a very delicate place in life."[cxxxiv] He later revealed in 2011 that he was still gay and is now married to his partner, Larry. Smid is portrayed in the film as "Victor Skykes" and played by the film's director and co-writer, Joel Edgerton. In an exclusive "first look" review of the film, *Entertainment* film critic Piya Sinha-Roy described the way Jared's parents, portrayed by Crowe and Kidman, played their parts, and how director Edgerton, portrayed them:

> Kidman wanted to bring love rather than maliciousness to the role of Nancy. "The way in which she and her husband feel about putting [Jared] into conversion therapy, I wanted that to come from a place of a mother thinking it's the right thing to do. Nothing that she did was vindictive, which is probably why they have such a strong relationship now" ... Edgerton says he hopes he's conveyed each person in the film the way he says Conley did on the page, "with a lot of empathy and compassion. My approach and treatment of this story was that there were no villains, that everyone thought they were doing the right thing."[cxxxv]

Considering past allegations of abuse, along with Smid's questionable behavior in his role as director, which had to have presented quite a conflict for his own unresolved homosexual attractions, one has to wonder how ethically the staff were treating youth at this program, and if any of the counselors were even licensed? According to the state of Tennessee, the facility was determined (in 2005) by the Department of Mental Health to have been operating

A very troubling aspect of the *Boy Erased* film is that it deviates from the facts of Conley's memoir in several ways, and, in Hollywood fashion, completely fabricates other parts of the story for dramatic affect. A critique published in *The Christian Post* by Family Research Council policy analyst, Peter Sprigg, points out these fictitious accounts:

> The filmmakers spiced up the film with completely fabricated scenes. The most dramatic—and most outrageous for its absurdity—is one in which an uncooperative Love In Action client is literally, physically *beaten with a Bible.*[cxxxvii]

Even more concerning was Smid's own response to those who questioned if the abusive methods in the film were accurately portrayed. In an article he wrote on his website, Smid did not explain what Love in Action did or why they used certain methods that were portrayed in the film as abusive, coercive, and shaming. Instead, he wrote an article on his website denouncing all "conversion therapy" efforts without taking responsibility for the harmful, ineffective methods he allegedly practiced at Love in Action:

> It is very well known today where I stand, and that I'm totally against any message, therapy, or religious organization or church that condemns LGBTQ people based on some interpretation of the Bible ... for 22 years I fell in line with the expectations, theories, philosophies, and religious dogma that lay underneath conversion therapy. I bought the rhetoric, I believed it. I attempted to apply it to my own life and lead others into it because it appeared to be the only hope any of us had.[cxxxviii]

The bottom line is that these two mainstream films are being used by gay activists to conflate unlicensed, unregulated religious programs with ethical, licensed therapy.[13] In fact (according to a recent post on Twitter), the National Center for Lesbian Rights, which is spearheading the campaign to ban "conversion therapy," was consulted by the producers of *Boy Erased* as they worked to perfect their script, leading up the filming of the movie.

Case in Point: Fake News and Bias Permeates the "Mainstream Media"

Not long after *The Miseducation of Cameron Post* was released, a reporter from CNN reached out to interview me to learn more about my work with clients who experience sexual and gender identity conflicts. Jen Christensen is a producer and editor with CNN's Health, Medical, and Wellness Unit. Since 2013, she has served as the president of the NLGJA, the association of LGBTQ journalists. She is an experienced and decorated journalist, having received multiple awards for her work.[cxxxix]

Unfortunately, she disclosed none of this to me after Peter Sprigg from the Family Research Council told her about my work as a psychotherapist and suggested she interview me for her story. It wasn't until after she interviewed me that I was able to find her online profile and discover who she was. After the article was published, I wasn't at all surprised by the level of bias in her coverage.

---

[13] It's important to note that I do not oppose unlicensed, religious and/or spiritual programs to help individuals struggling with sexual or gender identity conflicts. There are many well-designed, ethical, effective, and spiritually sound programs that are run by competent pastors and ministers providing effective spiritual and soul care ministry. What I am referring to here are religious fundamentalists who lack any specific counseling training and use methods like charismatic or ritualistic prayer, or even exorcism, to try and rid parishioners of homosexual demons, as they might describe it.

After mentioning that two "conversion therapy" films were hitting the "big screen" (by the way, she never acknowledged the fact that *Cameron Post* is a fictitious tale), she goes right into the unverified and unvetted story of Matthew Shurka's so-called "conversion therapy" experience:

> A therapist forbade 16-year-old Mathew Shurka from speaking to his mother and sisters for three years. The youngest child and only son in a tight-knit Long Island family, Shurka said that his mom wasn't physically or emotionally abusive. Instead, the therapist told the teen to give the women the silent treatment because it would help make him straight ... This is what's known as "conversion therapy," "reparative" or "sexual orientation change efforts," in which someone goes to therapy in order to change their sexual orientation or gender identity. It's often performed by religious leaders, but licensed clinicians are also engaged in the practice.

If you do a word count on the 1,600-word story, less than 4% of the piece (for a total of 61 words) is dedicated to the two movies in the title. Instead, Christensen focuses on describing what appears to be every single "conversion therapy" horror story she can find, ranging from fringe practices performed by unlicensed and unregulated counselors in the United States, to unfounded and unproven allegations of electroshock therapy for homosexuals in China. In fact, nowhere in the story does she describe mainstream practices among contemporary licensed psychotherapists until she quotes me:

> Therapist Christopher Doyle, a conversion therapy advocate working with conservative

groups like the Family Research Council to stop the government bans, disagrees. He experienced same-sex attraction but didn't want to, he said, but by addressing the trauma in his life through therapy, he was able to shift his attraction. He's married now to a woman and has five children.

He said he has dedicated his life to helping others who struggle with unwanted attractions. "I specialize in trauma and work with clients to resolve that trauma. People who want help. There's no electric shock or shaming," said Doyle, who practices in the Washington, D.C., area. He says he doesn't promise anyone that they will be straight. "Each individual is unique, but I try to give them realistic outcomes." He points to a new study in the *Linacre Quarterly,* the peer-reviewed journal of the Catholic Medical Association, in which 68% of the 125 religious men who underwent such therapy had at least some "heterosexual shifts in sexual attraction and behavior." Most scientific studies have shown the opposite. And while all the major mental health associations object to the practice, Doyle believes those objections are politically motivated. He believes that participants' horror stories involve practices that are not done by ethical mainstream practitioners.

After this story was published, I e-mailed Ms. Christensen to express my concerns about her ethics of not disclosing her role as president of the LGBTQ association of journalists and her biased reporting. While I will not quote the whole e-mail, I'll close this chapter with the final paragraph of my e-mail, which personifies my experience dealing with dozens of LGBTQ journalists over the last ten years, and the common problems of bias, lack of objectivity, and poor ethics:

> I find your whole approach and story to be very biased and your lack of disclosure to be unethical. I would expect more from a seasoned producer with such prestigious awards as you have listed in your biography. In my work, proper disclosure and fair balance and discussion of the research around sexuality and orientation is important to ensure the safety and legitimacy of the process. Your process, unfortunately, left out some crucial facts and disclosures that I believe are important—I wish I could say I expect more from CNN, but unfortunately, this is exactly what I have come to expect from CNN and LGBTQ journalists. Time and time again, I grant interviews to LGBTQ journalists and the story is almost never balanced, fair, or ethical.[cxl]

CHAPTER 6
THE WAR OF STRATEGY: BAIT AND SWITCH

You've heard of the golden rule, haven't you boy? Whoever has the gold makes the rules.

~ Disney's *Aladdin*

○ဩ

A common sales tactic that car dealers use with customers is to lure them in with great advertisements and sales pitches to market their newest, most expensive vehicles. The dealership purposely inflates the sticker price of the vehicle, so that after considerable negotiation, the customer believes he/she has received a great deal when the final sales price is agreed upon.

This is how it typically works: 1) The customer is lured in by the amazing sale, and then arrives to view the Manufacturer's Suggested Retail Price (MSRP) sticker on the side of the vehicle and determines that the price is too high; 2) The sales person then approaches the customer and praises the vehicle; 3) The customer listens, but inevitably tells the sales person that the price is too high; 4) The sales person then reassures the customer: "Don't worry, I'm gonna give you a great deal!" 5) Sales person and customer then sit down and begin to negotiate, usually on pieces of paper (for some reason, experience has shown that customers react better to prices written on paper, than verbal negotiations; 6) The MSRP magically drops to a considerably lower number, usually coinciding with other incentives such $1,000 cash back or 0% financing; 7) After several rounds of negotiations, most customers usually settle on a price and the sale is complete.

The consumer may believe he scored a great deal on his new vehicle. The reality is he merely participated in a game. The rules of the game were set up by the dealership in such a way that the customer inevitably ended up paying more for a vehicle than he/she wanted to. The price was intentionally inflated with incentives built in to make the deal sweeter, and if all else fails, the dealer reduces the price a little more, but only so much as to maintain a decent profit margin with the sale. This strategy has already been devised before the customer walks in. The dealer has instructed the sales person: "You may not sell this car lower than such and such number, and the higher the sales price, the more commission you receive on the sale." Thus, it's in the best interest of both the dealer and the sales person to sell the vehicle at the very highest price possible, and it will always be considerably lower than what the MSRP is listed at so to make the customer believe he/she got a good deal. This strategy has proven to be fairly effective in selling new vehicles. However, it doesn't work 100% of the time, and dealerships know it.

When the customer simply will not agree to a sales price that is too high and the negotiations are not going well for the sales person, the dealership instructs the salesman to immediately stop attempting to sell the new, shiny, expensive vehicle, and instead, begin to sell the customer a less expensive, but "reliable pre-owned" vehicle (by the way, the term used to be call "used"). The reason dealers do this is because they understand that the customer will eventually become fatigued or disillusioned with the negotiations, and possibly, leave the dealership without purchasing a vehicle.

At some point in the negotiation, the salesman has to realize that the customer is not going to buy the vehicle at the price he wants to sell it, and he now risks losing the sale. So the salesman immediately changes strategy and attempts to sell the customer a vehicle that is less expensive, with fewer features, and less, well, shininess. This strategy is called Bait and Switch. The dealer baits the customer with the amazing deal on the new, shiny vehicle, and then mid-way through the negotiations, switches the game.

LGBT activists have been using the Bait and Switch method for years in their work to ban licensed therapy for clients distressed by sexual and gender identity conflicts. The new, shiny, expensive vehicle they are trying to sell politicians is the myth that licensed, mental health practitioners are using abusive and harmful practices, such as electroshock therapy, and/or other aversive therapeutic methods to change gay-identified minors to a heterosexual orientation. But when politicians start to ask legitimate questions, such as: "Who/what/where/how did this abuse happen?" and: "Why is there not a complaint registered with the state licensing board on this abuse?" The activists switch the terms of the game in order to "save the sale"—which is a ban on "talk therapy," not "aversion therapy."

Talk therapy, like the pre-owned vehicle, is what they intended to sell (or ban) the whole time. But talk therapy isn't controversial enough to ban by itself, so the activists use the Bait and Switch method to lure politicians into a false narrative that professional therapy employs methods that are abusive and harmful. When these stories are exposed as unverifiable or challenged by a conservative politician in a committee hearing (i.e., the politician might simply ask: "Who performed this abusive therapy, and did you report this abuse to the state licensing board?"), the witness testifying, or the next of the 20-25[14] witnesses lined up to speak against therapy, might say something like this:

---

[14] Over the years I have testified in a number of hearings to ban "conversion therapy"; a common tactic gay activists use is to flood the hearing room with dozens of "conversion therapy survivors" and "conversion therapy" experts who testify of the horrors they experienced in so-called treatment. When questioned, 90% or more of those testifying have never actually undergone therapy or have any idea of the nature of safe and ethical therapy. They are typically gay advocates on the state level that work in public policy and are supported and/or funded by large national gay activist organizations.

Even though the abuse (e.g., electric shock, aversion therapy etc.) in the 'conversion therapy survivor's' story cannot be verified, talk therapy is just as harmful, and many more therapists are using talk therapy to harm clients, so that is why aversion therapy and talk therapy should both be banned!

This is exactly what happened in the state of Washington in 2014. Gay activists working with Democratic lawmakers introduced HB 2451. During the Senate committee hearing, Joseph Backholm of the Family Policy Council of Washington heard and reported the unbelievable testimony of one witness:

Proponents of the bill told stories about children being subjected to shock therapy and ice baths against their will. While that kind of aversive therapy is broadly condemned, there is little to no evidence that such therapy is done commonly if at all. The Washington State Department of Health said they have received no complaints about therapists performing coercive sexual orientation change therapy of any kind—much less ice baths and shock therapy—against the will of a client.[cxli]

The Republican-controlled Senate ultimately killed this bill in 2014. However, in 2015, the same bill was introduced and passed by the House, only to be amended in the Senate to ban all therapy (not only therapy intended to reduce or eliminate homosexual feelings or gender confusion) that used methods such as electroshock therapy. This bill would keep "talk therapy" of any kind legal. But when that bill was sent back to the House for consideration, something remarkable happened, again reported by Backholm:

> The same people who spent the last year talking about the need to protect children from ice baths and shock therapy suddenly and strongly opposed a bill specifically designed for that purpose. What was the problem? The bill didn't go far enough. "It must restrict talk therapy," they said. Last year, not a word was uttered about the need to ban talk therapy because everyone was so horrified by the stories of involuntary shock therapy. All they talked about was the need to protect kids from child abuse. But now that they have been given the chance to stop involuntary shock therapy without the ability to regulate conversations... suddenly shock therapy wasn't such a big deal.

There are two things we can learn from this recent development. First, the advocates of this bill have always been mostly interested in prohibiting conversations they dislike, not stopping physical forms of child abuse everyone opposes. The attempt to focus on stories of abuse was just part of the bait and switch. People suspected as much before, but now they have admitted it. Second, and maybe more importantly, the fact that they are willing to oppose a bill to stop child abuse in the hopes that they can pass a bill to ban conversations illustrates the depth of their conviction about this issue. From their perspective, telling kids same-sex attraction is not necessarily permanent is child abuse. The harm of involuntary shock therapy and the "harm" of a child being told change is possible are the same. If this tactic is successful now, it won't just be the therapists who are affected. If it were "child abuse" for a therapist to tell a child that sexual desires can be controlled or changed, why wouldn't it be child abuse for someone else to say the same thing?[cxlii]

This legislation was defeated again in 2015, was not introduced in 2016, and reintroduced again in 2017, only to fail once again. However, in 2018, the Republicans lost the majority in the Senate, and sadly, the bill was passed out of the legislature and signed into law by Democrat Governor Jay Inslee.[cxliii] As I discussed in the previous chapter, the power of the mainstream media has been especially helpful in advancing this false narrative, yet, when the stories of "therapy torture" are exposed as fraud, the mainstream media rarely, if ever, retracts the details of an article with false testimony because many of the authors of these stories are written by LGBT-identified journalists or writers very sympathetic to the gay political agenda. Even worse, far-left advocacy groups such as the Southern Poverty Law Center (SPLC) are often referred to in the media as "experts" or "watchdogs" for "conversion therapists" and transforma-tional ministries offering help to those distressed by sexual or gender identity conflicts. In that light, their written materials and opinions about the subject are reported as "objective" news, rather than what they really are—politically motivated and biased smear attacks.

Sleight of Hand, Opinion-Based Smears, and Innuendos
One of the strategies that far-left advocacy and gay activist organizations use to smear professional psycho-

therapists assisting clients distressed by sexual and gender identity conflicts is to intentionally conflate professional psychotherapy with religious practice and/or unlicensed, unregulated counseling. They do this by labeling all efforts—therapeutic, religious, or otherwise—to help clients distressed by sexual and gender identity conflicts "conversion therapy."

In May 2016, the SPLC published a paper on its website titled: "Quacks: 'Conversion Therapists,' the Anti-LGBT Right, and the Demonization of Homosexuality."[cxliv] The SPLC has a war chest of hundreds of millions of dollars and since it has the means to hire a multitude of attorneys and any other consultants it wishes, one can be rather sure this report represents what the SPLC considers the best case it has to offer against therapy that is open to a client's goal of sexual orientation or gender identity change. With all of the SPLC's resources, it should know whether its claims misrepresent current and scientifically accurate information or not.

The SPLC used the term "conversion therapy" about 250 times and never mentioned the terms actual psychotherapy providers use such as "sexual orientation change efforts (SOCE)," "sexual attraction fluidity exploration through therapy (SAFE-T)," or "heterosexual-affirming therapy." As I have discussed previously, "conversion therapy" is a term regularly used by opponents of real psychotherapy for clients distressed by sexual or gender identity conflicts, but even unlicensed religious practitioners generally do not use this term. They may however, speak of "religiously-mediated sexual orientation change efforts" or "transformational ministry" for the sexually and relationally wounded.

Why avoid the actual terms in usage for the very subject of the paper? Because the term "conversion therapy" deceptively associates religious practice, "conversion," with the term appropriate for licensed professions, "therapy."

This is yet another bait and switch strategy. The reality is that religious practices are not psychotherapy, and psychotherapy is not religious practice. The term "conversion therapy" also helps opponents lump unlicensed and licensed actors into one group. In this way, the SPLC can collect smears on a lay counselor, member of the clergy, or coach, none of whom are licensed psychotherapy professionals, and make it appear that such smears apply to all unlicensed and licensed actors.

This method is guilt by association, a sleight of hand, and it permeates the SPLC's paper. The high-powered and well-financed lawyers and professionals who work for the SPLC are aware of the difference between criticism that applies to some individuals in a group but not the whole group, between religious practice and psychotherapy, and between licensed and unlicensed, and they certainly know what they are doing when they use this deceptive practice.

The SPLC has also targeted organizations based on traditional values on a hate map leading to a gunman opening fire at the Family Research Council.[cxlv] It is doubtful that the SPLC would accept the accuracy of its smear-by-innuendo-and-association method if it were applied to itself. They convey deceptive perceptions indirectly not only about individuals who provide religious practices or professional psychotherapy, but also uses indirect methods to purvey false information about sexual orientation such as the falsehood that it cannot change.

Here are some examples:

- A Pew Research Center poll finds that 51% of Americans do not believe that gay men and lesbians can change their sexual orientation, while 36% think they can. Answering the same question for Pew a decade earlier, in 2003, 42%

said sexual orientation could be changed and 42% said it could not.[cxlvi]

- The National Gay and Lesbian task force... warned that the ex-gay industry was undermining the battle for LGBT rights by suggesting that homosexuality is a choice, not an unchangeable condition like skin color.[cxlvii]

The SPLC is careful not to put the generalization into its own mouth that sexual orientation never changes or is like skin color. Instead, it always presents the assertion from the mouths of others. There is a very good reason it is so careful. Research has established that the assertion is false. The organization may think if it cannot be pinned with actually stating a falsehood itself, it cannot be accused of being a purveyor of a falsehood. Thus, the SPLC shields its misrepresentations behind the assertions of others throughout the paper.[cxlviii]

"Conversion Therapy" Defined...or Ill-Defined

On February 14, 2018, Dr. Joseph Nicolosi, Jr., a clinical psychologist and son of the late Dr. Joseph Nicolosi, founder of reparative therapy, testified in front of the Maine state legislature against a bill seeking to ban "conversion therapy." Nicolosi Jr., like his father, has dedicated his career to helping men who experience conflicts around sexual and gender identity, heal the wounds that lead to homosexuality and transgenderism. Nicolosi Jr.'s testimony provides an excellent explanation why "conversion therapy" is not the same, or equivalent to, professional psychotherapy (including reparative therapy) open to a client's goal of sexual or gender identity change:

> Conversion therapy is broad, ill defined, there's no ethics code, no governing body, and it's pract-

iced predominantly by unlicensed individuals. Conversion therapy in some forms may be harmful to some people. The American Psychological Association has expressed legitimate concern about some of these approaches. In reparative therapy, the client is in the driver's seat. He sets his own goals, which the therapist helps him achieve. We use established, evidence-based treatments, the same treatments found in other clinics throughout the world, to treat trauma and sexual addiction. And as those underlying issues are resolved, the sexuality begins to change on its own. There is absolutely no documented evidence in the empirical literature showing that reparative therapy causes harm. None.[cxlix][15]

An important strategic weapon in the LGBT activist's tool belt is the need to frame the debate for banning therapy for clients distressed by sexual and gender identity conflicts in such a way that they control the language. By branding the term "conversion therapy" in the mainstream media—and by extension, the culture at large—activists are able to define the terms of the debate, and then control how the debate is argued. As Dr. Joseph Nicolosi, Jr. stated above, "conversion therapy" is not the same as reparative therapy or other forms of therapies to resolve conflicts around unwanted same-sex attractions or gender identity

---

[15] While the legislature in Maine ultimately passed this "conversion therapy" bill, on July 6, 2018 Republican Gov. Paul LePage became the first governor to veto a bill of this nature. In a statement about the veto, the governor labeled the bill "bad public policy ... (as) this bill attempts to regulate professionals who already have a defined scope of practice and standard of care per their statutory licensing requirement." Undoubtedly, Dr. Joseph Nicolosi Jr.'s excellent testimony helped to defeat this bill.

confusion; yet, activists and biased researchers often conflate the two for political and strategic purposes.

A perfect example of this conflation is a recent "study" out of the Williams Institute for Sexual Orientation and Gender Identity Law and Public Policy at UCLA School of Law. One need not read further than the executive summary to get an idea of how the authors frame the issue:

> Conversion therapy is treatment grounded in the belief that being LGBT is abnormal. It is intended to change the sexual orientation, gender identity, or gender expression of LGBT people. Conversion therapy is practiced by some licensed professionals in the context of providing health care and by some clergy or other spiritual advisors in the context of religious practice. Efforts to change someone's sexual orientation or gender identity are associated with poor mental health, including suicidality.

The Williams Institute estimates that:

- 698,000 LGBT adults (ages 18–59) in the U.S. have received conversion therapy, including about 350,000 LGBT adults who received treatment as adolescents.

- 20,000 LGBT youth (ages 13–17) will receive conversion therapy from a licensed health care professional before they reach the age of 18 in the 41 states that currently do not ban the practice.

- 6,000 LGBT youth (ages 13–17) who live in states that ban conversion therapy would have received such therapy from a licensed health care professional before age 18 if their state had not banned the practice.

155

- 57,000 youth (ages 13–17) across all states will receive conversion therapy from religious or spiritual advisors before they reach the age of 18.[cl]

As mentioned above with the SPLC, one of the main strategies LGBT activists' use—and the phony research they produce—involves the conflation of religious practice and licensed mental health therapy. This is perfectly illustrated with the Williams Institute "study" above. The authors assume that licensed mental health clinicians employ the same methods as religious or spiritual counselors, or that their clients, and corresponding goals, are identical. They also use an overly broad definition of "conversion therapy," and make large, unfounded estimates from the Generations Study, a national probability study of LGB individuals supported by a grant from the National Institutes of Health.

The fact that the authors released the "study" as a white paper, rather than submit their findings for peer review in a scientific journal, reveals that their findings are both unscientific and speculative, at best. Finally, the "study" was conveniently released in the month of January, right before the first of two dozen bills were introduced in state legislatures across the United States, and received wide-spread coverage in the mainstream media.

Making Conversion Therapy Culturally Inappropriate
In the first eight years of this war, the conflation of professional psychotherapy and religious practice was primarily a strategy used by activists to ban licensed psychotherapy for minors, and their families, distressed by unwanted homosexual and gender identity conflicts. Because there has never been a corrective action by a state licensing board against a licensed therapist in any of the United States for forcing or coercing a minor client into "conversion therapy," it became a necessary tactic for

activists to find examples of abuse or coercion outside of licensed therapy. They achieved this by highlighting a few isolated examples of parents who have sent their child to religious counseling or away to programs for "troubled children"—presumably to "cure" their son or daughter of homosexuality or transgenderism.[16]

While these examples are relatively rare, they do, however, exist; and although it's difficult to verify the accuracy of every single detail, I would be remiss, at best, for not mentioning these stories, and at worst, cruel and blind to the examples of real abuse or mistreatment of gay-identified youth. While much of this book has decried the shameful and fraudulent tactics of gay activists to achieve their political objectives, it is important that professionals speak out for the human rights of the LGBT community—and in doing so, remind readers that no one should ever be forced, pressured, or coerced into a therapeutic or mental health treatment against his or her will or volition.

It is a fundamental right of the client to consent to treatment, and when clients are below the legal age of consent, it is the responsibility of licensed professionals to work ethically with the child's family and make efforts to intervene in families where real abuse, coercion, or mistreatment occurs. Unfortunately, the following two examples illustrate what may happen when seemingly well-meaning parents try to help their LGBT-identified children with ineffective and/or harmful methods.

The first example is Leelah Alcorn. Leelah, whose birth name was Joshua, was from the small town of Kings

---

[16] Another method they use to achieve this indoctrination is by finding a religious fanatic or back-water religious program for "troubled youth"— as was discussed in chapter 5 in the *20/20* story —and portraying this as "conversion therapy" while conflating it with ethical, licensed therapy. Unfortunately, the general public is usually not sufficiently informed to make the distinction between ethical and unethical counseling.

Mill, Ohio. At the age of 16, she[17] told her parents she was transgender and depressed and wanted to get professional help for her depression. According to her suicide note, Leelah reported that her parents took her to a psychiatrist for depression medication and to several "Christian therapists (who were all very biased) so I never got the therapy I needed to cure me of my depression. I only got more Christians telling me I was selfish and wrong and that I should look to God for help."[18]

Leelah further writes in her suicide note that her parents took away her cell phone, access to social media, and isolated her from her friends and the public school she was attending. However, after five months, the parents changed their minds and let her have access to her phone and social media. But by that time, Leelah had grown away from her friends and realized they weren't really as close as she once thought. Eventually, her depression grew worse and she felt there was no way out and no way to be happy. On December 28, 2014 she ended her life by stepping in front of a tractor-trailer on I-71 in Warren County, Ohio.[cli]

The second example is taken from a memoir written by Alex Cooper, titled *Saving Alex*. At the age of 15, Alex revealed to her Mormon parents that she was sexually

---

[17] I use the pronoun "she" out of respect. While I do not believe persons are actually born in the wrong sex, I have found over the years in my clinical work with those struggling with gender dysphoria, and their families, that debating over pronouns is counterproductive and disrespectful to the person in their therapeutic process. In some of my clinical work, those struggling with gender dysphoria ultimately end up transitioning, while I have worked with others who de-transitioned. Ultimately, research shows that 85-95% of "trans" youth end up remaining in their biological sex, and of that population, the majority ultimately identify as gay or lesbian.

[18] It's also worth mentioning that Leelah's single source of stress was not her parents or the Christian community at large. In her suicide note, she laments about her struggle to ever feel happy, as well as her own friends, who she admitted didn't give a "s**t about me."

attracted to women. Vinton Rafe McCabe recounts the following in his review of the 2016 book:

> Once they are told that their daughter is gay, the parents fall silent and distant, only to finally come to their daughter with the suggestion that she go to stay with her grandparents in Utah for a while, while the family comes to grips with this new reality. Alex readily agrees, only to find that the trip is a ploy to deliver her not into the hands of her grandparents, but instead into the house of a Mormon couple who have declared themselves, although unlicensed and untrained, as experts in "Conversion Therapy." And the fact that she has been taken to Utah puts her fully in the Mormon Church's hands. As Alex is told again and again by the couple—their names, we are told, are Johnny and Tianna Siale—the fact that nearly everyone in the community was Mormon and had already been prepared for her arrival meant that no one would intervene to help or free her. After being placed in the couple's hands, the young woman is brutalized, threatened with her very life, and forced to undergo a series of gut punches, whippings, and systematic religious reprogramming—all while also being forced to act as an unpaid servant in the couple's home. She may not speak to any of the couple's many Mormon children. Nor may she do anything but stand with her face to the wall while wearing a knapsack loaded with rocks (to remind her of the burden of her aberrant sexuality) when not cleaning or preparing meals for the whole family.[clii]

What is, perhaps, the most disturbing part of Alex's memoir of abuse is not the actual physical harm or psychological coercion she underwent, but the fact that many people in the community came and went by the home and saw Alex standing in the front of the wall, being tortured, and felt no obligation to report it to the authorities.

It is tragic experiences like this that anger the LGBT community and create fuel for activists to fight for equality and right treatment. We should all be outraged. We should refuse to accept such ignorance. We need to learn from the mistakes of the past and not repeat them. These tragedies fall into what can really be considered forced treatment or "conversion therapy" and need to be understood for what they are: Abuse. They are not religious practice, and they are certainly not therapy.

Unfortunately, Alex's story was seized upon by the Human Rights Campaign (HRC) in their effort to make licensed therapy for minors illegal. In a recent video produced by the HRC, Alex tells her story of abuse by unlicensed "counselors" practicing "conversion therapy" on her at their Utah home. On their website, where the video is posted, HRC senior vice president of communications and marketing says the following:

> No child should be subjected to this practice that amounts to nothing less than child abuse. We're thankful for Alex Cooper's willingness to boldly share her story. It is our hope that this powerful new video will help fuel the momentum we are seeing across the nation as lawmakers on both sides of the aisle work with us to pass legislation protecting LGBTQ youth from this dangerous and discredited practice.[cliii]

The website says that 12 states plus the District of Columbia have passed laws to prohibit "conversion therapy" and that HRC has partnered with the National Center for Lesbian Rights (NCLR) and state equality groups across the nation to pass state legislation ending "conversion therapy."

However, what the HRC doesn't tell you is that the abuse Alex suffered from will not be prevented with the laws it is promoting. However, by conflating Alex's story with actual licensed therapy, it adds momentum and a real face to their cause, despite the fact that Alex was not actually receiving therapy that is regulated and sanctioned by the state and subject to ethical boundaries and disciplinary action, should actual abuse or coercion take place. This type of deceptive strategy permeates the campaigns to end therapy by the HRC, NCLR, and SPLC. Because of political pressure, over a dozen state legislatures and governors have gone along with this charade.

Lessons Learned: Perfect Love Drives Out Fear

If we can learn anything from the last eight years of legislation, as well as the decades of prior mistreatment, shaming, and in some cases, religious bullying of LGBT-identified persons, is that hearts and minds do not heal out of fear and shame-based messages. 1 John 4:18 says: "There is no fear in love. But perfect love drives out fear, because fear has to do with punishment. The one who fears is not made perfect in love." In the tragic examples described above, the tactics these parents used was not based on perfect love, but resembled more of punishment driven by their own fear. Clearly, this is not Christian, and its foundations are certainly not based on the Biblical concepts of grace and redemption demonstrated by Jesus Christ.

Religion, spirituality, and the church can and should be a safe place for healing, but it errs when it takes the place of qualified, mental health professions that understand how to work with individuals distressed by sexual and gender identity conflicts. As I write this chapter, LGBT activists have passed a bill in California that would essentially outlaw any form of counseling, therapy, or spiritual intervention—licensed or unlicensed —intended to help minors or adults that seek to leave homosexuality or transgenderism. This would include a book at the church's bookstore that told of a testimony of healing, or a simple behavioral choice to avoid homosexual practice.

Because of their deep wounding —some inflicted by misguided religious practice—activists such as Sam Brinton have gone so far as to admit that their goal is to make "gay conversion" in the church culturally inappropriate—meaning that even if the church were not regulated by the state—the culture at large would regulate the church not to offer spiritual guidance or pastoral support for those struggling with sexual and gender identity. How could this happen?

Look no further than the Metro City Church in Detroit, Michigan, which was bullied, harassed, and threatened after offering a six-week Bible-based workshop called "Unashamed Identity," intended for teenage girls struggling with their sexual identity. The church, which was partnering with FORGE ministries to offer the workshop to "Trans-Bi-Gay-or Other" girls, published a social media post that said: "Through thoughtful, relevant, and Biblical counsel, we will help your girl be unashamed of her true sexual identity given to her by God at birth."

But after word got out, church Pastor Jeremy Schossau received an onslaught of death and arson threats, as well as hundreds of angry phone calls (at some points as many as 40 per minute) by gay activists seeking to intimidate him. "People have literally threatened to kill me and my family, to burn our house down, to burn our church down, to assault the people of our church and our staff," the pastor said. According to an article on Life Site News, one man was charged by police after threatening the church: "Every member of the ANTIFA will show up 'armed and ready. This is not a joke.'" The workshop was reportedly cancelled at the last minute due to pressure from a protest organized by the LGBT community.[cliv]

Don't be naïve to think this is an isolated experience or spontaneous protest. Gay activists know that the church is protected by 1st Amendment freedom of religion laws and that by and large, they cannot shut down or make religious activity illegal. What they can do, however, is make it culturally inappropriate for the church to preach or offer services to help those distressed by unwanted homosexual or gender confusion. By spreading propaganda through the mainstream media or using tactics, as was seen with the persecution of Detroit's Metro City Church, they can essentially bully people through fear and intimidation, or even shame, by claiming that church teaching on sexuality is akin to "conversion therapy" or psychological torture.

This is exactly what Sam Brinton, former spokesman for the National Center for Lesbian Rights, now working with the Trevor Project, said at a recent presentation to employees of the Google Corporation. In the video, Sam explains how bans on licensed therapy are really intended to implement LGBT cultural values as a proxy to go after every pastor or church whose teachings go against homosexual practice.

In the presentation, a Google employee asked Sam about the scope of the California law (outlawing "conversion therapy" and regulating licensed mental health professionals) and questioned if he wished this regulation would be broader. Brinton responded, in kind:

> Yes, it is limiting. That is partially how you get some of these bills through, is by limiting it to licensed mental health professionals ... you can't take a license away from someone who doesn't have a license. Religious organizations will probably practice this for the rest of time ... unless I can figure out a way to stop it ... I may

not be able to find every little camp, right? I may not be able to find every pastor. But, I can make it something that culturally is unacceptable ... but that's a space, that as I see it, is that yes, it's directly addressing mental health professionals, but it's also by proxy, affecting everyone else because it's getting that reporting in.[clv]

You can see a video of Sam's presentation at https://youtu.be/WN3_eFIbZkU. If you pay close attention to the video, you can see that Brinton is taking his cues from Sam Ames (Ames is one of the chief strategist-attorneys behind the Born Perfect campaign with the NCLR). This strategy is intended to further the idea that one can make homosexuality not only illegal via means of licensed therapy, but also, culturally unacceptable for churches or pastors to suggest in their sacred spaces. If LGBT activists can successfully bully and intimidate the church every time she promotes an event that espouses a traditional Biblical view of sexuality, this strategy may prove to be successful.

The key point here is this: Activists understand they cannot eliminate certain deeply embedded ideas, especially when the source is from sacred documents that are revered by millions and passed down for generations.

But what they can do is destroy the practice and implementation of these ideas by persecuting and essentially killing the messenger. This is not a new strategy. It's been used against Christians for thousands of years. After all, following Jesus' death by crucifixion, at least ten of the apostles were martyrs who died for their faith.

CHAPTER 7
THE WAR IN THE COURTROOM

*Governments must not be allowed to force persons to
express a message contrary to their deepest convictions.
Freedom of speech secures freedom of thought and belief.
This law imperils those liberties.*

~ Supreme Court Justice Anthony Kennedy,
NIFLA v. Becerra

CR

Language is a powerful medium. It can frame and shape how
people view a subject. It has the ability to communicate
complex subjects in short sound bites. It has the capacity to
portray controversial issues in a particular way so as to
persuade a person how to think, feel, respond, and even act.
Politicians (especially liberals) love to use language to
communicate important ideas—they call these "buzz
words"—to sear a certain connotation, a suggestion, if you
will, into the minds of the general public so the population
will react a certain way.

The first presidential election I was eligible to vote
in was 2000. I was 19 years old and about to enter my first
year of undergraduate work in political science at Grove City
College, located just 60 miles north of my childhood home
in suburban Pittsburgh, Pennsylvania. I remember how
excited I was to cast my vote for former Ambassador Alan
Keyes, a staunch African-American social conservative, in
the primary. Unfortunately, Keyes didn't stand a chance, but
Texas Governor George W. Bush's stock was rising at the
time, and he ended up winning the Republican nomination.

The mainstream media hated Governor Bush, and
they sought to brand him from day one as an inexperienced,
uneducated, hick from the Deep South riding on his father's

165

(George H.W. Bush, the 41st President) coattails to presidential power. When Governor Bush announced his running mate, Dick Cheney, shortly before the Republican National Convention that summer, liberal politicians went wild with a rarely heard phrase to communicate the relative weight that Cheney brought—presumably to offer more substantial experience and wisdom—to the ticket. The word was "gravitas," and the mainstream media swallowed it whole!

Discussing the word "gravitas," well-known conservative columnist Thomas Sowell summed it up nicely in an op-ed he wrote for *Townhall*:

> Before Dick Cheney was announced as Governor George W. Bush's choice for vice presidential candidate, practically nobody used the word. Now everybody and his brother seems to be using it ... Democrats follow tried and true principles of propaganda, using the same phrases again and again, to drive the words into the heads of the public.[clvi]

Principles of Propaganda

Using buzzwords to communicate propaganda is an effective means of portraying an issue a certain way and branding your opponents in the most unfavorable light. One of the most powerful aspects of propaganda is that no matter how loose the facts, the narrative is usually based on a loose fabric of truth, and therefore, becomes believable in the minds of unsuspecting consumers. No issue is more appropriate to illustrate in this discussion than the "born that way" myth.

For the last 30 years, tens of millions of dollars of funding has gone into researching a biological basis for the origins of homosexuality. First it was the gay gene, then the gay brain, and finally, gay hormones. When each of these

166

fields of study failed to produce quality replication to their original dubious studies, funding didn't dry up—it increased! Why? The propaganda machines of the mainstream media and liberal politicians kept repeating the lie over and over and over again: Homosexuals are born that way! For example, I discussed research in Chapter 4 by Dr. Dean Hamer, a gay-identified scientist, who published a famous genetic study on homosexuality in 1993. Newspapers were quick to make conclusions: "Report Suggests Homosexuality Is Linked to Genes," said the *New York Times*.[clvii] But in actuality, Hamer commented in the study that he did *not* find a gay gene. Yet, that didn't stop reporters from exaggerating the results of the study in the mainstream media.

In truth, research has never made this determination, and even the most liberal of trade associations for mental health professionals, the American Psychological Association (APA), has said that scientists cannot conclude that people are born with a sexual orientation—and that nature and nurture both play roles in how individuals develop sexual attractions.[clviii] In fact, the most recent data compiled by the APA's 2014 *Handbook on Sexuality and Psychology* cites recent data that states: "[W]e are far from identifying potential genes that may explain not just male homosexuality but also female homosexuality" and that there are "associative or potentially causal links between childhood sexual abuse and ever having same-sex partners, especially for some men" as well as family dynamics, including the "loss of a same-sex parent (such as through death, divorce, end of parent cohabitation, not living with the same-sex parent, or unknown paternity) that are associated with a greater likelihood of entering a same-sex marriage."[clix]

Yet, the phrase: "You're born that way" or "You're born gay" still gets repeated over and over by the mainstream media, far-left academics, and liberal politicians. One would think that the very idea of spreading this "born gay" propaganda would be considered fraudulent, yet, the very opposite is now happening. Those who suggest, write about, or provide therapeutic assistance to individuals with sexual and gender identity conflicts are being sued, legislated against—and if the courts don't intervene soon, they may even be criminalized! Think I'm joking? Look no further than a small, non-profit organization that offered counseling and coaching to the Orthodox Jewish community in New Jersey.

Accused of Consumer Fraud: JONAH

Jews Offering New Alternatives to Healing (JONAH) was a small, Jewish non-profit (and the only, to my knowledge) organization offering counseling and coaching to members of the Jewish religious community struggling with unwanted same-sex attraction and gender identity conflicts. In 2012, four former clients of JONAH filed a lawsuit against Arthur Goldberg, the organization's codirector, and Alan Downing, a life coach employed by JONAH. The four plaintiffs (and two of their mothers)—Michael Ferguson, Benjamin Unger, Sheldon Bruck, Chaim Levin, Jo Bruck, and Bella Levin—were represented by three well-funded law firms, chief among them, the Southern Poverty Law Center (SPLC), infamous for its far-left advocacy and direct mail fundraising off of far-left social causes that has banked them tens of millions.

The charge of consumer fraud was brought against JONAH for allegedly promising that its clients would go from "gay" to "straight" with its counseling and coaching services, and in so doing, that its services should be considered an unconscionable business practice that caused irrevocable harm. The New Jersey Consumer Fraud Act protects consumers from deceptive, false, or fraudulent business practices. Particularly vague in its description, the law had historically been used to protect customers from "snake-oil" salesman, or from companies that sold faulty appliances or used cars that turned out to be lemons. But because of the loose interpretation of the law by Superior Court Judge Peter F. Bariso, Jr., the trial was allowed to go forth. In fact, this was the first time ever that the New Jersey Consumer Fraud Act was applied to prosecute a religious non-profit organization.

Because of the controversial nature of JONAH's work, gay activists wanted to make a high-profile example out of the Jewish organization. It's clear from court affidavits that the lawsuit against JONAH was well thought-out and coordinated, in conspiracy-fashion, by certain gay activists. In fact, court documents indicate that the SPLC actually recruited these plaintiffs in order to take down JONAH. For example, in a pre-trial deposition, gay activist Wayne Besen, notorious for his efforts to take down what he calls "ex-gay therapy," testified to having worked with two of the plaintiffs, Chaim Levin and Benjamin Unger, to produce a video that included their alleged harmful experiences in counseling. Besen subsequently helped connect them with the SPLC to explore a civil lawsuit. In fact, Levin told Besen that he deserved "half the credit" for bringing the suit against JONAH.[clx]

Because of the judge's loose interpretation of the New Jersey Consumer Fraud Act, as well as what some may consider unorthodox counseling methods employed by a few of JONAH's referral coaches and counselors, it was relatively easy to bring the lawsuit. While some of the allegations of unorthodox counseling methods were true, the SPLC and its plaintiffs basically threw the book at JONAH, hoping for as many charges as possible to stick, regardless of whether or not the allegations were based on facts. For example, in court affidavits, plaintiff Sheldon Bruck, who received a total of four counseling sessions with Thaddeus Heffner (a licensed therapist contracted by JONAH), alleged that Mr. Heffner:

169

. . . instructed him to wear a rubber band around his wrist and snap himself each time he felt attracted to a man [and this] self-inflicted pain matched other aspects of conversion therapy, which focused on magnifying painful or traumatic experiences from Bruck's past on the baseless assumption that by re-experiencing hurt and anger, he would become straight.[clxi]

While the SPLC never proved that Heffner actually used this method on Bruck (it should be emphasized that Bruck received only four counseling sessions before he terminated his relationship with JONAH), by sensationalizing the ineffective, fictitious "rubber band" technique, the SPLC used it as a way to conflate other counseling techniques used by JONAH that actually helped clients resolve past trauma by reprocessing the emotions that occurred during the traumatic events. In fact, in emotion-focused therapy, reprocessing painful emotions based on past traumas is a very common technique to help clients heal, regardless of their issue or goal for seeking counseling. But by describing the counseling in such a way, the SPLC and its plaintiffs were able to cast a shadow on any effective or otherwise mainstream counseling methods employed by JONAH, rendering all of their services as harmful pseudoscience.

Another effective technique used by the SPLC was the conflation of JONAH's work with that of Journey Into Manhood (JIM), a peer-led experiential retreat for men struggling with unwanted same-sex attraction that was run by the organization People Can Change (PCC) (now called Brothers on a Road Less Traveled). JONAH referred many of its clients to attend JIM retreats as an auxiliary to its individual and group sessions, and while JONAH and PCC were clearly separate organizations, SPLC continued to refer retreat experiences by the plaintiffs as actual counseling sessions by JONAH during pre-trial and trial court proceedings. I wrote about this strategy during the trial proceedings:

> ... it's a classic bait and switch tactic of the left. Accuse JONAH of doing harm to its clients by throwing every accusation possible at them, including insinuating that they run "weekend in the woods" retreats that are similar to the "conversion therapy camps" that were reported in 2013 when transgender activist Brielle Goldani testified at a New Jersey Senate hearing that she was electroshocked and tortured... Then, after it'ss revealed that these weekends are not really JONAH's counseling, the other side changes its tune to describe all efforts to help men with unwanted same-sex attractions as "cults" to implicate the defendants ... the "weekend in the woods" camps ... are actually part of Journey Into Manhood, a 48-hour experiential healing retreat for men with unwanted same-sex attractions. JONAH endorses and refers their clients to voluntarily attend the retreat, but is in no way affiliated. Yet, the SPLC continues to attempt to confuse the jury by referencing experiences the plaintiffs (JONAH's former clients) had at the Journey Into Manhood retreats with the counseling of JONAH, all the while distorting the intent and processes of Journey Into Manhood in order to make the small, Jewish non-profit look bad.[clxii]

The SPLC did this intentionally to confuse jurors and sensationalize Journey Into Manhood retreat processes (labeling them "weekend in the woods retreats") so that any perceived negative experience a JONAH client had during counseling, whether it occurred in or outside of a session with a JONAH-referred coach/counselor, would thus be used as ammunition during the trial. Ironically, one of the chief plaintiffs, Chaim Levin, wrote on the JONAH list serve:

> . . . saying how much the work he was doing with Downing was helping him, and how profoundly impacted he was by Journey Into Manhood ... Levin wrote multiple messages on the JONAH list serve about his joy and gratitude for Arthur, Elaine (Berk, codirector), and JONAH and testified to his brothers of the powerful and helpful aspects of JIM and the JONAH program, saying it greatly helped him reduce shame, improve self-esteem, and understand himself.[clxiii]

Despite the many contradictions by the plaintiffs, along with the lack of evidence that Goldberg and JONAH ever promised the former clients they would go from "gay" to "straight",[19] it wasn't the actual facts of the case or violation of the law that implicated JONAH. Rather, it was the effective use of propaganda, persuasion, and citation of scientific inaccuracies by the SPLC and their army of lawyers that convinced the liberal judge to allow the proceedings to go forth, and eventually, hamstring JONAH and its lawyers from effectively defending themselves. They did this by capitalizing on one very controversial practice and then generalizing all of JONAH's counseling, and their expert witnesses, in guilt-by-association fashion.

The Bait: Low-Hanging Fruit
As an expert witness named in this case, I was among several colleagues, including the late Dr. Joseph Nicolosi

---

[19] All the plaintiffs also signed informed consents which stated that JONAH made no promise of their counseling/coaching outcomes. Yet, this fact was ignored by the judge at trial.

(founder of Reparative Therapy) and Dr. James Phelan (well-known clinician and researcher of sexual orientation change efforts) who was asked to produce testimony that JONAH's services had a scientific basis. My particular emphasis on the expert witness team was to defend the use of certain psychodramatic and experiential processes that JONAH used in group (and in some cases, individual) therapy sessions. Because of my experience using some of these experiential processes in practice with clients struggling with sexual and gender identity conflicts, I was asked to write an expert report, undergo depositions by the plaintiff's lawyers, and eventually, testify during trial.

As I began to read through thousands of pages of court affidavits and depositions, it became increasingly clear that the toughest technique to defend would be the use of nudity in Alan Downing's coaching sessions with some of the plaintiffs. To be abundantly clear, I was not asked by the defense team nor JONAH to promote the use of nudity in coaching or therapy, nor have I employed or ever practiced any form of nudity in a therapeutic context with any client. I would also like to state, for the record, that I do not recommend using nudity with a client for any mental health or therapeutic reason. Nonetheless, my task was to merely inform the court, based on my knowledge of what the research and anecdotal evidence shows, if there were any scientific evidence to support the use of therapeutic interventions that incorporated nudity. To say I was skeptical of this practice, and any science behind it, would be a huge understatement.

After a great deal of research, I was surprised to find an abundant amount of support, both in the scientific literature, and in anecdotal reports, to support the use of interventions incorporating nudity with general population clients and for those experiencing sexual identity conflicts. While many may consider nudity in a therapeutic environment bizarre and unorthodox, it has been used for

decades in some therapeutic circles, including therapists by
who practice gay-affirming therapy, a therapy that
encourages and affirms homosexual men and women to
become comfortable and open with their gay or lesbian
identity.[clxiv, 20]

The use of nudity in psychotherapy dates back to
1967, and was originally designed as a form of group
therapy, where a group of participants were encouraged to
"disrobe" in order to facilitate "emotional intimacy [and]
transparency" and decondition "distortions ... associated
with body image". Historians examining the practice noted
it was important to emphasize that therapeutic nudism has a
distinguished academic pedigree in academic psychology,
most notably in the humanistic psychology of Abraham
Maslow.

> Maslow's concept of 'peak experiences,' a
> psychological term for a mystical experience (is
> important in the development of nudity in
> psychotherapy). Likening the experience to a
> 'visit to a personally defined heaven, Maslow
> described peak experiences as moments of
> maximum psychological functioning. 'He feels
> more intelligent, more perceptive, wittier,
> stronger, or more graceful than at other times.'
> Not only was a person generally enhanced during
> a peak experience, but he also felt a heightened
> sense of oneness with himself and the world
> around him. 'The person in the peak-experiences
> feels more integrated (unified, whole, all-of-a-

---

[20] The importance of citing this author is to compare his report of six
clients he treated with nude psychotherapy to help affirm their
homosexuality with the type of work done by JONAH-referred
counselors/coaches, who helped clients with unwanted same-sex
attraction reduce body shame and increase self-acceptance. The intent of
both processes was similar.

piece) ... and is more able to fuse with the world.' [clxv]

Paul Bindrim developed Maslow's concept of peak experience to further his work in nude psychology. Using nudity in what he called Encounter Groups, Bindrim's concept was that physical nakedness could facilitate emotional nakedness and, therefore speed up psychotherapy. Bindrim was convinced that the 'natural state' of humanity had been lost and that disrobing would peel back layers of modernist artifice and alienation and reestablish a healthy connection with one's body and the true self."[clxvi] According to those familiar with Bindrim's work, it was essential for Bindrim's participants to be physically open in order to facilitate emotional openness:

> Freely blending psychoanalysis and Maslovian theory, Bindrim told his participants that they needed to reenact the hurt and frustration in their life in order achieved a psychologically hallowed state. 'The idea is to regress, if possible, to the trauma that caused the distortion. That's the way to start toward a peak experience' ... Nude therapy was based on the idea of the naked body as a metaphor of the psychological soul ... For more pragmatically minded clients, nude therapy was simply a new technique to achieve old, earthbound aims: a happier marriage, better communication, greater self-acceptance. For more spiritually restive clients, nude therapy promised not only a new self, but a 'higher' self with a richer and more fulfilling emotional life and an enduring connection to a transpersonal power.[clxvii]

In recent years, historians and social commentators have promoted nudity as a means of enhancing social equality, body acceptance, and a natural way of being.[clxviii] In fact, some self-help, peer-led organizations such as the Mankind Project (MKP) and Body Electric (both of which are very similar to People Can Change), offer experiential healing weekends to help gay-identified men, and incorporate the use of nudity to reduce body shame and enhance social and gender quality among its participants. In fact, MKP is a very gay-affirming organization, and prides itself on its cultural diversity. On their website, MKP boasts that it welcomes men of all sexual orientations to participate in their weekend:

> We create trainings and circles in which all men are welcome to discover their deepest truths. We welcome men of all sexual orientations: gay, straight, and bisexual, including those who identify as having unwanted same-sex attraction, to do their own work as they define it, to respect the identity and value of others, and to take responsibility for the impact their words and behaviors have on others.[clxix]

The exercises involving nudity at MKP retreats are very similar, in intent, to that which Downing used in his coaching sessions with some of the plaintiffs. Although the methods are not identical, the purpose for their use is to reduce body shame and challenge negative messages and perceptions that men have about their bodies.

In order to achieve a sense of trust among men and to feel comfortable around each other while nude, during the second night of the MKP retreat, the men being initiated were blind folded and marched a few hundred yards to a remote location outside of the retreat center, where they were instructed to keep their blind folds on and remove all of their clothes, including under garments. The men were then placed back in a single-file line and marched nude together while listening to the beat of distant drums and individuals chanting and screaming. When they arrived at their destination, they were greeted by dozens of initiated men (some of whom were staffing the weekend, others comprised of formerly initiated brothers) and instructed to dance around a large bonfire while fully nude.

The men were then instructed to sit around the fire while the leaders called them up one-by-one where they were honored in front of the entire group for their work and bravery thus far in the retreat. After experiencing a sense of bonding and group cohesion from the nudity exercise, the following morning the men were once again instructed to undress and form a circle, where the leader engaged them in a discussion on sexuality, body shame, and manhood while holding a wooden phallus. This activity is often called "Cock Talk" and is meant to demystify the men of any body shame and promote a sense of equality and brotherhood. Gay and bisexual men (as well as straight men) were celebrated within these circles and encouraged to accept their bodies and sexuality without any shame or pretense. According to an article on its website, MKP describes this process:

> The male body, in its many forms, is beautiful, normal, ridiculous, natural. We use nudity in our training to reveal and confront shame about the male body and to challenge our negative self-images ... Honest and affirming dialog about male sexuality is still taboo. Today's young men are raised in a stilted, secre-tive culture where their expectations of the male body may be almost exclusively formed by viewing pornography. This presents a deeply warped view of the male body (and we cannot help but also notice and confront the often harmful,

degrading, warped and objectified view of the female form and female sexuality). The rest of the time we see men in the media who are either the 'idealized' athlete, soldier, comic book hero, or the ridiculed overweight slob. None of these are healthy or typical representations. Deeply ingrained homophobia, self-hatred, and fear of being ostracized or teased have funda-mentally altered the fabric of male development. Many men carry painful memories of locker-room torment, self-consciousness and shame. As adult men, the preoccupation with sexual prowess, sexual function (E.D., penis enlarge-ment) or sexual orientation forms constant stream of meta information in our culture. The message is usually that we're not OK, not good enough, or not acceptable to society. Our intent is to create safety to reimagine a man's relation-ship to his own body and to his sexuality. Men have the opportunity to begin constructing a sexuality that will help them deepen their relationship to themselves and their wives or partners. This exercise helps men create the intimacy that they want in their lives.[clxx]

In his defense, Alan Downing (himself, a former same-sex attracted man now married to a woman) described the purpose and intention for his use of nudity in coaching as originating from his experience in MKP's *New Warrior Weekend* and the desire to take the nudity exercises that helped many gay-identified men (at the MKP weekend) achieve a sense of equality with their heterosexual brothers, and incorporate these concepts in healing for men with unwanted same-sex attractions in order to gain a greater sense of self-acceptance and reduce body shame:

Its primary intended purpose in my opinion based on my observations and conversations with other New Warriors (including leaders), is to create a sense of equality between all the men on the weekend, and to heighten one's vulnerability and openness ... I also found it to be a powerful tool for demystifying stories that I told myself about my body and the bodies of other men ... Demystifying and desexualizing male anatomy go hand in hand since with repeated exposure to non-sexual, non-isolating same gender nude experiences, my perceptions around men and me began to expand and then change. That which used to be exotic and therefore erotic became much more common place ... My own use of nudity in individual sessions grew out of the recognition that many of the men with whom I was working were experiencing serious envy towards other men. This usually grew out of deep shame that they felt about themselves and a belief that they were less than the men with whom they compared themselves. I wanted them to be able to grow beyond these self-limiting perceptions but not all of them could wait for, or afford the next NWTA weekend ... In these latter situations I began to notice that nudity could be used not only as a way of literally changing perceptions around one's physical body, but it was equally effective as a metaphor for changing one perception of one's internal power and the ability to manifest that power by walking through fear and the old self-limiting stories.[clxxi]

Downing then described how he specifically incorporates the use of nudity in his coaching sessions, such as his

179

work with Chaim Levin, one of the leading plaintiffs in the lawsuit:

> The process consists of a man identifying his self-limiting beliefs, the things that hold him back from living his life fully, freely, and without shame. Once the self-limiting beliefs are identified, the client is given the option of discarding those old beliefs or holding on to them. If he chooses to discard them, then he identifies an article of clothing that he will associate with that belief and then consciously states his intention to shed that belief as he removes the article of clothing. After the article of clothing is removed, then the client is instructed to feel what it is like to "be" without the burden of the former belief. The physical association of one less piece of clothing whether because of exposure of skin to air, or because of less weight/pressure on the body, or even feeling the sensation of the ground on ones bare or stocking feet creates a physical association and metaphor which drives home the point. This is a multi-step process. After each step the client is given time to orient himself to his new state of awareness and asked if he wants to proceed further or if he wants to stop the process. The client is always in charge and has the option of stopping at any time. They are reminded of this before and throughout the process. As with any kind of process, resistance to going forward is acknowledged, processed, and challenged, however if the client chooses not to proceed then as a facilitator I look to acknowledge the accomplishment of where they came to, leaving open the possibility that they can revisit this

another day, or that it is very possible that this is far as they need to go. It is essential that the client not experience any shame around how far they took the process or any decision they made. Once the client has reached his end point which may or may not include full nudity, then he is given time to acclimate to his new sense of self and find positive messages about himself that will eventually replace his recently released negative, self-limiting beliefs. In most cases he is also given the opportunity to explore his body visually or tactilely as suits his need. Once this second phase of the process is complete, then the client is instructed to put his previously discarded clothing on, one article at a time and to associate that article of clothing with a new, positive message about himself. The client is given the assignment to follow this ritual for the next week or more every time he gets dressed ... To the best of my knowledge the clients who experienced this process, including the three plaintiffs prior their going public, found it to be enlightening, empowering and free of shame. It was in this spirit and with this intention that it was delivered. [clxxii]

In court affidavits and in testimony delivered at the trial, the attorneys and plaintiffs described these processes as humiliating, abusive, and exploitive. They also alleged that Downing instructed them to touch their genitals during the sessions, and that they felt this harmed them. Even though no physical evidence was ever submitted to prove these allegations, the judge allowed the testimony to remain on the record. The details were sensationalized at trial and in the media and had to have caused an indelible mark of guilt against Downing and JONAH in the minds of the jurors.

Despite all of this controversy, it is important to understand how nudity work may be beneficial to some individuals with unwanted same-sex attractions. In his book: *A Bigger World Yet: Faith, Brotherhood, & Same Sex Needs*, author Tim Timmerman (himself a man with unwanted same-sex attractions) takes the reader inside of what it means to be a man with these unwanted attractions, and how nudity with other men in a non-sexual, safe, and healing atmosphere, has greatly benefitted him:

> You may wonder, 'How on earth can getting naked with another man be helpful? Wouldn't that just trigger sexual desires all the more?' I'm not equating this resolution with attempting to solve a heterosexual man's issues of lust by exposing him to a lot of naked women, an absurd notion at best. The key comes from the obvious physicality of the matter. Men are men, women are women, and there are biological differences between the two. Men who have difficulty seeing themselves as men need to learn how to self-identify as being part of the brotherhood in often the most basic of contexts: equal and the same as gender-mates. The nudity that has been healing to these men is far from erotic and is always in a brotherly context, free from sexual overtones. It is an inclusion of being 'one of the guys' that this community of men has felt so estranged from. Men who struggle with sexualizing their same gender have a false sense that men are 'the other' rather than women, so when naked in a non-sexual context, they are confronted with the fact that they have the same equipment and they are part of the larger community of men. In the right context, that camaraderie dilutes and negates any sexualizing that could take place. In our fear of

the opposite, we inhibit what would bring health, and make the situation more problematic, more of 'the other,' more mystery. When confronting the truth that their body is basically like other men, much of the power of that lie is taken away.[clxxiii]

It is important to note that for Timmerman, a core aspect of being nude in the presence of other men in a safe, non-sexualized manner was to gain a sense of equality and belonging in the presence of other men, to feel a sense of belonging and brotherhood.

While I must restate that I do not condone or support any nudity as a best practice in psychotherapy, I think it's important to respect the legitimate experience of Timmerman and others that have described these processes as helpful to their healing and growth, while at the same time, recognize the double standard that existed with JONAH's prosecution:

Nudity is acceptable and helpful if men want to become more comfortable in their homosexuality, but harmful and illegal for those to practice in their efforts to help clients with unwanted same-sex attractions or gender identity conflicts.

Trial of the Century: David v. Goliath

By now you may have surmised that JONAH was found guilty. In my opinion, the straw that broke the camel's back and ultimately caused the jury to side with the plaintiffs was the SPLC's ability to sensationalize the use of nudity in Alan Downing's coaching in the media and convince the jury that it was exploitive and abusive. While no particular therapeutic technique was on trial (or was found guilty), the SPLC's use of propaganda and misuse of science effectively hamstrung the small non-profit from defending itself. I wrote about this in the first few days of the trial at *The Christian Post*:

> Even before the trial began, the far-left media began spreading the SPLC's lies and actively distorting the evidence of what actually happened in sessions between Downing and some of these clients. One of the worst purveyors of this spin is blogger Scott Bixby, who writes for Mic.com, a fringe liberal website that has recently been heavily funded by far-left millionaires seeking to indoctrinate millennials, most of whom have two-minute attention spans and are easily impressed by the website's colorful graphics and tabloid-style headlines. For example, Bixby only reported the side of SPLC when writing of the case, spinning key disputed details of a coaching exercise Downing has been criticized for using to heal body shame. In a later article after the trial got underway, Bixby used the SPLC's angle and portrayed Downing as a pervert who was "collecting shirtless photographs" of his client. In actuality, Downing snagged the photos from the client's (Benjamin Unger) Facebook page after the lawsuit was filed and sent them to his lawyers at the Freedom of Conscience Defense Fund to prove that Unger, who took half-nude photos of himself in New York City, had no problem baring his half-naked body. Truly, Unger's public exhibitionism was much more vulnerable and exposing than the body shame exercise Downing employed.[clxxiv]

While the media bias was a huge obstacle to overcome, the liberal bias within the court system was an even bigger hurdle. Only months before the trial began, the

SPLC petitioned the judge to dismiss all of JONAH's expert witnesses on the grounds that science has settled the issue that people are born gay and cannot change, and therefore, any so-called experts were akin to "flat earthers," denying the existence of reality. In a crushing blow to their defense, the judge agreed and dismissed all but one (five out of six) of JONAH's expert witnesses, including yours truly. The SPLC claimed that the dismissed experts were providing "scientifically refuted testimony that was outside the mainstream opinion of professional mental health organizations, chief among them that we all considered homosexuality to be a mental illness."[clxxv] [21]

On the other hand, the SPLC was allowed to keep all of its expert witnesses, none of whom had ever practiced therapy for clients with unwanted same-sex attractions. In fact, all of these witnesses believed that gay-affirming therapy is the only method a counselor should employ, whether a client's homosexuality is wanted or undesired, despite the fact that there is no compelling scientific evidence that suggests gay-affirmative therapy is more effective than efforts to resolve unwanted homosexual feelings. In fact, as the trial progressed, the expert witnesses on the plaintiff's side actually contradicted the arguments put forth by the SPLC:

> Under cross-examination ... Dr. Carol Bernstein, an expert witness for the plaintiffs and a well-known psychiatrist and vice chair of the New York University School of Medicine, conceded that sexual orientation is fluid and can change. She went on to state that she has not conducted any research on the effectiveness of sexual orientation change effort therapy or familiarized

---

[21] For the record, I have never publicly called or labeled homosexuality a mental illness.

herself with any studies looking at harm from such efforts. Additionally, when asked about the particular type of counseling, psychodrama, that JONAH uses in its practice, Dr. Bernstein replied that it was not a well-respected counseling modality, despite that fact that Columbia University, where she attended, offers a course for undergraduate students on the method, a fact of which she was unaware.

As the trial rolled onto a third week, it seems as if the defense was gaining momentum and actually winning. Several witnesses for JONAH testified on how they were helped by similar services they underwent that were also offered by the Jewish non-profit, including Journey Into Manhood and other counseling for unwanted same-sex attractions. Not only that, but testimony delivered by plaintiffs on the stand cast a considerable doubt as to their credibility.

> ... [O]ne of the clients who claimed he was harmed by JONAH's counseling (Benjamin Unger) testified on the stand that he was a virgin, yet when cross-examined, he was confronted with the fact that in his initial client intake documents, he had stated he had been having oral and anal sex since he was 16 years old. Unger's response to the inconsistency was that he did indeed have anal sex, but didn't ejaculate.

Even more contradictions among the plaintiffs caused considerable doubt to their legitimacy, honesty, and mental stability:

> ... former JONAH client Chaim Levin said he was distressed by the counseling he underwent, yet multiple times during his counseling he wrote

enthusiastically of the help he was receiving, so much so that he wanted to become a public spokesman for JONAH as a testimony of change. He even went on the record in depositions and admitted during the trial that at times, he was attracted to women and the girl he was dating at the time he was undergoing counseling. Even more bizarre was testimony from Levin's mother, who was questioned why she accused codirector Arthur Goldberg and life coach Alan Downing, in depositions, of molesting her son. Even the SPLC didn't take Levin's strange rant seriously. Another client's mother, Jo Bruck, was forced to admit that JONAH never made any guarantee that her son would go from "gay" to "straight" when it was brought to her attention that she signed an informed consent document that expressly said there was no guarantee, and that she initialed several paragraphs, one of which discussed the controversial nature of JONAH's services and that there was no guarantee of success.[clxxvi]

Guilty Until Proven Innocent

Because of the severe restrictions Judge Peter Bariso placed on JONAH's defense, the organization was essentially pronounced guilty before the trial. Because of the lack of respect by Judge Bariso for JONAH's spiritual practices, it was practically impossible for the jury to hand down a not guilty verdict. At nearly every point before, during, and after testimony was given, the judge undermined JONAH's freedom of religion. Potential jurors who believed homosexuality is a sin were screened out; defense attorney Charles Limandri was not allowed to discuss JONAH's First Amendment freedom of religious expression in his closing arguments; and Judge Bariso effectively handicapped

187

JONAH's ability to defend itself by cutting out the ability to argue with a synthesis of faith and science, which would have been a true reflection of their religious counseling program.

Even more troubling was the absolute control the judge placed on the jury in its deliberations. He controlled all aspects of evidence and testimony delivered, allowing the jurors to consider only certain "facts" while instructing them not to consider other aspects of the trial he either dismissed or found not to be credible. According to his deliberation instructions, the jury was instructed to consider: 1) Did JONAH make "misrepresentations in connection with the sale, advertisement, or the subsequent performance" of its counseling program; and 2) Did they engage in "unconscionable commercial practices in connection with the sale, advertisement, or the subsequent performance of the JONAH Program?"

In its defense, JONAH maintained it made no misrepresentations and engaged in no unconscionable commercial practices, and contended it referred to homosexuality as disordered from a religious perspective, not as a mental disorder. JONAH also argued that clients were provided a detailed informed consent document before counseling began, which outlined the controversial nature of the services and that there was no guarantee any of the plaintiffs would succeed in overcoming homosexuality.

Foundational to the argument of whether JONAH misrepresented its services was Judge Bariso's pre-trial determination that "it is a misrepresentation ... to describe homosexuality, not as being normal, but as being a mental illness, disease, disorder, or equivalent thereof." Specifically, Bariso ordered the jury before deliberating: If you "determine that the Plaintiffs have demonstrated that any of the Defendants said that homosexuality was a mental illness, disease, disorder, or something equivalent when advertising, selling, or providing the JONAH Program to the Plaintiffs, then you must find that the Defendants have violated the Consumer Fraud Act."

This determination by the judge was the factor that tipped the scales against JONAH, and it is important to discuss the implications of this decision.

First, Judge Bariso is not a mental health expert, nor did he conduct an exhaustive review of the peer-reviewed scientific literature on same-sex attractions, their fluidity, and/or ability to change through counseling. Instead, Bariso relied on so-called mainstream opinions from non-licensing and non-binding mental health trade organizations, such as the American Psychological Association, which contains LGBT task forces and committees dedicated to advancing the political objectives of gay activists through mental health policy. As such, Bariso's determination in declaring these trade organizations' opinions supreme was prejudiced. Rather, he should have considered the many other profes-sional mental and medical health guilds that recognize the efficacy of SOCE therapy and support the client's right to self-determine their response to unwanted same-sex attractions.

This decision also allowed Bariso to disqualify five out of six expert witnesses that JONAH selected to defend its practices, because these experts practiced under the premise, according to Bariso, that homosexuality is a mental disorder. Meanwhile, the SPLC was able to keep all three of its experts, despite the fact that it was demonstrated during trial that none had ever practiced, and in many cases, had very little knowledge of the type of counseling JONAH was conducting. Additionally, since the judge constricted JONAH's ability to defend its practices from a mental health perspective, the validity of any outcome statistics used to inform clients of their relative chance for success in counseling to overcome same-sex attractions was severely limited.[22]

For example, JONAH relied on certain peer-reviewed studies documented in the scientific literature to estimate the chance of success for the Plaintiffs (e.g., Spitzer, 2003). But these outcomes primarily came from psychological and mental health counseling, not religion-based interventions. Because some of JONAH's referral counselors were licensed mental health providers, while others were unlicensed life coaches, it would have been appropriate to cite these statistics. But because of the judge's pre-trial determination, JONAH would have only been found not guilty if they relied on the few published studies (e.g., Jones and Yarhouse, 2007) that reported successful outcomes from religion-based interventions to inform clients.

Understanding JONAH's responsibility to inform clients of these outcome statistics, it was unfair of the judge to disqualify mental health techniques and practices that have been shown to be effective in helping clients overcome sex attractions, just because those practices are not inspired by the Bible or the Torah. In fact, this also shows the inherent bias and ignorance of Judge Bariso, whose underlying assumption must have been that mental health disorders should be treated with mental health counseling alone, while spiritual disorders should be treated with religious interventions alone.

---

[22] Judge Bariso ruled in pre-trial decisions that all of the so-called mainstream mental health trade associations had concluded homosexuality is not a mental disorder needing treatment; therefore, using studies and citing statistics of clients benefitting from mental health treatment for homosexuality were disallowed from JONAH's arguments, and only studies showing religion-based positive outcomes for individuals distressed by unwanted same-sex attractions were allowed to be presented as evidence.

Relying on this premise, Judge Bariso undermined a foundational Judeo-Christian principle of ascertaining truth, that God reveals Himself both in His word (special revelation) and through His works (general revelation). As such, people from a Judeo-Christian background recognize that all truth, whether revealed in sacred documents such as the Torah or Bible, or demonstrated in the principles of science and psychology, is God-inspired and therefore, this synthesis guides their faith and practice. In fact, Arthur Goldberg speaks of this synthesis in his book, *Light in the Closet: Torah, Homosexuality, and the Power to Change.*[clxxvii,23]

In the aftermath of JONAH's loss, the small non-profit was unable to mount an appeal, mostly because of the millions of dollars it would have taken to retry the case, and the fact that their original defense team, Chuck Limandri and the Freedom of Conscience Defense Fund, represented JONAH *pro bono* and couldn't afford to take the case on a second time. In an undisclosed settlement, the judge ordered JONAH to shut down, liquidate all of its assets, and permanently cease operations.

We Lost the Battle, Not the War

Despite the huge loss of JONAH and the ongoing negative publicity and propaganda that the case has generated, the war against the SPLC and other gay activist organizations continues to rage, and intensify, in recent years. Shortly after JONAH was found guilty in the summer of 2015, the SPLC, Human Rights Campaign (HRC), and National Center for Lesbian Rights (NCLR) filed a complaint with the Federal Trade Commission (FTC) (citing the JONAH case as precedent) against People Can Change (now called Brothers on a Road Less Traveled), accusing the

---

[23] For more information on many of the technical aspects of the trial that produced what JONAH and its defense considered to be an unfair outcome, see Appendix A.

Virginia-based non-profit organization of committing consumer fraud, namely, by offering, marketing, selling, and performing services that purport to change a person's sexual orientation or gender identity, commonly referred to as "conversion therapy." This complaint was a part of the SPLC, HRC, and NCLR's ongoing effort to curtail the therapy rights of individuals, and their families, who experience sexual and gender identity conflicts by enacting legislation to ban licensed psychotherapy on the state and federal level.

At the foundation of their complaint to the FTC, the SPLC, HRC, and NCLR said that People Can Change:

> . . . offers, markets, sells, and performs services that purport to change a person's sexual orientation or gender identity, commonly refer-red to as "conversion therapy." The practice is based on the false premise that being lesbian, gay, bisexual, or transgender is a mental illness or disorder caused by a developmental deficiency, trauma, and/or unmet emotional needs. Proponents of conversion therapy, including PCC, assert that addressing those underlying issues will heal the disorder and cause the person to no longer be LGBT.[clxxviii]

The most obvious flaw in this complaint to the FTC is the accusation that PCC is offering therapy. One only needs to visit the organization's website to find that Journey Into Manhood, and their other programs, are all peer-led coaching, not professional psychotherapy from licensed counselors. Thus, to call any of the services offered "conversion therapy" is to grossly distort the nature of their work. But this type of distortion is so common among the SPLC and their counterparts that it has become acceptable to them—after all, any attempt to help people who experience unwanted same-sex attractions or gender identity conflicts is, in their eyes, evil, and therefore, the end justified the means.

Because of their egregious lies, slanders, and material omissions, the National Task Force for Therapy Equality, a coalition of licensed psychotherapists, doctors, public policy organizations, and clients—which I co-founded—submitted a comprehensive report and counter-complaint to the Federal Trade Commission against the SPLC, HRC, and NCLR. Titled: *In Their Own Words—Lies, Deception, and Fraud: The Southern Poverty Law Center, Human Rights Campaign, and National Center for Lesbian Rights' Hate Campaign to Ban Psychotherapy for Individuals with Sexual and Gender Identity Conflicts*, the complaint provides scientific evidence against the claims that therapy and coaching for unwanted same-sex attraction is harmful and ineffective, while at the same time, documents the false claims and fraudulent testimony being supported by the three organizations. Among the many findings of the report are the following fraudulent actions performed by SPLC, HRC, and NCLR, including that they:

> ... actively and knowingly engaged in deceptive and fraudulent marketing practices of the kind the FTC considers malicious, which are particularly deceptive and misleading to consumers and the general public ... pursuant to the FTC's definition of unfair practices, demeaned as those that "cause or are likely to cause substantial injury to consumers which is not reasonably avoidable by consumers themselves and not outweighed by countervailing benefits to consumers or to competition."

> ... supporting witnesses on the state, federal, and international level that have delivered unveri-

fiable and fraudulent testimony in front of law-making bodies in the effort to persuade legis-lative action to ban psychotherapy. Through multiple examples, it has now been proven these witnesses have lied and engaged in a variety of deceptive practices.

... through their marketing campaigns, are actively raising large sums of money in the effort to ban psychotherapy by using deceptive and fraudulent practices. These practices are misleading to the general public, and, as this report documents, it is highly unlikely that the three [organizations] are unaware of the false and misleading nature of how their statements distort the facts and research around psychotherapy to help clients with sexual and gender identity conflicts. As such, they are knowingly mis-leading consumers in their efforts to profit from such activities.

... through their marketing campaigns, have actively and knowingly distorted the research to promote efforts to ban psychotherapy for clients with sexual and gender identity conflicts, including misleading statements regarding the 2009 American Psychological Association task force Report on Appropriate Therapeutic Responses to Sexual Orientation, as well as other research (e.g., Ryan et al., 2009).

... [they] use these misleading statements to make false and misleading claims that psycho-therapy is harmful and ineffective for minors who experience sexual and gender identity conflicts.

... through their marketing campaigns, have actively distorted the scientific research in promoting the "Born Gay" hoax, a notion that has been disproved and refuted by organizations such as the American Psychological Association through their 2008 Position Statement and 2014 *APA Handbook of Sexuality and Psychology. . .* [they] have perpetrated this lie to further their respective political agendas, and in so doing, have raised untold sums of money from unsuspecting consumers and the general public.

... engaged in smear and defamatory attacks on licensed psychotherapists and faith-based ministries providing help and assistance to those who experience sexual and gender identity conflicts.

... Until recently [the] SPLC included an interactive "Hate Map" that identified nearly 100 therapists and ministries on its website ... (they) recently removed this map in the aftermath of the crime of Floyd Corkins, a gunman who was inspired by the SPLC's "Hate Map" to enter the Family Research Council in 2013 and attempt to murder conservatives.

... the [SPLC] was also reported to the Internal Revenue Service (IRS) in 2017 by the Federation for American Immigration Reform (FAIR) for engaging in practices of using "opinion-based smears and innuendos" as though they were educational while violating governmental regulations and using tactics that it claims shields it from liability lawsuits ... [which is a] blatant engagement in political activity (and) a clear violation of their 501(c) (3) status with the IRS.

The National Task Force for Therapy Equality accused the three organizations of using these tactics to perpetrate undue harm to millions of consumers and the general public, hundreds of licensed mental health providers, and thousands of clients and potential clients that experience sexual and gender identity conflicts.

Their hate campaigns have already resulted in therapy bans enacted in 14 states and 45 cities and jurisdictions. The report, therefore, asked the FTC to review these fraudulent and deceptive practices and to promptly order the three organizations to cease their activities in the effort to protect therapists, clients, consumers, and the general public from further harm, as well as issue press releases, correct inaccurate statements on their websites, and actively work with legislators across the United States to reverse legislation that has been passed into law so that further harm can be avoided.[clxxix]

To date, the FTC has not ruled on either complaint.

The War is Heating Up

When gay activists first began to propose laws on the state and federal levels, their talking points were very specific. Laws prohibiting "conversion therapy" are needed to project vulnerable LGBT youth from being subjected to coercive, dangerous, and ineffective practices to change their sexual orientation and gender identity. In order to achieve this, gay activists distort what the actual scientific research reports; they lie and commit fraud in front of political bodies where testimony is delivered; and they indoctrinate the mainstream media, their colleagues, and other vulnerable youth (and adults) that may be likely to seek out help for unwanted sexual or gender identity conflicts.

As this book has already described, these activists share strategies to streamline their fraudulent practices, and have even developed a "tool kit" (see Figure 7.1) to help advocates of their work pass legislation in other jurisdictions. While this "tool kit" has not been made public, I was able to obtain a copy from a source close to the National Center for Lesbian Rights and the Trevor Project, two of the leading organizations supporting "conversion therapy" ban legislation. In their "tool kit," a playbook for how to pass legislation to ban therapy for minors, they claim the following:

> There is an overwhelming scientific consensus that these practices have no scientific basis, contradict the modern scientific understanding of sexual orientation, and put young people at risk of serious harm, including severe depression and suicide. In addition to harming youth directly, the therapists who engage in these practices prevent parents from obtaining accurate information about their child's sexual orientation and gender identity, including the critical importance of family acceptance and support to a child's long term health and well-being. Youth in the child welfare and juvenile justice systems may be especially vulnerable to these practices. Some researchers estimate that as many as one-third of LGBT youth may encounter these practices in some form.
>
> This document draws upon successful efforts to enact state laws protecting youth from these dangerous practices. It also incorporates lessons learned from successfully defending these laws against legal challenges filed by anti-LGBT groups. The sample legislation, based upon bills

197

introduced in several states and successfully defended in court, is both comprehensive and adaptable to the existing law and legislative climate in your state. This tool kit also contains talking points and other messaging tools used in other successful state campaigns as well as the most common opposition arguments.

The most effective and legally appropriate way to enact legislation protecting LGBT youth from so-called "conversion therapy" is through amending state laws that regulate professional counselors and empower governmental bodies to enforce those regulations. Each state has professional licensing boards with the authority and responsibility to regulate the practice of medicine to protect public health and safety. Laws protecting youth from so-called "conversion therapy" fit squarely within this legal framework. They simply require licensed mental health practitioners to follow professional standards and to refrain from using practices that have no basis in science or medicine and that pose serious risks to young people's health and safety. While these practices are potentially harmful to all patients, the risks they pose to minors are particularly great. For example, research has shown that youth experience these practices as a form of family rejection, making them more likely to engage in unprotected sexual intercourse, use illegal drugs, suffer from depression, and attempt suicide.[clxxx]

Nearly all of the statements in these paragraphs above are either false or contain factual inaccuracies that most people in the general public, and sadly, many mental health professionals, would not be able to prove otherwise. Most important to recognize is the lack of outcome-based research among minors that have undergone any sort of therapeutic efforts to change, alter, or eliminate homosexual attractions or gender identity conflicts. The research simply doesn't exist. Yet, these activists distort other research and then conflate its findings and outcomes with professional psychotherapy.

A good example of this tactic is their use of the *Ryan et al.,* 2009 study, which found that family rejection of LGB youth can lead to increased depression, increased suicidal ideation, increased illegal drug use, and unprotected sex. However, the *Ryan et al.,* 2009 study never examined the therapeutic outcomes of LGB youth, but only found that increased family rejection led to greater negative outcomes.

It is not the case that gay activists are unaware of what the actual research says and does not say. The reality is that they simply don't care. The truth is inconvenient, and they will justify whatever means they use in order achieve their ultimate end—to make therapy illegal for anyone, minor or adult, that seeks to reduce or eliminate same-sex attractions or gender identity conflicts. For years, they have said such laws were needed for protection, and would not affect consenting adults, nor would they seek to prohibit faith-based organizations, churches, or unlicensed religious counselors from offering spiritual counseling or religious education on sexuality, sexual orientation, or gender identity. I have sat in multiple state legislative hearings and listened to these very words come of their mouths in order to "project youth" from harm. It's a lie!

Witnesses offering testimony to political bodies to pass this legislation are frauds. They distort the science. They cry and tell emotional, unverifiable stories of torture and claim that youth are being coerced into therapy, against their will, and being electroshocked in the process. Yet, they leave out the inconvenient fact that no licensed therapist in the United States has ever had a state licensing board take action against his or her professional license for using coercion or forcing an LGBT youth into therapy. But all of those "facts" do not matter. The only thing that matters is that their political agenda is achieved, and that political agenda was clearly shown in 2018 when AB 2943 was introduced in California's state legislature. If you don't believe me, just ask Dr. Michael Brown, a leading culture warrior against LGBT activism, who wrote:

> Assembly Bill 2943 would make it an "unlawful business practice" to engage in "a transaction intended to result or that results in the sale or lease of goods or services to any consumer" that advertise, offer to engage in, or do engage in "sexual orientation change efforts with an individual ... The California Assembly [bill] tells churches and other[s] with traditional beliefs about gender and sexual orientation that advocating for their views could get them sued [and] declares advertising, offering to engage in, or engaging in sexual orientation change efforts with an individual" is illegal under state's consumer fraud law ... Yes, AB 2943 bans books, conferences, counseling advocating Muslim, Jewish, and Christian views on gender and sexual orientation.[clxxxi, 24]

Never mind what they said—that these laws were intended only to "protect youth" from abuse and coercion. We knew all along, and we tried to warn all those who would listen that this was coming. But such was as we often hear; "sometimes it has to get worse before it gets better." Despite

---

[24] A revision of AB 2943 removed the sale of books as a material good, while keeping the rest of the bill intact.

Figure 7.1: Trevor Project/NCLR "Conversion Therapy" Ban Tool Kit

TERMINOLOGY

The practices used by therapists who falsely claim to be able to change a person's sexual orientation or gender identity are known by different names, such as so-called "conversion therapy," "reparative therapy," "ex-gay therapy," "conversion efforts," and "sexual orientation change efforts." These terms all refer to the same harmful practices, but there are some contexts in which using a particular term may be preferable or even necessary to advance legislation protecting youth from these practices.

For example, while the terms "conversion therapy" and "reparative therapy" are the most recognized and best understood by the general public, they mischaracterize these harmful practices as therapy, providing false legitimacy. Moreover, they imply that LGBT people can or should be "converted" or "repaired," when in fact modern science recognizes that being LGBT is not a disorder that requires treatment, and that these practices are ineffective and harmful. "Sexual orientation change efforts" (often abbreviated to SOCE) is a more clinical term for these practices that is well-understood in the mental health profession, but it has little recognition among the general public.

There are great benefits to using the term "sexual orientation change efforts" in legislation. This is the neutral, professionally accepted term used by mental health professionals and organizations, including in research and policy statements that describe why SOCE is unsafe, inappropriate, and should not be used by ethical practitioners. When speaking to the general public, however, it is advisable to use other terms to describe what the bill does so that its purpose can be clearly understood.

PURPOSE OF THIS DOCUMENT

This toolkit provides sample legislation and best legislative practices for state LGBT, mental health, and child welfare advocates who seek to protect young people from so-called "conversion therapy," also known as "reparative therapy," "ex-gay therapy," and "sexual orientation change efforts." There is an overwhelming scientific consensus that these practices have no scientific basis, contradict the modern scientific understanding of sexual orientation, and put young people at risk of serious harm, including severe depression and suicide. In addition to harming youth directly, the therapists who engage in these practices prevent parents from obtaining accurate information about their child's sexual orientation and gender identity, including the critical importance of family acceptance and support to a child's long term health and wellbeing. Youth in the child welfare and juvenile justice systems may be especially vulnerable to these practices. Some researchers estimate that as many as one-third of LGBT youth may encounter these practices in some form.

This document draws upon successful efforts to enact state laws protecting youth from these dangerous practices. It also incorporates lessons learned from successfully defending these laws against legal challenges filed by anti-LGBT groups. The sample legislation, based upon bills introduced in several states and successfully defended in court, is both comprehensive and adaptable to the existing law and legislative climate in your state. This toolkit also contains talking points and other messaging tools used in other successful state campaigns as well as the most common opposition arguments.

Please refer to the included Resources Section for additional information. Note that every state is different, and it is best to reach out for support in drafting or advocating for legislation. If you are planning on developing a law protecting LGBT youth from these dangerous practices, please contact The Trevor Project, Government Affairs Department (202-204-4730 or Advocacy@TheTrevorProject.org) and Samantha Ames, Staff Attorney at the National Center for Lesbian Rights (415-365-1308, SAmes@NCLRights.org).

2 **TREVOR** NCLR

Figure 7.2: Trevor Project/NCLR "Conversion Therapy" Ban Tool Kit

the fact that AB 2943 was withdrawn on the last day of the legislature (August 31, 2018), LGBT activists in the state of California are likely to continue their mission to declare any counseling for unwanted same-sex attractions—for a minor or adult, licensed or unlicensed—fraudulent.

But there have been several encouraging developments. First, hundreds of pastors, men and women of faith, and dozens of former homosexuals and "ex-gays" lobbied the state capitol in Sacramento in the spring of 2018 against this oppressive bill. According to the California Family Council:

> Over 350 people, including over 20 "once gay" individuals testified in the California Senate Judiciary Committee June 12 against AB 2943, a bill that would ban churches from providing fee-based resources, counseling, or conferences to those wanting help with unwanted same-sex attraction. "California legislators have publicly claimed that change is impossible and those people simply don't exist," said a press release in advance of the hearing. "While the state celebrates those who embrace an LGBTQ+ identity, this bill will deny such choice and fluidity from anyone seeking to move in the opposite direction."[clxxxii]

If you view the citation at the end of the quote above, it will direct you to the video footage on YouTube, (https://www.youtube.com/watch?v=S78rgepocJw) which shows the overwhelming opposition to this bill, and despite the physical evidence of former homosexuals who said their lives were changed, many of whom show photos of their spouses and children, the bill's chief sponsor, a gay-identified man, refused to acknowledge them![25]

A Silver Lining

But there is a silver lining. On June 26, 2018, the Supreme Court of the United States (SCOTUS) handed down a momentous decision that may have huge implications for the constitutionality of "conversion therapy" bans across the nation. In *NIFLA v. Becerra,* SCOTUS ruled that the state of California via *"The California Reproductive Freedom, Accountability, Comprehensive Care, and Transparency Act"* could not force pro-life crisis pregnancy centers (National Institute of Family and Life Advocates) to provide information on free or low-cost abortion services to their patients since it would be a violation of their First Amendment speech protections.

Before reaching the high court, a federal district court and the Ninth Circuit Court of Appeals ruled against NIFLA, with the rationale that because practitioners were licensed medical professionals, the state could regulate their speech under what is described as professional speech, or medical conduct speech. But Justice Clarence Thomas, who delivered the majority opinion, said there could be no such distinction in protections for free speech versus professional speech:

> The dangers associated with content-based regulations of speech are also present in the context of professional speech. As with other kinds of speech, regulating the content of

---

[25] On August 31, 2018—the final day of the legislature—Assemblyman Evan Low withdrew the bill, which easily passed the Senate (by a vote of 25-11), despite heavy opposition from the legislature Republicans, thousands of members of the faith community in California, and dozens (if not hundreds) of former homosexuals that testified against the bill. The reasons Low withdrew the bill, which was expected to be passed by the Assembly and signed into law, are unclear.

professionals' speech pose[s] the inherent risk that the Government seeks not to advance a legitimate regulatory goal, but to suppress unpopular ideas or information. Take medicine, for example. Doctors help patients make deeply personal decisions, and their candor is crucial. Throughout history, governments have manipulat[ed] the content of doctor-patient discourse to increase state power and suppress minorities.

What Thomas did not eloquently say was brutally communicated by 81-year-old Justice Anthony Kennedy, who had announced his retirement from the court at the end of July 2018:

The so-called learned professions, acting in their professional capacities, are among our most valued participants in the marketplace of ideas. It is one thing to require professionals to exercise due care and competence in the provision of their services. It is another thing entirely to draft them to advance the ideological priorities of an activist state. By requiring pro-life professionals to advertise for free abortions, the state uses its immense power to undermine the very purpose of their professional work.

Kennedy then went onto ridicule the state of California:

The California Legislature included in its official history the congratulatory statement that the Act was part of California's legacy of "forward thinking." But it is not forward thinking to force individuals to be an instrument for fostering public adherence to an ideological point of view

205

[they] fin[d] unacceptable. It is forward thinking to begin by reading the First Amendment as ratified in 1791; to understand the history of authoritarian government as the Founders then knew it; to confirm that history since then shows how relentless authoritarian regimes are in their attempts to stifle free speech; and to carry those lessons onward as we seek to preserve and teach the necessity of freedom of speech for the generations to come. Governments must not be allowed to force persons to express a message contrary to their deepest convictions. Freedom of speech secures freedom of thought and belief. This law imperils those liberties.

The ramifications that come with the *NIFLA v. Becerra* decision are paramount for these counseling bans, because both the Ninth Circuit (*Pickup v. Brown*) and Third Circuit (*King v. Christie*) courts upheld bans on "conversion therapy," precisely because they established what the SCOTUS just struck down—professional speech—a category of speech that is not found in the Constitution, but was invented out of thin air as a means to regulate unpopular, politically charged ideas.[clxxxiii]

As gay activists continue to work across the country to ban "conversion therapy," the implications of this recent SCOTUS decision may prove to be the kiss of death for their attempts to silence professional counseling for unwanted same-sex attractions and gender identity conflicts. Now that the court has struck down the state's right to regulate "professional speech," it is highly likely that *Pickup v. Brown* or *Christie v. King* will be reconsidered in the near future by the high court, bearing in mind that Justice Kennedy retired in July 2018, and President Trump's nominee, Judge Brett Kavanaugh (a strict Constitutionalist), will fill the vacant seat and tip the balance of the SCOTUS even further to the right.

In fact, in early 2019, a federal magistrate judge in Tampa, Florida ruled to partially block the city's ban on SOCE therapy for minors, agreeing that the free-speech rights of the plaintiff counselors had been violated and that the city presented no evidence of minors being harmed by "conversion therapy" within the city of Tampa.[clxxxiv] The *Washington Post* reported:

> [Amanda] Arnold Sansone recommended a limited injunction against enforcing the ban on "non-coercive" sexual orientation conversion efforts that consist entirely of "talk therapy." Under her recommendation, conversion-therapy techniques that are "aversive," such as electro-shock therapy, would still be banned. Her report will be sent to a federal district judge, who will issue a ruling.[clxxxv]

In fact, in early 2019, a federal magistrate judge in Tampa, Florida ruled to partially block the city's ban on SOCE therapy for minors, agreeing that the free-speech rights of the plaintiff counselors had been violated and that the city presented no evidence of minors being harmed by "conversion therapy" within the city of Tampa.[clxxxvi]

But let's say this didn't happen, and gay activists were to continue to pass consumer fraud laws and legislation to restrict therapy and counseling in additional liberal jurisdictions, the overwhelming power of testimony may be great enough for many consumers to still engage in psychotherapy. Despite the negative publicity that certain controversial therapeutic methods have garnered over the years, there still exists a sizeable minority of individuals who will seek out professional services for their unwanted sexual or gender conflicts.

If these services were truly what gay activists made them out to be—consumer fraud—the free market would act as a regulating mechanism, and ultimately, counseling of this nature would no longer be viable or profitable.

But the fact is, those professional counselors who are highly trained, ethical, and offer effective treatments will find themselves with plenty of work, while those truly offering "snake-oil" or "pray away the gay" services will ultimately go out of business. In other words, the cream will rise to the top; and that's not consumer fraud—it's just good old capitalism.

CHAPTER 8
THE WAR IN PUBLIC EDUCATION

I don't think children can grow unless they are accepted just as they are. I think those who try to make you less than you are—that's the greatest evil.

~ Fred Rogers

ℭ

The public education system has been a vehicle for homosexual indoctrination for many years, beginning in elementary school and into higher education. For example, *Heather Has Two Mommies*, a book about two lesbian women raising children together, has been on the classroom shelves for over 35 years. LGBT activists have infiltrated the system through key positions of power to strategically advance their political agenda—and it's gone far beyond issues such as tolerance, equality, and anti-bullying—it's gotten to the point of promotion and recruitment. "Gay is OK—in fact, if you experience same-sex attractions—it's the only way, and if you dare to try and leave, don't even think about it, because you'll become anxious, depressed, and most likely kill yourself"—they say. Later in this chapter, I'll discuss how LGBT activists are waging their battles against "gay conversion therapy" in higher education. But first, I want to paint a picture of how they reach and indoctrinate vulnerable students before they reach college age. This chapter does not cover the entire history or current detail on what's going on in the grade school and secondary school environment. It focuses on the high school and university settings—where young people are making enduring life choices and are in the final stages of preparing for adulthood.

Trade Associations and Labor Unions

Making in-roads in the educational policies of public schools requires the successful indoctrination of decision makers at the local, state, and national levels. LGBT activists know this is how a "deep state"[26] becomes embedded within the public education system, and to achieve their ends, they have worked hard to lobby key institutions and have their members continuously elected into these bodies to become a part of the leadership. One of the most effective ways a deep state is constructed in the education system is for powerful and influential political organizations, labor unions, and trade associations (such as mental and medical health associations) to partner with and infiltrate national agencies, such as the federal Department of Education, and state education agencies, which exist in every state (and vary by structure). They do this by banding together and forming a coalition with each other, and then with their overwhelming numbers, put forward policy statements that influence controversial issues.

Once they have established themselves in leadership, their next objective is to create a permanent structure for their policies to be advanced via special committees and caucuses, designed to indoctrinate the bureaucratic public education leadership and membership at large, so their causes can be incorporated into the collective consciousness for all schools, teachers, students, and parents. An excellent example of how this is achieved is the issue of sexual orientation and youth.

In 2008, a coalition of 13 liberal organizations, including the American Psychological Association, American

---

[26] The "deep state" is a political science term used to describe "influential decision-making bodies believed to be within government who are relatively permanent and whose policies and long-term plans are unaffected by changing administrations." For more information, see: Ambinder, Marc; Grady, D.B. (2013). *Deep State: Inside the Government Secrecy Industry*. Wiley.

Academy of Pediatrics, and the National Association of Social Workers, published a white paper titled: "Just the Facts About Sexual Orientation and Youth: A Primer for Principals, Educators, and School Personnel." In the primer, these 13 organizations, representing 480,000 mental health professionals, all espouse their position statements against so-called "conversion therapy" and brand all those that support therapeutic efforts that are open to change in sexual or gender identity as "political" or "religious" organizations. They state:

> Because of the aggressive promotion of efforts to change sexual orientation through therapy, a number of medical, health and mental health professional organizations have issued public statements about the dangers of this approach. The American Academy of Pediatrics, the American Counseling Association, the American Psychiatric Association, the American Psychological Association, the American School Counselor Association, the National Association of School Psychologists and the National Association of Social Workers together, representing more than 480,000 mental health professionals, have all taken the position that homosexuality is not a mental disorder and thus is not something that needs to or can be "cured."

> The potential risks of reparative therapy are great, including depression, anxiety and self-destructive behavior, since therapist alignment with societal prejudices against homosexuality may reinforce self-hatred already experienced by the patient. Many patients who have undergone reparative therapy relate that they were inaccurately told that homosexuals are lonely,

unhappy individuals who never achieve acceptance or satisfaction. The possibility that the person might achieve happiness and satisfying interpersonal relationships as a gay man or lesbian is not presented, nor are alternative approaches to dealing with the effects of societal stigmatization discussed. [clxxxvii]

Very interesting! For some reason, when you look at the appendices of this document, no survey is ever cited that lists all the clinician's opinions and their therapeutic approaches to sexual and gender identity conflicts, nor is it ever listed how each therapist stigmatizes LGBT persons or what specific advice they provide to their clients. Hmmm... seems like a broad generalization to me! The fact is that there is no actual science that says reparative therapy is dangerous and causes depression, anxiety, and self-destructive behavior among youth. It doesn't exist, because there is no outcome based research on the experiences of minors who have undergone therapy that is open to sexual orientation change or gender fluidity!

In response, the American College of Pediatricians, which was subsequently branded by the famous 13 above as a "small, right wing, anti-science, religiously bigoted" organization of pseudo-professionals, released its own report (with each bullet point fact cited by scientific research) about sexual orientation and youth. It is called: "Facts About Youth." It reads as follows:

- Homosexuality is not hard wired by DNA.

- Homosexual attraction is determined by a combination of familial, environmental, social, and biological influences.

212

- Most students (75% to over 85%) who question or have same-sex attractions will ultimately adopt a heterosexual orientation if not otherwise encouraged. Most questioning students are experiencing temporary sexual confusion or are involved in experimentation.

- The homosexual lifestyle, especially for males, carries grave health risks.

- Declaring and validating a student's same-sex attraction during the adolescent years is premature and may be personally harmful.

- For many youth, homosexual attraction develops due to negative or traumatic experiences, such as sexual abuse. These students need therapy for the trauma, not affirmation of a "gay identity."

- Sexual reorientation therapy has proven effective for those with unwanted homosexual attractions.

- There is no evidence that pro-homosexual programs, such as on-campus student clubs, ease the health risks or emotional disorders suffered by homosexuals.

- Regardless of an individual's sexual *orientation*, sexual *activity* is a conscious choice.

- It is in the best interest of all students to refrain from any sexual activity until adulthood, optimally until they enter a life-long faithful marriage.

- The school's responsibility is to provide a safe environment for respectful self-expression for all students. It is not the school's role to diagnose and attempt to treat any student's medical condition, and certainly not the school's role to "affirm" a student's perceived personal sexual orientation.[clxxxviii]

Of course, the American College of Pediatricians fact sheet was not embraced by the 13 liberal trade associations or the powerful labor unions that give big money to the big gay activist organizations. The reason is that these labor unions have deep financial and special interests tied to the activists. In fact, three of the biggest culprits pushing this agenda (who signed onto the "Just the Facts" statement) in the public education system are the American Federation of Teachers and the American Federation of Labor and Congress of Industrial Organizations (AFL-CIO) with the National Education Association (NEA), who together have a Labor Solidarity Partnership among their nearly 16 million members combined.[clxxxix]

The NEA has been advancing the radical homosexual agenda for decades. In recent years, targeting ex-gays and eliminating any support for so-called "gay conversion therapy" has been on their hit list. The fact that thousands of individuals who once experienced same-sex attractions or gender identity confusion have now resolved those conflicts through therapy is very inconvenient for the LGBT lobby within the NEA, so much so, that in years past they have sought to exclude the Ex-Gay Educators Caucus from exhibiting at their annual convention, held each summer in a major city across the country.

In 2002, a non-profit ex-gay advocacy group, Parents and Friends of Ex-Gays and Gays (PFOX), was denied an exhibitor booth at the NEA's annual conference. The rationale for denial was that booth space was limited and preference would be given to organizations that exhibited in the past. PFOX filed a discrimination claim in 2005 with the D.C. Office of Human Rights (OHR) against the NEA for refusing to provide public accommodation to ex-gays. When the OHR sided with the NEA, PFOX appealed the decision several years later and filed a lawsuit in the Superior Court of Washington, D.C. In his decision, Superior Court Judge Ross upheld the NEA's right to discriminate against PFOX:

> The Court affirms OHR's ultimate determination that PFOX's application was denied legally. In NEA's judgment, PFOX is a conversion group hostile toward gays and lesbians. Thus, even though PFOX vehemently disagrees with NEA's characterization, it is within NEA's right to exclude PFOX's presence at NEA's conventions ... Indeed, the HRA would not require NEA to accept an application from the Ku Klux Klan or a group viewed by the NEA as anti-labor union or racist ... Similarly, military organizations and the Boy Scouts of America are excluded from renting exhibit space at the NEA Annual Meetings because of the positions those organizations take with regard to gay and lesbian rights ... The NEA did not reject its application because PFOX's members include ex-gays, homosexuals, heterosexuals, or members of any other sexual orientation. Rather, NEA rejected PFOX's application because PFOX's message and policies were, in NEA's opinion, contrary to NEA's policies regarding sexual orientation.[cxc]

While Judge Ross did not reverse the OHR decision to allow NEA to discriminate against PFOX, his decision *did* recognize ex-gays as a protected class of individuals in the District of Columbia, which was a rather landmark recognition![27] Because the OHR's stated rationale in siding against PFOX was that the characteristic of the person must be an immutable trait to be protected against discrimination, Judge Ross disagreed:

> OHR's determination that a characteristic must be immutable to be protected under the HRA is clearly erroneous as a matter of law ... Indeed, the HRA lists numerous protected categories such as religion, personal appearance, familial status, and source of income, which are subject to change ... Pertaining to sexual orientation, moreover, the HRA in §2-1401.02(28) defines sexual orientation as "male or female homosexuality, heterosexuality and bisexuality, by preference or practice." Thus, the HRA's intent and plain language eschews narrow interpretation.[cxci]

After the Superior Court of D.C. ruled former homosexuals as a protected class, the leadership within the NEA continued its efforts to silence PFOX and the Ex-Gay Educators Caucus. In 2010, the Ex-Gay Educators Caucus spoke at the Resolutions Committee Open Hearing asking that in Resolution B 14a "ex-gays" be added to the list of individuals (gays, lesbians, bisexuals, transgenders) needing protection from discrimination. The request was denied. Additionally, the caucus wrote a letter (as they had in years past) to President Dennis Van Roekel, requesting ex-gay representation on the NEA Sexual Orientation and Gender Identification Committee. It was also denied.[cxcii]

At the 2017 annual convention, another attempt to remove the Ex-Gay Educators' Caucus was made by radical

---

[27] No other jurisdiction outside of the District of Columbia in the United States officially includes "former homosexuals" as a protected class against discrimination.

activists within the NEA. Sue Halvorson, chair of the caucus wrote:

> New Business Item 86 was written by a delegate from Massachusetts to try to remove our exhibit from the convention. The wording stated: NBI 86—Be it moved that the NEA implement its own rules and regulations on "Becoming an Exhibitor" to NEA caucuses Ex-Gay Educator and immediately remove the exhibit from the exhibit hall on the grounds that this exhibit violates existing NEA exhibitor standards. These standards state that exhibitors may not distribute materials that are offensive, distracting, or discriminatory.[cxciii]

In 2018, another official resolution was introduced at the annual convention to condemn "conversion therapy" as harmful. New business item 121 reads:

> Using existing resources, NEA will release a public statement in opposition to conversion therapy. The American Psychological Association reaffirms that homosexuality is not a mental illness or developmental disorder and opposes the use of conversion therapy. Dozens of cities, states, municipalities, have banned the practice as a form of child abuse.[cxciv]

Linda Harvey, whose organization Mission: America, acts as a watchdog against the radical activities of the NEA, commented on this resolution in an article published at WorldNetDaily.com, describing how the NEA leadership actually violated its own rules when debating the resolution, effectively silencing anyone who opposed the resolution and wished to speak against it:

NBI 121 stated this: "Using existing resources, NEA will release a public statement in opposition to conversion therapy, repairative [sic] therapy, reorientation, or any other process to alter a student's orientation or identity." Come on. If you are an "educator" who can't even spell "reparative," maybe you've missed some other key facts about this issue. One observer in attendance, who wants to remain anonymous, made this observation about the "stacked deck" on the therapy ban issue: "While NEA, to its credit, has relentlessly enforced Robert's Rules of Order, NEA president Lily Eskelsen Garcia caught on that the RRO process was being sabotaged, but she went along with the ploy. Normally, delegates are taken in the order of one speaker 'for' and one speaker 'against.' That was not the case here. One person who called in to submit an argument 'against,' in fact spoke 'for,' and when Eskelsen Garcia caught the error, she said, 'Oh, but that's okay.' "Then a third person submitted an 'against' position to speak to NBI 121, but he simply said, 'I'm against it.' Eskelsen Garcia said, 'No reason?' And then she passed it off with, 'Oh, I'm beginning to figure this out.' When a delegate got up and asked if she could close debate, Garcia said, 'Yes,' so in essence, no one spoke against NBI 121, though at least one conservative delegate had submitted her slip of paper and stood at a microphone prepared to do so. It was a slap in the face of the democratic process."

Harvey then went onto comment about the NEA's long history with LGBT activism in the public education system, and how insane it is that the organization opposes therapy but supports children who wish to change their gender:

> The union is open about its long partnership with GLSEN, the Gay, Lesbian and Straight Education Network, and with the Human Rights Campaign and its corrupting "Welcoming Schools" grade school "LGBT" curriculum, featured at an NEA exhibit booth. Yes, these "educators" are totally fine with seven-year-olds who identify as homosexual, or who are tragically confused about gender.[cxcv]

While the opportunity to speak against this resolution was not offered in 2018, two years prior (2016), Sissy Jochmann of the Ex-Gay Educators Caucus delivered a defense in front of the NEA delegation for former homosexuals and students with unwanted same-sex attractions, while fighting against a similar resolution:

> Distinguished Members of the National Educators Association:
>
> My name is Sissy Jochmann. I am a teacher and a mother, and today I am speaking on behalf of the NEA Ex-Gay Educators Caucus. We represent thousands of teachers who formerly identify as lesbian, gay, bisexual, or transgender (LGBT), as well as the tens of thousands of youth who experience unwanted same-sex attractions, or unwanted SSA.
>
> I want to be clear from the start: Youth with unwanted SSA *do not* always identify as LGBT. Many of these youth are in the process of

working through conflicts with their sexual identity and family, spiritual/religious values, and life goals. While these youth may experience homosexual attractions, they may also have opposite-sex attractions, or their sexual identity may not correspond with their unwanted sexual feelings. Meaning, they may believe in their heart and identify themselves as heterosexual, but due to various unresolved issues, experiences, and sometimes, trauma, they struggle with attractions that do not correspond with who they believe they are at their core.

Because of the complex nature of human sexuality and identity development, scientific research shows that sexual attractions are especially fluid and subject to change during adolescence. Young people are especially vulnerable, due to the immature pre-frontal cortex in their brain, to take sexual risks during this developmental period that could have lasting and harmful effects on their future.

Because of the nature of these risks and the immaturity of their bodies, as well as their emotional and psychological fragility, we believe youth have the right to be provided with the medical and psychological risks associated with homosexual and transgender behavior, and that school counselors, teachers, and educators can act as supportive adults to provide a safe place for youth to discuss these risks and receive help and information to make the best decision for their lives.

Presently, well organized attempts are under way to block youth from being given both the appropriate scientific knowledge and counseling about homosexual and transgender behavior. Activists labeling this counseling "conversion therapy" are using scare tactics to silence teachers, counselors, parents, and students who seek help for their sexual and gender identity conflicts. Let me remind this body of three important facts:

1. The American Psychological Association said in 2008 that although much research has been conducted, scientists cannot conclude that homosexual orientation is innate, or that people are born gay.

2. While activists have made strides in a handful of states to ban therapy for youth who experience sexual and gender identity conflicts, the majority of states, *which now totals 20 in the last three years,* have voted not to take away the rights of youth and parents.[28]

3. Finally, there are *no* (meaning, zero) out-come-based studies on youth who experience unwanted same-sex attractions and seek therapy to resolve their conflicts. Therefore, the role of the NEA should be to promote research efforts to study and *support* youth that seek therapy, not pre-maturely ban their

---

[28] These states include: Connecticut, New Hampshire, Arizona, Georgia, West Virginia, Nevada, Minnesota, Rhode Island, Pennsylvania, Ohio, Iowa, Colorado, Virginia, Washington, Florida, Texas, New York, Massachusetts, Maryland, and Hawaii.

efforts. Recommending a ban sends a message to these students and parents that they are unwelcome at the NEA, and at a time when we are seeking inclusion and tolerance for all, this would be a step backwards.

The NEA can play an important role in supporting *all* youth who experience sexual identity conflicts, not just those who identify as LGBT. I hope this body makes the right and fair decision to support all youth and respect the wide range and diversity of sexual values they hold.

Respectfully yours,
Sissy Jochmann
NEA Ex-Gay Educators Caucus

The Gay–Straight Alliance Strategy

One particularly insidious tactic in use by the opponents of support for young people who are questioning their sexual orientation is to create events and structures within the school system which help to normalize the transition to homosexual identity and behavior. In both secondary and higher education, "safe spaces" and "safe zones" are vehicles of indoctrination where questioning or sexually confused adolescents are "educated" and then enrolled into the LGBT identity. These safe zones provide a physical meeting place for like-minded young people, and some school administrations have gone so far as to sponsor events specifically for self-identified LGBT students, including gay proms.

Their most powerful and widespread method, however, is the Gay-Straight Alliance (GSA). Initiated by the Gay Lesbian Straight Education Network (GLSEN), the GSA is a very clever machine, in that it recognizes that

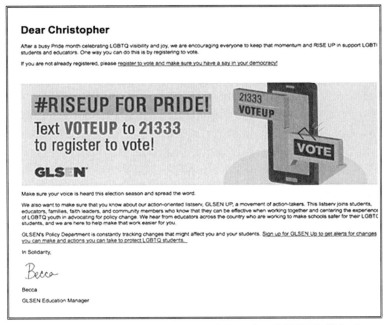

Figure 8.1: E-mail from GLSEN Encouraging LGBT Political Activism

access to children is dependent the GSA is a very clever machine, in that it recognizes that access to children is dependent upon successful indoctrination from within; so in order to spread its propaganda, it must recruit sympathetic staff—teachers and administration—to wield its power.

After administrators are on board, the campaign to end bullying LGBT students (which may or may not actually be happening in a particular school) is initiated, and teachers, often LGBT-identified, are recruited or volunteer to host a "safe space" in their classrooms. After the safe space is initiated, the next step is to form a GSA as an extra-curricular activity, similar to a club like the National Honors Society or an after-school sport. But unlike football or basketball, the objective is not teaching kids a skill or facilitating fun and competition. No. GSAs exist to normalize and advocate for homosexual and transgender-identified students and to encourage questioning or confused students to "come out of the closet" and identify as LGBT, and then help advance LGBT political goals. Don't believe it? See Figure 8.1 to see just one of the many political e-mails GLSEN routinely sends to its educators' network.

While their stated goals are usually about tolerance, anti-bullying, and safe schools, the GSAs are organized and promulgated by organizations like GLSEN and the Trevor Project, which became nationally known for its "It Gets Better" campaign to prevent LGBT suicides. These groups cooperate with larger, well-funded gay rights organizations that oppose therapy for young people struggling with sexual and gender identity conflicts.

Case in point: In 2013 my wife and I were guests on the nationally syndicated talk show, *The Dr. Oz Show*. The subject was Reparative Therapy and California's SB 1172 law to ban "conversion therapy" for minors.

While I have to give credit to Dr. Oz and his producers for giving me and my colleagues ample air time to tell our stories and explain our work, the second half of the show was essentially a setup to denounce our work by gay rights advocates. Who do you think they invited to do this? None other than Eliza Baird, the executive director of GLSEN (who is also a lesbian) and the Gay and Lesbian Alliance Against Defamation (GLAAD). Both Baird and GLAAD gave a song and dance about how all schools and adults should be "supportive" and "embracing" of LGBT kids and that encouraging "change" was harmful and abusive.

Did anyone find it odd that neither the representative from GLSEN or GLAAD was a mental health expert, nor did they even advocate for the population of clients (unwanted sexual and gender identity conflicts) that my colleagues and I worked with? Of course not, because it didn't matter! What was really important was that some "compassionate" bully buster and media thought police were given equal air time to denounce a therapy they didn't understand, but was threatening enough for them to show up and spew their canned talking points. Funny enough, former American Idol Clay Aiken, who appeared on the show to promote his failing singing career, agreed with my stated opinion—that all sexual and gender minorities should be supported (not just some).

One of the biggest, if not the most prominent, Trojan horse for LGBT activism within secondary public education has been anti-bullying programs and the creation of "safe spaces" in schools. In secondary schools, safe spaces function as a place where LGBT-identified or questioning students can find protection from harassment from those who might discriminate or intimidate them on the basis of their sexual orientation or gender identity. They are usually identified by a rainbow sticker, placed on a particular teacher's door or class window, and represent an inviting and affirming place for the student to retreat. The problem with anti-bullying and safe spaces is that they do not stop at protection, and tend to operate as indoctrination breeding grounds for a variety of LGBT political causes. For example, in 2016, the American Federation of Teachers (AFT), a big supporter of safe spaces, adopted a resolution titled: "School Safety and Educational Opportunity for Lesbian, Gay, Bisexual, Transgender, Queer and Questioning (LGBTQ) Students."

On its face, the resolution's call for safe schools seems reasonable, but it goes far beyond issues of safety when it advocates expansive LGBT initiatives, including: 1) Professional development opportunities on issues affecting LGBTQ students; 2) Extracurricular clubs such as Gay-Straight Alliances; 3) Family engagement and support for families of LGBTQ students; 4) Respect for human rights, including LGBTQ rights, across the curriculum; 5) Developmentally appropriate resources on LGBTQ issues (e.g., in libraries, faculty resources); 6) The collection and review of data to identify disparities and barriers for LGBTQ students; 7) Staff people who are conversant in issues relating to sexual orientation, gender identity and gender expression; and finally, here's the most controversial; it calls schools to:

Adopt specific policies for ensuring transgender students are treated in a manner consistent with their gender identity, including:

1. Using chosen name and pronouns;
2. Changing name and gender in school records;
3. Ensuring student privacy and confidentiality in disclosing private student information;
4. Providing access to facilities and programs according to the student's gender identity;
5. Implementing gender-neutral dress codes; and
6. Reviewing all gender-based activities.[cxcvi]

As is seen by trade associations like the AFT and NEA, when radical LGBT activists first arrive in public schools, they begin very innocuously. They call for tolerance, understanding, compassion, and love. What kind of person would be against those ideals? The problem is that it never stops there. Once they get their foot in the door, they establish a culture within the system by aggressive lobbying—disguised as "educational campaigns"—to influence key decision makers, while at the same time, recruiting sexually confused children into their scheme. What happens next is heavy indoctrination.

LGBT activists tell children, usually in very subtle ways (but sometimes overtly) that their parents, school, and church are the enemy; and in order to be free of this discrimination, kids must become activists to push forward the LGBT agenda. Of course, it all sounds very noble—Fight for equality! Oppose oppression! Be who you are! But what sounds like freedom and liberation, is really a cover for cult-like behavior; and once you're a member of the cult, you no longer can think or act independently. You must group think!

A Case Study on LGBTQ "Safe Zones"

In 2013, I founded a non-profit organization called Voice of the Voiceless. I was genuinely distressed by the recently passed therapy ban law in the state of California—as well as the systematic oppression I began to witness across many sectors of society—for former LGBT persons and individuals with unwanted same-sex attractions and gender identity conflicts. I knew I could not properly advocate for this in my role as a licensed psychotherapist; after all, if I were going to criticize the mainstream mental health field's political activism within their ranks, I had better put my money where my mouth was! So, I created a place for myself to do this work, and recruited about a dozen like-minded individuals, most of them former LGBT-identified individuals who had experienced transformation in their lives, much as I did.

One of the first projects we undertook was to examine how higher education so-called "safe zones" treated students that were distressed by their sexual and gender identity conflicts. We wanted to know if colleges would make appropriate referrals to culturally competent therapists, counseling centers, referral agencies, or faith-based ministries for students who may not have identified as LGBT and sought healing or change from their unwanted attractions, behavior, or identity. In order to do this, we had to go under cover and pose as graduate students at the university and actually speak with someone at the safe zone. One of my colleagues and I visited seven public higher education institutions in the state of Virginia to explore this issue.

The results of our project are described and summarized below and in Appendix B. Let me caution you as you read. The entire report is available as a PDF document that can be downloaded on our website (www.VoiceoftheVoiceless.info), and what is described below is a condensed summary. The summary below will give you a taste of what is going on at public universities, and our assumption is that this project is a small sample of what is happening at public universities across the country. Now that I am actually employed by a private college as a licensed mental health therapist, I can attest that the procedures that were followed at these universities were extremely unprofessional, inadequate, and in some cases, dangerous.

My colleague and I were able to make an appointment (in some cases, with a licensed clinician) without ever providing any proof whatsoever that we were a student at the university. We were able to video and audio record the entire conversation with relative ease. We were granted access to books, libraries, and videos, without any censorship or thought from employees that some of the material might not be appropriate or suitable. In some cases, the materials we examined were borderline or overtly pornographic! But what is worse, the university employees were deceptive, ignorant, and ill-informed! They operated as group think cattle that took their talking points from those who had indoctrinated them. Many of them, when posed with difficult questions, could not think clearly or critically, or provided canned and biased answers with no regard to the actual diversity of their student population. In summary, if these safe zones were supposed to be inclusive and diverse, they were anything but that!

Campus Climate Report:
An "Unsafe" Zone for Students with Unwanted SSA

In order to assess the Virginia University system's LGBTQ resource centers' attitudes and services toward QU students, we selected seven state-funded four-year higher education institutions: George Mason University, James

228

Madison University, University of Virginia, Virginia Commonwealth University, Old Dominion University, Christopher Newport University, and the College of William and Mary. In September 2013, two representatives from Voice of the Voiceless (VoV) visited these campuses over a 2.5-week period to document the services rendered by LGBTQ resource center counselors and information given or provided in the resource center. We documented each meeting by using concealed audio or video equipment, and have made these recordings available on our website (www.VoiceoftheVoiceless.info) and via YouTube. We also took notes and photos to document the materials in each LGBTQ resource center to determine what, if any, information was made available for QU students. As a note of caution, these universities do not represent a random sample nor should be viewed as representative of all LGBTQ resource centers in Virginia or across the United States.

What is Happening at the Universities?

As adolescents enter the college years, they continue to explore their identities while experiencing a greater level of autonomy, develop a more meaningful sense of self, and realize greater levels of intimacy in social and romantic relationships. Developmental psychologist Erik Erikson described youth in this critical period as transitioning between two significant life stages: *Identity vs. Role Confusion* and *Intimacy vs. Isolation*. In the former, adolescents develop a sense of self and personal identity. Successful completion of this stage leads to an ability to stay true to oneself, while failure leads to role confusion and a weak sense of self. In the latter stage, young adults need to form intimate, loving relationships with other people. Success leads to strong relationships, while failure results in loneliness and isolation.[cxcvii]

Universities provide an ideal social context for young people to begin making the transition from childhood to adulthood. Professors, coaches, counselors, and mentors have a profound impact on adolescents as they negotiate conflicts during this process. It is essential that young people are given time and space to explore these challenges with proper guidance to help them come to terms with their identity. Sexual orientation and identity is one of those challenges, especially as it concerns adolescents who are lesbian, gay, bisexual, transgender, intersex, questioning, or experience unwanted same-sex attractions (LGBTQIU).[29]

For a number of reasons, LGBTQIU students may experience greater challenges than their heterosexual classmates in transitioning from adolescence to adulthood. Thus, resource centers specifically tailored to the needs of these vulnerable populations may provide the necessary knowledge, support, and skills required to help these youth develop a strong sense of self and form loving and intimate relationships. Many state-funded universities in Virginia have realized the benefit of such LGBTQ resource centers and have set aside funds to support sexual minority students as they negotiate the unique challenges that heterosexual students do not encounter.

In recent years, many of these LGBTQ resource centers have also developed or infused the concept of a safe zone, which works to promote a welcoming atmosphere for sexual minority students on campus. For example, Virginia Commonwealth University "educates members of the University community LGBTQ issues to create a network of allies who, together with members of the LGBTQ community, work to create community of safety and full inclusion for all its members."[cxcviii] Similarly, Virginia Tech's Safe Zone Manual states "some students may be hesitant to come out to everyone on campus. Safe zones are

_____

[29] While we recognize that Intersex students should be included in this list of sexual minorities, we found no resources specifically dedicated to this population among the LGBTQ Resource Centers visited.

expected to uphold an individual's privacy and treat information gained from that student in a confidential manner."[cxcix] Thus, these programs are primarily meant to provide support for sexual minority students in the effort to help them feel safe and to experience acceptance, love, and intimacy in relationships.

Virginia universities have developed a number of supportive mechanisms for sexual minority youth, including designated safe spaces, staff/faculty that serve as on-campus allies, and educational programs, seminars, and workshops to help further tolerance and understanding for LGBTQ students. Such programs serve as a place for students to feel welcome and supported in their sexual identity, but they may also be a place where youth come to receive counsel over various conflicts. In that case, an LGBTQ resource center or safe zone may provide information, options, and referrals for the student to seek out mental health services within their university counseling center or local community to help them negotiate these challenges.

In Virginia, the state has appropriated funds to assist students in need of counseling, regardless of sexual orientation and/or identity, through a program called Counseling and Psychological Services (CAPS). For example, at the University of Virginia, CAPS primarily utilizes a brief psychotherapy treatment approach with students. Duration of psychotherapy is generally six to ten sessions. Clinical efforts are focused on assisting students to returning to the level of functioning required for successful academic achievement. When students' needs do not fit a brief therapy approach, referrals are made to alternate clinic sites or to psychotherapists within the Charlottesville community. In situations in which a community therapist referral may be problematic or contraindicated, exceptions to a brief treatment approach are made on a case-by-case basis.[cc]

In the referral process, LGBTQ resource centers and safe zones play an important role by helping students identify services, programs, and allies that may support them in their unique challenges. Therefore, it is vital for LGBTQ resource centers and safe zones to correctly identify a student's sexual identity and/or orientation so they can be linked to a competent professional that can help them reach their goals. While it appears that the needs of lesbian, gay, bisexual, and transgender (LGBT) students are being adequately served in Virginia university LGBTQ resource centers and safe zones, there exists a population of individuals that are either questioning their sexual orientation and/or have unwanted same-sex attraction (SSA) that may not be receiving equivalent support.

Students that experience homosexual feelings but do not identify as LGBT may be questioning their sexual identity or have unwanted same-sex attractions (QU). It is inappropriate to label such students LGBT or refer them to churches, programs, organizations, or counselors that adhere only to a gay affirming approach. Such mislabeling may be offensive and harmful, and should be avoided. Alternatively, QU students may self-identify as a former homosexual or ex-gay. In 2009, the Superior Court in the District of Columbia ruled that ex-gays or former homosexuals are a protected class against sexual orientation discrimination.[cci] Because Virginia is located in a neighboring jurisdiction to Washington, DC, it is especially appropriate for state-funded universities to recognize such individuals as separate and distinct from the LGBT population, and therefore, provide information and services that are sensitive to their values and unique needs.

Due to the nature of state-funded services, LGBTQ resource centers and safe zones are obligated to provide QU students competent referrals and assistance that are sensitive to their values and unique needs. Because LGBTQ resource centers and safe zones are publicly funded entities, they are considered a limited public forum, and as such, must provide equal access to views and/or organizations that may serve the unique needs of QU students.

By forming an LGBTQ resource center and/or safe zone, Virginia universities have established a limited public forum for the purpose of providing non-university resources for issues surrounding sexual orientation. These universities provide resources from and web links to organizations espousing the belief that an individual should express his or her same-sex attractions. Therefore, they cannot discriminate against the viewpoint of those who have provided resources to the university for those questioning their homosexual attractions and feelings and/or offer sexual orientation change services. Since government may not regulate speech based on its substantive content or the message it conveys, in the realm of private speech or expression, government regulation may not favor one speaker over another.

Discrimination against speech because of its message is presumed to be unconstitutional. When government targets not subject matter but particular views taken by speakers on a subject, the violation of the First Amendment is all the more blatant. Viewpoint discrimination is thus an egregious form of content discrimination. The government must abstain from regulating speech when the specific motivating ideology or the opinion or perspective of the speaker is the rationale for the restriction.[ccii] When a government opens a forum for literature distribution, it must treat all persons and groups seeking to use the forum equally, regardless of their viewpoint.[cciii]

The actions of the universities found in our investigation, in their refusal to mention the existence of ex-gay resources or offer appropriate therapy and/or competent referrals, when repeatedly requested by an individual ostensibly experiencing confusion over his sexuality, or conflict between his sexuality and his faith, demonstrate that the universities favor the speech of the LGBT community over the ex-gay community. The universities have thus suppressed and deemed the viewpoints of ex-gays on human sexuality and sexual orientation as unworthy of exhibition and distribution, while the viewpoints of the LGBT community are favored and deemed worthy by the university.

In this context, presenting only one viewpoint on the issue of sexual orientation not only constitutes viewpoint discrimination, but it may also constitute sexual orientation discrimination. Additionally, it may also be harmful to the student's self-identity, as it presents a scenario of isolation (versus intimacy), described above in Erikson's developmental model. This in turn could lead to feelings of anxiety, depression, and hopelessness (among others) at the thought of having to live in such a way that is incongruent with the individual's spiritual/religious values and/or moral ideals.

Despite the suggestion by several counselors and administrators in Virginia university LGBTQ resource centers, Sexual Orientation Change Effort (SOCE) therapy is neither illegal in Virginia, nor is it unethical or harmful for clients who voluntarily take part in such therapeutic processes. Professional psychological associations have varying opinions as to the efficacy of such interventions.

The American Psychological Association (APA) formed a task force in 2009 that issued a report on the outcomes of SOCE therapy in the research literature. In their systematic review of SOCE literature, they concluded that "research on SOCE (psychotherapy, mutual self-help groups, religious techniques) has not answered basic questions of whether it is safe or effective and for whom," and that there are "no scientifically rigorous studies of recent SOCE that would enable a statement to be made about whether recent SOCE (interventions) are safe or harmful and for whom."[cciv] However, this report has been criticized for insisting that SOCE outcome research exhibits high methodological research standards while not demanding the same criteria be used to evaluate the efficacy of gay-affirmative therapy, which the task force (as well Virginia universities) recommend for all clients who experience homosexual feelings, whether LGBT or QU identified.[ccv]

Another comprehensive review of SOCE literature by the National Association for Research and Therapy of Homosexuality (NARTH) in 2009 came to a diametrically opposed conclusion. Reviewing 100 years of research and clinical literature, the report concluded that it is possible for some men and women to change from homosexuality to heterosexuality, and that efforts to change do not invariably result in harm.[ccvi]

Misstatements by LGBTQ Resource Center Counselors

VoV's investigation of the seven institutions of higher education that maintained resource centers or help programs found viewpoint discrimination across the board.

In some universities, the locations that assist sexual minority students are not specifically called LGBTQ resource centers. At Virginia Commonwealth University, the Office of Multicultural Student Affairs houses their LGBTQ efforts. At Old Dominion University, sexual minority issues are given space within the Division of Student Engagement and Enrollment Services, called the ODU Safe Space program or ODU Out. At the College of William and Mary, the Center for Student Diversity is the home for LGBTQ activities. Nonetheless, all of these offices provide anonymous counseling and guidance to sexual minority students in need of assistance and/or resources. The offices also maintain a website where LGBT-affirming web links are available for students seeking referrals, constituting an additional (limited) public forum for the purpose of providing non-university resources for issues surrounding sexual orientation.

Additionally, Christopher Newport University did not maintain an actual LGBTQ resource center staffed by university employees, nor did they host LGBT-affirming resources on a public website available for students. While we did meet with the president of their Gay-Straight Student Union on campus, and speak with a counselor at their Health and Wellness Services program, these meetings did not constitute a limited public forum. However, we have included the recordings of our meetings with them and their statements for the purpose of documentation. Liberty Counsel, the litigation firm representing VoV, did not send a letter to this university due to the fact that one counselor and student-run group did not qualify as a limited public forum.

In addition to inaccurate statements about the legality, efficacy, potential harm, and ethicality of SOCE therapy, LGBTQ resource center counselors and administrators also made a number of common misstatements about the nature of SOCE therapy, ex-gay organizations, and religious ministries, as well as the etiology of homosexuality.

Specific statements will be examined in detail in this report, and include:

- **Improper terms for SOCE therapy, including names such as "conversion" and "reparation" therapy.** Such expressions are used pejoratively by those who oppose SOCE, are offensive, and should be avoided in a value neutral setting where public funds are utilized.

- **Simplified explanations of the nature of SOCE therapeutic interventions.** Explanations of SOCE therapy ranged from being described as "not valid" or an "invalid" form of therapeutic treatment, while others referred to it as an attempt to "pray away the gay" that relies on purely behavioral methods of distraction and/or suppression. Such descriptions are based on negative portrayals by activists and opponents of SOCE, and do not reflect the work of licensed mental health practitioners who practice SOCE therapy.

- **Inaccurate outcomes of clients who undergo SOCE, including the use of scare tactics as a means of discouragement.** Some counselors went so far as to suggest that SOCE therapy is inherently harmful and will ultimately cause a client to become anxious, depressed, and/or commit suicide. Such statements are inaccurate and rely on anecdotal evidence and/or studies that have used convenience samples.[ccvii] While SOCE therapy carries with it a level of risk, so does any form of medical or psychological treatment; and there is no scientific evidence that suggests it is more harmful than other forms of psychotherapy.

- **SOCE therapy is illegal and unethical.** While laws have recently been passed to prohibit minors from undergoing SOCE therapy in California and New Jersey, it is still legal for adults to undergo SOCE therapy in these two states and is permitted for all clients in the other 48 states. Although some professional trade associations (i.e., American Psychological Association, American Counseling Association) caution and/or discourage the use of SOCE, none of these organizations have gone as far as to regard the practice as unethical. Additionally, organizations such as the American Association of Christian Counselors (AACC) and the National Association for Research and Therapy of Homosexuality (NARTH), which comprise over 50,000 licensed mental health practitioners collectively, support a client's right to pursue SOCE therapy.

- **Parents force their homosexual-oriented children to undergo SOCE therapy, and in some cases, isolate them by requiring them to attend "conversion therapy camps" in order to become heterosexual.** Some anti-ex-gay activists have made accusations that parents have forced their homosexual children to undergo SOCE interventions, which include camps that rely on aversive (i.e., electroshock) methods for conversion.[ccviii] Such claims are myths and have been investigated and disproven, yet nonetheless were repeated by some LGBTQ resource center counselors as scare tactics to discourage students from pursuing SOCE therapy.

- **Individuals who claim they have experienced sexual orientation change have only changed their behavior. SOCE therapy does not change an individual's sexual attractions and desires.** Such statements are not scientific and are impossible to verify. Research has demonstrated that some homosexual-oriented individuals can and do experience change, on a continuum, in their homosexual feelings and develop heterosexual attractions and desires.[ccix] Thus, counselors making this assertion are making unsubstantiated claims that are not grounded in science and is in direct violation of the APA's "Leona Tyler Principle."[ccx, ccxi]

- **Homosexual feelings are biological and/or genetic.** While there may be some biological pre-dispositions to the development of same-sex attractions, scientists have not been able to determine

238

a simple biological explanation for the development of same-sex attractions. In 2008, the APA said: "There is no consensus among scientists about the exact reasons that an individual develops a heterosexual, bisexual, gay, or lesbian orientation. Although much research has examined the possible genetic, hormonal, developmental, social, and cultural influences on sexual orientation, no findings have emerged that permit scientists to conclude that sexual orientation is determined by any particular factor or factors. Many think that nature and nurture both play complex roles; most people experience little or no sense of choice about their sexual orientation."[ccxii]

- **Homosexual feelings are hard-wired and impossible to change.** While no one simply chooses to experience homosexual feelings, they are not hard-wired and research indicates that some individuals may experience change or fluidity.[ccxiii] A recent study indicated that while heterosexual feelings are more stable in both genders, women might have even more fluidity in their same-sex attractions than men.[ccxiv] Similarly, previous research has found that heterosexual attractions are 17 times more stable in men and 30 times more stable in women than homosexual attractions.[ccxv]

- **Homosexual sexual activity is no more risky than heterosexual sexual activity as long individuals practice "safe sex."** Data from the Centers for Disease Control and Prevention found that in 2011, 94.9% of HIV diagnoses among young men ages 13–19 were linked to men who have sex with men (MSM) and 94.1% of HIV cases among young men ages 20–24 were from MSM.[ccxvi] While condoms may reduce the risk of contracting and spreading HIV through anal sex, the Food and Drug Administration has advised the following on their website: "Condoms provide some protection, but anal intercourse is simply too dangerous to practice... condoms may be more likely to break during anal intercourse than during other types of sex because of the greater amount of friction and other stresses involved. Even if the condom doesn't break, anal intercourse is very risky because it can cause tissue in the rectum to tear and bleed. These tears allow disease germs to pass more easily from one partner to the other."[ccxvii]

Findings and Conclusions

The VoV investigation established that QU students were marginalized and discriminated against at every university visited in Virginia. While some LGBTQ resource centers simply lacked the necessary knowledge and information to offer students who might want to pursue SOCE therapy, others, unfortunately, were actively suppressing ex-gay resources and discouraging QU students by using scare tactics, misrepresenting the facts of SOCE, and portraying those who have experienced sexual orientation change in a negative light. For the LGBTQ resource centers that made a concerted effort to suppress information, misrepresent SOCE therapy, and portray those who have experienced sexual orientation change in a negative light, not only are they engaging in viewpoint discrimination, but sexual orientation discrimination as well.

While former homosexuals have existed as a sexual minority for quite some time, only within the last five years have they been recognized as a distinct sexual orientation that needs protection from harassment and discrimination under nondiscrimination laws.[ccxviii] When an LGBTQ resource center staff favors certain sexual orientations (i.e.,

LGBT) over others that may be unpopular or politically incorrect, such as former homosexuals or ex-gays, this is unlawful. For example, transgender individuals are celebrated by the university centers or changing their gender identity, but ex-gays who change their sexual orientation from homosexual to heterosexual are disfavored, maligned, and discredited. This conduct may also be against the university's policies on sexual orientation nondiscrimination, because such actions defeat their own mission statements on sexual orientation diversity, tolerance, and inclusion.

Some university LGBTQ resource center employees may feel justified in suppressing information on SOCE therapy due to their beliefs that SOCE is harmful, damaging, and/or ineffective. While those beliefs may not be grounded in scientific fact, it is understandable why they may feel justified in withholding this information. However, it is important to note that the PFOX brochures that were rejected by many of these university centers were not even about SOCE therapy, but rather, discussed anti-bullying, tolerance, and respect for former homosexuals (see http://www.pfox.org/resources/students-and-schools-2/).

Regardless of one's viewpoint regarding SOCE therapy, reasonable individuals can still agree that tolerance, respect, and bullying prevention for former homosexuals and individuals with unwanted same-sex attractions is a worthy goal that promotes diversity and appreciation of sexual orientation. Yet, many of the LGBTQ resource center employees still refused to make these brochures readily available for interested students. Instead, they contributed to the intolerance and bullying of former homosexuals by saying negative things and repeating stereotypes in the effort to discredit the ex-gay community and discourage QU students from seeking resources that align with their spiritual/religious values.

In a 1994 paper titled "Hate Speech on Campus," the American Civil Liberties Union provides an excellent discussion on the problem of censoring unpopular and/or politically incorrect viewpoints on college campuses:

> Many universities, under pressure to respond to the concerns of those who are the objects of hate, have adopted codes or policies prohibiting speech that offends any group based on race, gender, ethnicity, religion or sexual orientation. That's the wrong response, well-meaning or not. The First Amendment to the United States Constitution protects speech no matter how offensive its content. Speech codes adopted by government-influenced state colleges and universities amount to government censorship, in violation of the Constitution. And the ACLU believes that all campuses should adhere to First Amendment principles because academic freedom is the bedrock of education in a free society. How much we value the right of free speech is put to its severest test when the speaker is someone we disagree with most. Speech that deeply offends our morality or is hostile to our way of life warrants the same constitutional protection as other speech because the right of free speech is indivisible: When one of us is denied this right, all of us are denied. Since its founding in 1920, the ACLU has fought for the free expression of all ideas, popular or unpopular. That's the constitutional mandate. Where racist, sexist and homophobic speech is concerned, the ACLU believes that more speech—not less—is the best revenge. This is particularly true at universities, whose mission is to facilitate learning through open debate and study, and to

enlighten. Speech codes are not the way to go on campuses, where all views are entitled to be heard, explored, supported or refuted. Besides, when hate is out in the open, people can see the problem. Then they can organize effectively to counter bad attitudes, possibly change them, and forge solidarity against the forces of intolerance. College administrators may find speech codes attractive as a quick fix, but as one critic put it: "Verbal purity is not social change." Codes that punish bigoted speech treat only the symptom: The problem itself is bigotry. The ACLU believes that instead of opting for gestures that only appear to cure the disease, universities have to do the hard work of recruitment to increase faculty and student diversity; counseling to raise awareness about bigotry and its history, and changing curricula to institutionalize more inclusive approaches to all subject matter.[ccxix]

LTBTQ resource centers routinely hold campus wide events in order to educate students on sexual orientation. Accordingly, their bias and outright discrimination against the ex-gay community reaches the student population at large and affects the entire student body. Thus, it is clear that this discrimination and marginalization go beyond assisting so-called queer and questioning (QU) students and offering them resources and referrals for SOCE therapy. Through the recordings and descriptions in this report and the FOIA's listed in the appendices, it is evident that discrimination at the hands of Virginia LGBTQ resource centers is very broad-based and affects the entire university, including those students who do not have same-sex attractions but are educated by LGBTQ resource centers, their campus wide events, and additional educational programs. Therefore, in addition to the specific policy recommendation changes suggested for each LGBTQ resource center in this report, tolerance training for the entire university campus staff and student body is necessary in order to achieve meaningful reform on Virginia university campuses

The Acception Project

If an anti-bullying program is a good excuse to get LGBT activism in public schools, why can't that program also promote tolerance and acceptance for students who experience unwanted same-sex attractions or gender identity conflicts? That's exactly what I thought. So, in 2010, I began a project called *Acception*. Conceived as a short film and bullying prevention curriculum for middle-school students, *Acception* (see Figure 8.2) tells the story of four students who are given a classroom project to investigate the history of bullying, and why sexual minority students are bullied so much. In their homework assignment, the students researched on line and find several two-minute vignettes of young people, one gay, one lesbian, and one young women with unwanted same-sex attractions, as well as two animations, one explaining the origins of bullying with funny cavemen, and another cartoon that debunks the "born gay" myth in an Albert Einstein laboratory scene. The stories are heart-wrenching, while the animations are educational and provide comic relief.

The 20-minute film was accompanied with a five-lesson curriculum, wristbands, and classroom poster. After test piloting the program in several Bronx, New York middle schools, I worked with officials in Prince George's (PG) County, Maryland, one of the largest school districts in the United States, and was granted permission to conduct training and implementation in its roughly 30 middle schools.

But as soon as the program was beginning to be rolled out, I received several threatening messages on Facebook from a PG County employee, and within two days of notifying the superintendent of the school district about the harassment, *Acception* was thrown out of the curriculum.

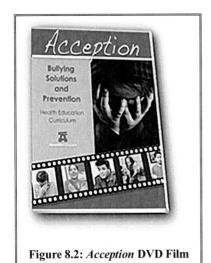

Figure 8.2: *Acception* **DVD Film**

I was shocked. I had spent years developing the content, writing the film's script, hiring actors, directing and editing the movie, creating the curriculum, and promoting the educational campaign in our community. I suspect the PG County employee that harassed me had also leaked the story to major media outlets in the Washington, D.C. metro area: An ex-gay therapist was trying to "convert" and "cure" gay students with his anti-gay bullying program. *Washington City Paper* reported the following:

> Prince George's County Public Schools has pulled from six middle-school health classes a controversial video that discusses therapy as a tool to help gay teens become straight ... A roughly five-minute segment also discusses whether people are born gay and describes reparative therapy as an option for gay people who want to be straight. If you're attracted to members of your own sex, you can get therapy to change that. It's an idea mainstream medical organizations have described as dangerous—and, it turns out, it's also a message that's been taught to some middle schoolers in Prince George's County since last year. Starting last fall, some seventh-grade health classes in the Prince

George's County Public Schools system were shown an anti-bullying video that promoted gay-to-straight therapy as an option for LGBTQ youth. When City Desk started asking questions about the video this week, the school system pulled it from classrooms.[ccxx]

The *Washington Examiner* reported the following:

Prince George's County Public Schools has pulled from six middle-school health classes a controversial video that discusses therapy as a tool to help gay teens become straight ... A whether people are born gay and describes reparative therapy as an option for gay people who want to be straight. The film came under fire for this apparent advocacy of reparative therapy.[ccxxi]

What an absolute farce! There is no mention of reparative therapy, and any objective person viewing the film and curriculum would see the film actually portrayed LGBT students sympathetically and compassionately. Heck, the "born gay" cartoon scientist actually says that "suggesting that happy gays and lesbians should change can be harmful" and "we must accept and appreciate differences!" But that didn't matter. The very fact that one character in the film described her experiences of having unwanted homosexual feelings and finding a man she loved and got engaged to, sent gay activists through the roof (see Figure 8.3).

In the aftermath of *Acception*, I was able to meet with the county's assistant superintendent and express my dismay. He admitted that several employees were dis-

Figure 8.3: Maria from *Acception*

gruntled about the message of the film and my connections with "conversion therapy" and told me that the politics of it caused the district to back away, and ultimately throw it out of the program.

Several months later, I submitted a Freedom of Information Act (FOIA) request in order to determine if district employees were targeting me due to my former homosexual status. Hundreds of pages of e-mails were eventually turned over to me, and the results were disappointing. Some employees made derogatory comments over e-mail about me and my work. They were judgmental and disrespectful, and made assumptions about me and my motivations for *Acception*.

The evidence I obtained from the FOIA e-mails was enough for me to contact several religious liberty law firms, one of which tried to work with me on filing a discrimination case against the school district. Ultimately, we never proceeded with the lawsuit, mostly because there was no legal precedent in Maryland to protect against discrimination against former homosexuals, combined with the recent laws that were prohibiting "conversion therapy" for minors. The legal battle to justify such a program—even though the amount of content for sexual orientation change was miniscule—was too tall an order. In the end, I learned a good lesson. The theme of *Acception*—to accept and appreciate differences—was simply not possible in an educational setting that is biased towards LGBT propaganda. Gay activists fight for acceptance and toleration, but in reality, they are some of the least accepting and tolerant people among us. When it comes to education, they've marked their territory, and you're not getting in!

CHAPTER 9
THE WAR ABROAD

Progress is impossible without change, and those who cannot change their minds cannot change anything.

~ George Bernard Shaw

☞

In my work over the last ten years as a licensed psychotherapist, I have counseled clients from all over the world. Along with the many clients in the United States, individuals and families struggling with sexual and gender identity conflicts have reached out to me from Central and South America, Europe, Asia, Australia, and the Middle East—and while I have never worked with a client from Africa, I have received requests from faith-based leaders and churches seeking information and help. I don't say these things to make you think I am some kind of international phenomenon—my wife would quickly remind me that I am not. I mention this because the most common reason I hear for why these families and persons reach out to me is that they cannot find help, at least good help, in their own country.

The vast majority of therapists in these countries are either untrained or uneducated in how to work with clients who experience sexual and gender identity conflicts, or they are so biased against anyone who may seek to change, they discourage them from seeking healing. I have even had clients tell me that their therapist mocked them, insulted them, or were offended they would have a goal of change. In many other cases, the therapist provided them with ineffective solutions, and in most circumstances, encouraged the client to simply embrace an LGBT identity and get on with his or her life. How utterly sad and unethical!

Outside of a few well-trained and vocal practitioners, I have not come across many international therapists who know how to work with this client population and have much success. So, when I hear horror stories of client abuse from abroad, I immediately assume one of two things: 1) The therapist or counselor was not licensed or sufficiently trained in ethical, effective practice; or 2) The story is fabricated from LGBT activists. In some cases, a gay newspaper or media outlet may sensationalize some form of family or societal rejection or abuse of their LGBT-identified child and conflate this with licensed, ethical therapy. One particular case in South Africa stands out in particular.

Making Men Out of Boys or Converting Gay Kids to Straight?

On April 29, 2013 *Gay Star News* reported: "Gay teens starved, tortured, killed at camp to turn them into 'men.'" Raymond Buys was one of those boys, and his parents sent him to a residential program camp for troubled boys to help them grow up and become men. When the story broke in 2011 of the boy's torture, abuse (and eventual death) at the hands of the camp's leaders, the *Daily Maverick* reported the following:

> [Raymond was] cast away due to his rebellious nature, by his mother and her boyfriend. They dropped him off at the gate of the Leader [De Koker]...They were willing to pay thousands of rand just to be rid of him. The group known as X—Military Leaders (7,000 members) took him in and cared for him. The young man's behavioural deviations were noticed imme-diately. Exactly what these "behavioural devia-tions" were (other than a physical inability to carry out certain tasks) is unclear. Buys was believed to have had some sort of learning

disability, as, reportedly, did Calitz and Van der Walt, two other young men who previously suffered similar torture, and eventually died as a result.

However, gay activist Melanie Nathan filled in the blanks to make her own conclusion. This boy and other boys were gay. The camp intended to turn them straight, and if it failed, the boys would die. The problem with Nathan's analysis is that it assumes too much. For example, none of the major newspapers in South Africa, nor on the television news broadcasts, was there ever any mention that these teenagers were gay or that their deaths are related to their homosexual orientation.

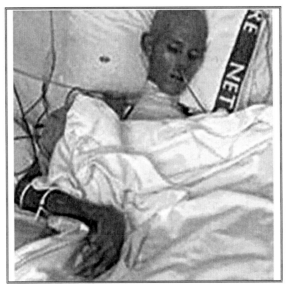

Figure 9.1: Raymond Buys, a Tortured Young Man in South Africa, on Life Support

André Bekker, a former homosexual, licensed counselor, and native South African native, commented on this ruse in an investigative article. While gay activist reporter Melanie Nathan tried to connect the camp's brutality with some sort of "conversion therapy" and even suggested that the leader's words to the parents of the child, which are translated into "We will make a man out of him" were meant to say "we will convert him to heterosexuality," Bekker comments that Nathan's translation is not only culturally incorrect, but that she purposefully intended to deceive the public to make this tragedy about sexual orientation politics, not merely the abuse of teenagers.

> It was reported that [camp leader] De Koker told Calitz that he wasn't a "moffie" (like saying "fag") and he "would make a man out of him." Interestingly, that remark is made to suggest that the death of previous camper Calitz was as a result of mistreatment. It is worth mentioning that this was never brought up as the motive for this crime in the 2007 trial. Of more importance is the fact that among the Afrikaners, to say someone is not a "moffie" is a saying, "you are not a sissy." In this context it has no reference to a person's sexual orientation. For example, a boy would for instance dare his friend to do something risky, and if the friend didn't have the courage to take up the challenge, his friend will then say; "come on man do it, you are not a moffie." What De Koker then said to Calitz is that he is not a sissy, he will make a man out of him, with no reference to his sexual orientation. This clearly means, "making men out of boys," not changing gays into straights. What is troubling is that Melanie Nathan "suggested" that "they were all perceived as 'gay and clearly effeminate'."[ccxxii] *Gay Star News* quotes her as saying the same and goes one step further with her quotation by suggesting this was a "gay conversion camp" and "with a little bit of digging

[into the story], the gay reparative undertones start to emerge." Just what those "gay reparative undertones" are, is not clear. Although activist Nathan does not mention "gay conversion camps," there has never ever any mention made in any of the court hearings or news reports of any "gay conversion camp." This is entirely the *Gay Star News* reporter's own invention.[ccxxiii]

Eager to paint the "gay conversion camp" picture, activists posing as journalists, such as Melanie Nathan, do not report the facts, but concoct an ideological narrative to spread around the world: "Gay conversion therapy is not only 'talk therapy', but also includes a set of barbaric practices ranging from discredited theories, to shaming, to electro shock therapy and vomit-inducing techniques, to even castration and lobotomies."

If you support it, you are actually condoning torture! This is what is being fed to international activists from very well-funded sources in the United States, and it is done via brainwashing and indoctrination.

Beirut, Lebanon:
They Will Torture You to Turn You Straight

In 2016, I had an amazing opportunity to travel to Lebanon at the invitation of a dear colleague, a devout Catholic and pro-life activist, who was working to support vulnerable populations around the city of Beirut, including women who had unwanted pregnancies and were seeking help to avoid abortion, and men who had sexual and gender identity conflicts. Part of the mission was to hold a seminar tailored to help gay, transgender, or men who experienced unwanted same-sex attractions. I was told by my friend and others in the country that I was the first person to ever hold such a healing seminar, not only in Lebanon, but also in the entire Middle East. While I cannot confirm those details are true, I can tell you that seminars specifically tailored to help gay, transgender, or men who experience unwanted same-sex attractions are not openly publicized, if they do in fact occur. While we marketed the seminar for all men with sexual and relational conflicts, about ten men attended, all ended up being on the spectrum of LGBTQU.

Leading up to the seminar, my friend found it terribly difficult to recruit men to attend. They were frightened to death! "No one holds therapy weekends for men like us! What if someone finds out I have these attractions? What if they tell my parents or church?" Half of the men were Muslim, half Christian. The Muslim men, in particular, were very homophobic. If internalized homophobia ever existed, this was it! As an aside, I came to discover that Lebanon is actually the most liberal country in the Middle East. Imagine if this seminar was held in Saudi Arabia, Jordan, or the United Arab Emirates! Can you imagine how much internal torture these men experience? Sadly, I can. I have worked with more than one man from the Middle East, and they have no place to go for help; if they come out as gay, the face intense persecution, even death! Their psychologists don't know how to help them, and in fact, are also very homophobic and afraid to talk about the issue publicly (I'll speak more about this at the end of my story).

One man that attended the seminar stands out in particular. He was a gay-identified young man who also struggled with some feelings of gender dysphoria. We'll call him Mohammad, a very common name in Lebanon. Mohammad came from a broken home. His father and mother were emotionally and verbally abusive to him, and he was very much an outcast at his secondary school. Now in his early twenties, Mohammad worked odd jobs, and spent much of his time surfing the Internet and talking with other gay men in Lebanon, including some local gay activists. Mohammad was a part of an organized group of gay men that were loosely affiliated with an unknown international operation of gay activists. He was paid a few bucks here and there to participate in gay events and spread what can only be thought of as propaganda in the country.

While Lebanon is known as the most liberal country in the Middle East, it is still a relatively conservative country. Driving through the streets of Beirut, you will see nothing overtly sexual—no gentleman's clubs (aka strip clubs), no pornography, no suggestive advertising of any sort. The most scandalous activities men are known to take part in Beirut is poker! As one drives down the road, poker and gambling advertisements crowd together. To come out of the closet as gay in Lebanon would not be highly unusual, but it would be highly stigmatizing for men who were very religious or wished to be well respected in public. For example, homosexual establishments (bars/night clubs) are still technically illegal in the country, as they are in most Middle Eastern countries, and would result in a fine or possibly even prison time. Mohammad's "low-profile" work was to essentially recruit other young men and then normalize their experience among the general population.

So when my friend invited him to attend the seminar, he consulted with the "higher ups" in his circle, and they warned him that the "conversion therapy" he was considering would traumatize him! He should by no means attend! But on Friday night, Mohammad bravely traveled the long road up the mountain to the convent that hosted our seminar. After he was ushered into the room to meet me before we began our group retreat, I asked him (just as I asked each of the other men): "Who are you, and what is your idea of a man?" Mohammad, who was trembling with fear, nervously blurted out:

"I do not know, but I do not wish to have 'the conversion therapy'."

"What is conversion therapy?" I questioned.

"It is when they turn you straight by electric shock." Mohammad answered.

"You will not experience that here." I reassured him, and then sent him out of the room.

That night, I led the ten men into several exercises that helped them release the shame they were holding onto for having homosexual feelings. As each man stood up on a chair in our circle and confessed a shameful behavior or attraction he experienced (some had been with prostitutes, others had lust towards children, while one had sex with an animal), tears of sadness and relief poured down their faces. When Mohammad finally got the nerve to stand up, he smiled and remarked that this was the first time he felt loved and accepted by other men for his gay feelings. Even among the activists that paid him, he felt "less than" and used. As the weekend unfolded, I led the men into deep experiential healing exercises that helped them resolve years of emotional and relational wounding from their fathers, brothers, and male peers. It was an amazing experience for them, and for me.

On Sunday, we debriefed and had a final lunch together. The men expressed their gratitude that I came all the way to Lebanon to work with them. I invited all of them to attend a symposium I was holding that night at a local Christian Orthodox church to talk of my upcoming book, and a few of them accepted. Among them, was Mohammad. At six o'clock, the young Mohammad walked into the church, smiling from ear to ear. He sat toward the front and listened as I told my story and the work I described in my book. After I spoke, a local psychologist and priest shared their experiences with sexual minority persons in Beirut. Sadly, only one brave Christian woman out of dozens and hundreds

Men's Breakthrough Healing Seminar

18-20 November 2016
Beirut, Lebanon*

Location and registration details provided upon registration

Come experience a life-changing experiential healing seminar for men that desire to overcome hurts and wounds from the past. Together we will process relationship issues, sexual and gender identity conflicts, unwanted behaviors, masculinity problems, and unmet love needs. Whatever wounds you have experienced in the past, this seminar will help you breakthrough to a healthier and happier future! All are welcome, regardless of race, religion, sexual orientation, gender identity, or socioeconomic status.

What to expect:

Our group of men will be immersed in a weekend of experiential healing, processing, reflecting, and sharing our lives with each other. Each man will leave with concrete action steps to assist him in his continued growth into manhood.

The group will work through:

• Discovering your authentic self and real needs

• Processing pain and hurts through experiential exercises

• Learning ways to engage in healthy relationships with men and women to get your deepest needs met

• Healing wounds from the past and present

• Male bonding through physical and emotional exercises

Christopher Doyle is a licensed psychotherapist in the Washington, D.C. area. He is the author of several books and curricula on sexuality, writes frequently on sexuality, and has been published in numerous media outlets. He has been a guest on the Dr. Oz. Show, Fox News Radio, National Public Radio, Christian Broadcasting Network, and many more. His work has been featured in USA Today, AP, NBC, AOL, BuzzFeed, Washington Post, and many more. Christopher earned a Master's Degree in Professional Counseling from Liberty University and is a certified EMDR Therapy Provider. As a childhood sexual abuse survivor and recovering sex addict, Christopher is blessed with a beautiful wife of ten years. Together they have three biological children and two adopted toddlers from China!

Testimonial from a past participant:

I was able to accept myself for the first time in my life in my own skin, down to my core. I know now that I was created to be artistic and sensitive, passionate and beautifully unique! My heart feels warm as if light is shining in places that have never seen the light before, almost like the first day of a new life! A wall came down.

Schedule for the Weekend		
Friday: 18 November	Saturday: 19 Nov.	Sunday: 20 Nov.
4:00pm – 5:30pm	9:00am – 5:00pm	8:30am – 12:00pm
Check-in	Seminar	Seminar
5:30pm – 10:00pm	12:30pm – 1:30pm	12:00pm – 1:00pm
Seminar	Lunch	Lunch and final blessing

The healing seminar will be free of charge and facilitated by Christopher Doyle, a licensed psychotherapist from Washington, D.C. (USA) who specializes in sexual and relational conflicts. For more information and to register, contact Carol by e-mail to: c***@***.com

All participant identities will be kept strictly confidential!

Figure 9.2: Sexual Integrity Healing Seminar (Beirut, Lebanon)

of mental health professionals we invited, agreed to attend and speak. So many clinicians were scared to attend the talk due to the controversial topic. After the panel discussion ended, there was time for audience questions and answers. Mohammad's hand shot up immediately. He said he wished to tell the story of his therapy experience with me. We invited him to stand on the stage and speak from the microphone:

> My gay friends, the activists, warned me not to attend this 'conversion therapy' weekend. They said I would be hurt. That it would harm me. They said I would be tortured and electroshocked and I would be made to feel bad for who I am. They lied. I felt more loved and accepted this weekend than I ever have in my entire life. This therapy helped me. It was healing. Everyone should attend this therapy. It was very helpful to me. Thank you!

The crowd of about 50–60 people stood and cheered for Mohammad, and one of the country's Christian television stations broadcast the entire symposium on their station! After the talk, several monks and nuns embraced me and asked me to return to educate their bishops and help them. I hope to go back to Lebanon very soon. It is a beautiful country, rich with art and culture, whose people are warm and sincere! Unfortunately, their mainstream psychologists are being indoctrinated from outside—most likely from United States activists and the United Nations—that therapy for persons struggling with sexual and gender identity is torture! In fact, not long ago, Samuel Brinton and the National Center for Lesbian Rights testified as much in Geneva, Switzerland.

United Nations Special Committee on Torture

Samuel Brinton is one of the National Center for Lesbian Rights' most prominent (former) spokespersons. Now working on behalf of the Trevor Project to end "conversion therapy," Brinton has testified on multiple occasions in state legislatures and, in 2014, traveled to

November 18, 2014

Samuel Brinton: "A Therapist Told Me I Was Sick"
By NCLR Staff

#BornPerfect Campaign Leader Samuel Brinton Addresses U.N. Co...

I never imagined I would be in Geneva, Switzerland, but last week there I was. I was no tourist. I was there to testify before a United Nations Committee. To say this was surreal would be a vast understatement.

In the two minutes that I was given to address the U.N.'s Committee Against Torture, I fought back tears as I described how a psychotherapist, at the request of my parents, tried to change my sexual orientation through conversion therapy when I was 10 years old.

You can help NCLR's #BornPerfect protect LGBT kids with your donation. Will you support us in our fight to end this dangerous and discredited practice?

I told the Committee how the therapist said I was sick, that God hated me, and that the government was exterminating all LGBT people. My voice shook as I detailed the physical abuse I endured in an effort to make me straight, including being restrained and physically hurt.

But last week, as part of NCLR's #BornPerfect campaign delegation, I was finally vindicated. Our testimony resulted in the Committee addressing the issue of conversion therapy with the U.S. State Department for the first time in history. We brought international awareness to conversion therapy, a dangerous and discredited practice that is still wreaking havoc in the lives of youth across the country.

As co-chair of the #BornPerfect Advisory Committee, I hope that my testimony will save other children across the U.S. and around the world. No one should ever be told that they need to change who they are. WE ARE ALL BORN PERFECT.

Will you help us in our fight to end this practice in the next five years by donating today?

Samuel Brinton
#BornPerfect Advisory Committee Co-Chair

Figure 9.3: Sam Brinton/NCLR 2014 Fundraising Letter

Geneva, Switzerland to speak at the United Nations about his "therapy torture." When Washington, D.C. considered (and ultimately passed) a bill to ban therapy for minors in 2014, one witness, Dr. Gregory Jones, included this quote (in part) from a *TIME* magazine article telling Brinton's story, in his testimony in front of the city council:

Sam Brinton says that his father first tried physical abuse to rid his young son of homosexual feelings. When that didn't work, Brinton's parents turned to something called reparative therapy. Some of the memories are hazy more than 10 years later, but Brinton does remember the tactics the counselor used. There was talk therapy, about how God disapproved, and there was aversion therapy, during which pictures of men touching men would be accompanied by the application of heat or ice. "It was pretty much mental torture," Brinton says. "To this day, I still have light pain when I shake hands with another male."[ccxxiv]

On November 14, 2014, Brinton spoke at the United Nations in Geneva, Switzerland to testify to the alleged abuse he suffered from an unnamed, licensed therapist. According to CNSNews.com, Brinton "testified about the licensed psychotherapist who tied his arms down, wrapped his hands in hot copper coils, and stuck needles in his finger to channel electric shocks whenever he was shown a picture of men kissing."[ccxxv] Even more troubling, Brinton later authored (with the help of NCLR staff) a fundraising letter that was published on the NCLR blog of his experience at the United Nations (see Figure 9.3).

While Brinton's story sounds compelling, it has yet to be confirmed by any legitimate source or news outlet. According to a 2014 article, some pro-gay media tried to verify this report—and couldn't.[ccxxvi] Even Wayne Besen, the most rabid anti-ex-gay activist, declared, "[U]ntil he [Brinton] provides more information to verify his experience, he makes it impossible for us to use him as an example. Indeed, it would be grossly irresponsible for us to do so."[ccxxvii]

Brinton Exposed

The tables turned on Brinton in 2019, however, when a new independent website was released to expose the questionable nature of his testimony. This website (www.sambrintonhoax.com) sheds light on some of the inconsistencies in the story Sam has told in front of many different national and international audiences about his alleged "conversion therapy torture." A quick glance at the samples of the website on the next page provides an abundant store of information on Brinton's current activities. The website also provides testimony of Brinton's involvement with violence against women and bestiality.

Figure 9.4: A Sample of Brinton's Campaign Against So-called "Conversion Therapy."

Figure 9.5: Another View of the Sam Brinton Hoax Website: Brinton Leads Young Boys in Bestiality Practice.

Figure 9.6: Home Page of Brinton Hoax Website: Brinton Leads Young Boys in a Dress-up Session.

Clean Water or Gay Rights:
Choose Both or You Get Neither

Austin Ruse is a culture warrior, and his organization, the Center for Family and Human Rights (C-Fam) acts a watchdog over the United Nations' (UN's) liberal policies on sex, sexuality, and gender. In 2017, Ruse and C–Fam warned in an e-mail of the upcoming arrival of a totalitarian LGBT enforcer at the UN:

UN OFFICIAL COMING FOR YOUR CHURCH...
COMING TO INDOCTRINATE YOUR CHILDREN...
HELP US STOP THIS...

2:00 a.m. June 26, 2017

Dear Friend of the *Friday Fax*,

There is a new UN office to enforce a radical view of gay rights. It is headed by a man named Vitit Muntarbhorn.
He met last week with the UN Human Rights Council and what he told them should frighten anyone with children, any practicing religious believer, and anyone who cares about freedom of religion. First, he lied. He said his mandate is based on established international law. That is false and he knows it. There is no existing international law that even mentions LGBTs, or "sexual orientation and gender identity." But, then he went further. Much further. He talked about how to deal with "the hostile element," that is, those who may oppose the imposition of radical sexuality on traditional people and reluctant governments and especially the Church. He said there is a primacy of "human rights" over religion!

This gentleman apparently has never read the Universal Declaration of Human Rights which guarantees freedom of religion, which understands RELIGION IS A HUMAN RIGHT!

Practically speaking what this means is that any person who believes what the Bible teaches on human sexuality, any person who believes what the Church teaches on human sexuality, and any Church that teaches Bible-based human sexuality is in violation of human rights and he is coming for them. And, in the past, this gentleman has also said that he is going to target children for indoctrination! For good measure, he also called for censorship of the Internet to shut down those who may oppose him and his sexual rights agenda.

Do not be afraid of these people. We aren't.

Yours sincerely,

Austin Ruse
President/C–Fam
Publisher/*Friday Fax*

Figure 9.7: Austin Ruse/C–Fam E-mail on LGBT Enforcer

Culture War at the United Nations

Ruse was right on target. In 2017, the United Nations appointed Muntarbhorn as the "independent expert on sexual orientation and gender identity." Despite the fact that 77 countries opposed this measure, Muntarbhorn was nonetheless tasked to travel the globe in the effort to promote LGBT human rights. A 66-year-old international law professor from Thailand, the "LGBT Enforcer" planned to use his mandate to pressure countries into advancing LGBT rights, and even wants to ban therapy for those who struggle with their unwanted same-sex attraction of their gender identity.

He also plans to recommend the educational systems in every country mainstream controversial concepts of sexual "rights" and lifestyles, and we can be certain he will be promoting radical comprehensive sexuality education. The key to his 'strength' as a UN appointee is the funding of various programs to particularly third world countries. "Do as I say or your funding may be withdrawn" ... imagine you lived in a country suffering drought, starvation, war, or any other crisis situation where the lives of millions are supported by UN programs and funding?[ccxxviii]

As we have come to expect, enforcing LGBT human rights rarely stops at the issue of equality. Once the LGBT identity is established as a protected class against discrimination, the activists use this position to suppress all those who disagree with their practice, including those who struggle with unwanted attractions or gender confusion and may want out! Muntarbhorn's successor, Victor Madrigal-Borloz, who was appointed in December of 2018, went on record and was reported by *Reuters* as saying that banning the "barbaric" practice of giving people electric shocks and injections to "cure" them of homosexuality is a key priority of his:

> We need to create awareness that no diverse sexual orientation or sexual identity is a pathology ... The objective at the end is that people live free of violence and discrimination against who they are and what they love ... We're talking about barbaric actions that give people great suffering. The reason why this form of violation is deeply disturbing is because of the participation oftentimes of the family.

Incredibly, the *Reuters* article stated that therapy, often conducted in "religious settings, can involve psychoanalysis, injections and electric shocks. In some cases, people undergo beatings, solitary confinement, and even 'corrective rape' aimed at changing their sexual orientation."[ccxxix] Shockingly, there was no counterpoint in the article to discuss the many mainstream psychological methods licensed counselors most often use to help clients with unwanted sexual or gender identity conflicts.

Banned in Ecuador, Malta, ~~Brazil~~ and England?

According to the International Lesbian, Gay, Bisexual, Trans and Intersex Association (ILGA), "Conversion therapy" is banned in Ecuador, Malta, and Brazil, although a recent court decision struck down Brazil's law as unconstitutional. In September of 2017, Brazilian Judge Waldemar de Carvalho ruled in favor of Rozangela Justino, a psychologist and evangelical Christian who had her license revoked in 2016 for offering the therapy and referring to homosexuality as a "disease." Overturning the 1999 ban by Brazil's Federal Council of Psychology, the judge ruled that "people who want help in relation to their sexuality should not be prevented from voluntarily pursuing the therapy."[ccxxx]

While most reasonable judges, such as Carvalho, believe that willing clients should be able to pursue help if they want it, thankfully no one seems to be in favor of involuntary therapy forced on clients without consent. Yet sources have reported that some rogue clinics in countries such as Ecuador continue to offer "barbaric" treatments to reverse homosexuality for teenagers. In a February 2018 article, *Reuters* reported that while the practice is officially illegal, gay people are being admitted to secret clinics where they are forced to undergo treatments to go from gay to straight, despite what the minister of health, Maria Jose Espin, claims:

. . . no "conversion therapy" was found in the more than 60 clinics it has shut since mid-2016 for insanitary conditions or operating without a license. None of the closures were due to human rights violations. We frequently verify with our teams that these types of establishments do not exist, where rights violations can take place. There are no de-homosexualization clinics. They shouldn't exist ... homosexuality is not a disease.

However, it is difficult to determine if the government is really being honest when "eye witnesses" in the country report that:

Gay people, mostly lesbians, are typically admitted to clinics by their parents or other relatives and held against their will for at least three months, with therapy costing up to $1,500 a month ... Taller de Comunicacion Mujer documented testimonies of four victims who said they were locked up against their will and underwent conversion therapy from 2014 to 2016. This included psychological and physical abuse—beatings, solitary confinement, being chained to a bed for days, force-feeding of medicine and being made to wear makeup and high heels. Victims also reported "corrective rape" by fellow patients and staff with the aim of changing their sexual orientation. About 200 unlicensed clinics are operating across Ecuador, rights groups estimate. No one regulates or monitors them.[ccxxxi]

Such stories are tragic and heart-breaking, yet hard to verify. One would think that if this were truly happening, more major media outlets would be covering it and providing more detailed documentation and reports. Yet, when performing an online search of "gay conversion therapy" and "Ecuador," I found only LGBT media outlets that have published stories, and these reports cite the original *Reuters* story above. With all of the outcry and abuse, one has to wonder why the Human Rights Campaign doesn't open up shop in Ecuador to investigate and put a stop to this torture.

Does It Exist?

Do organizations and counselors exist that mistreat vulnerable homosexual and gender confused youth? I'm sure they do. But the descriptions of these gay activist organizations are so far overblown, and in the vast majority of situations, the abuse is carried out by rogue, unlicensed, and untrained pseudo-professionals. But if you looked at the false narrative promoted by the likes of the National Center for Lesbian Rights and the Human Rights Campaign (HRC, (two of the largest pushers of "conversion therapy" ban legislation, you might think these "conversion therapy" camps are a widespread practice among licensed therapists!

When one peels away the layers of the onion on the "gay conversion therapy" torture stories, what usually turns up is a pretty ordinary, old, white guy driving the narrative, kind of like *The Wizard of Oz*. If you recall, Dorothy and her compadres, the lion, scarecrow, and Tin Man, were so excited to meet the wizard that they sung, skipped, and jumped their way along the yellow brick road to the magical land of green people, only to find that "The Great and Powerful Oz" wasn't really what they thought he was.

Behind the deep, dark scary voice, spitting out green smoke, with giant arms flailing back and forth was a disillusioned, wounded old white man. If you have been fortunate enough to see the hit Broadway show *Wicked,* you discover that the Oz, not the Wicked Witch of the West

(Elphaba, is the real villain of the story. He only uses Elphaba to continue the good vs. evil narrative to remain in power. As we learn, Elphaba is the real victim!

It's kind of interesting to note that HRC, the largest gay activist organization in the world, did an internal evaluation a few years ago about the structure of their organization and found major diversity and organizational problems, chiefly that the LGBT rights organization operated more like a white, gay male club that excluded transgender, women, and effeminate gay men among their leadership. Indeed, while the HRC positions itself as a diverse, multicultural, hate-fighting organization, behind the scenes, its own staff described itself as:

> "judgmental," "exclusionary," "sexist," and "homogeneous." Based on a series of focus groups and surveys with the staff, conducted by outside consultants, the report detailed systemic problems within HRC—ranging from treatment of employees, including those who are trans-gender, to concerns about human resources and organizational commitment to diversity and inclusion.[ccxxxii]

The internal report detailed, among HRC's many shortcomings, the following:

1. Transgender and genderqueer staffers reported being mis-gendered often, "even after repeated attempts to educate." One staffer overheard another coworker use the word "tyranny."
2. Feminine men and women were not considered as important [as more masculine staffers].
3. The top executives are exclusively, white, gay males.

4. The Human Resources department and promotions are rules by favoritism.
5. While diversity is often a rallying cry at the organization, there is no real push for diversity among its employees. Employees claim that "a lot of folks are personally invested in diversity inclusion, but their voices have been smothered or pushed away."[ccxxxiii]

By reading this report and observing the way HRC operates, it sounds very much like a "do as I say, not as I do" club that is more interested in members' privilege and salary than the actual work they are doing. Sounds a lot like the big old Wizard of Oz spinning a lot of "diversity speak" while in actuality, they are the least diverse (and tolerant) among us! Is it any concern that, in their efforts to ban so-called "conversion therapy," HRC and others fail to see and acknowledge the former homosexuals and ex-gays among them that have left their club? Are they so lost in their own ideology that they cannot accept the fact that some individuals—both men and women—have experienced sexual fluidity (which LGBT activists openly acknowledge exists) and that ethical psychotherapy could have possibly helped some people achieve that?

Some People Are Gay, Get Over It!
Rather than acknowledge that change is possible and recognize the many persons that have experienced a shift in their sexual attractions, the HRC and other gay activists choose to focus on the few stories of client abuse or unethical conduct, instead of recognizing that for some people, perhaps their desire to choose their faith over their feelings, their life goals over their attractions, might be more important! In this sense, is it any surprise that the intolerance and hate for former homosexuals, and the therapists that help them, would be exported to other prominent countries? But

that's exactly what we're seeing in some of the current campaigns to ban "conversion therapy" across the pond. Most notably, the United Kingdom.

Figure 9.8: A Billboard Touting Stonewall's "Some People Are Gay. Get Over It!" Campaign

In April 2012, right around the time the first "conversion therapy" ban bill was circulating in the California legislature, Stonewall, the largest gay activist organization in the United Kingdom, ran an advertisement on the sides of buses throughout London, England. It read "Some people are gay. Get over it!"

While the gay rights group intended the advert (as the Brits call it) to encourage equal rights for gay couples and anti-bullying, some saw the slogan as a confusing, "in-your-face" campaign with unintended consequences. For example, an article in the *Guardian* asked:

> Who exactly was that exclamation mark meant to jolt out of an unthinking stupor, and teach that homosexuality is a fact of life? ... I'm not sure what a project like this brings to the table. But when I saw the advert it occurred to me that it,

and that supercilious exclamation mark in particular, could in fact give people an excuse to express their homophobia. Stonewall's good intentions might simply end up making gay people's lives more difficult ... And so, it came to pass. The Core Issues Trust ... and Anglican Mainstream, a group of hyper-conservatives within a generally quite gay-friendly church, took the bait. They booked space on buses to display a different tagline: "Not gay! Post-gay, ex-gay and proud. Get over it!" Slightly baffling, but definitely homophobic, and obviously intended as a riposte to Stonewall.[ccxxxiv]

As it turned out, gay people's lives did not become more difficult because of that advertisement. In fact, not long after the ad appeared on London buses, Transport for London, the public bus authority, removed the ad, and Core Issues Trust sued, only to be ruled against by the British Court of Appeals and ordered to pay £100,000:

The judge found that Transport for London properly cancelled the ad under the Equality Act requiring all public agencies to promote equality and reduce discrimination, but should have canceled the Stonewall ad for the same reason ... "It is bizarre," Davidson told *Life Site News*, "that the very idea of seeking change is now viewed as impermissible." But Davidson has treated many clients successfully. We don't say we can cure. But some people can go on to lead heterosexual lives while others have to be satisfied with living their lives in a way that is consistent with their Christian beliefs. This needs to be respected as a reasonable and good outcome."

An important outcome of the court of appeal case, which went before the Master of the Rolls, one of the highest judges in the land, was the fact that then Equalities Minister Maria Miller intervened through her lawyers in the case arguing that ex-gays are in fact protected against discrimination in the UK under the Equality Act 2010:

> As Mr. Squires says, it would be surprising if less favourable treatment because a person in the past was homosexual, but is now heterosexual, was not equally prohibited. This does not require that "ex-gays" are to be regarded as a separate category of sexual orientation. Discrimination against a person because of his or her past actual or perceived sexual orientation, or because his or her sexual orientation has changed, is discrimination "because of ... sexual orientation." There is no requirement in the EA that discrimination must relate to a person's current sexual orientation. All that is required is that the discrimination is "because of sexual orientation."[30]

Clearly this is important case law, indicating not only that discrimination for "ex-gays" is illegal but also recognizing that sexual orientation may change in the course of a person's lifetime. Given that the Royal College of Psychiatrists issued a revised statement on sexual orientation shortly after this, in April 2014,[31] the case may have been more significant than it is given credit for. Moving from a position of genetic causation, the college now says: "sexual orientation is determined by a combination of biological and

[30] Paragraph 98 Judgement: 27 January, 2014.
http://www.bailii.org/ew/cases/EWCA/Civ/2014/34.html <28 September 2018>
[31] https://www.rcpsych.ac.uk/pdf/PS02_2014.pdf

postnatal environmental factors." Cushioned with many cautions, the statement crucially continues: "It is not the case that sexual orientation is immutable or might not vary to some extent in a person's life."

In 2013, the Church of England's Pilling Commission Report had stated that homosexual people experience an "elevation of risk for anxiety, mood and substance-use disorders and for suicidal thoughts and plans ... [and, for men] high risk sexual activity" (para 205 and notes that the Royal College attributes this to "discrimination in society and possible rejection by friends, families and others" (para 206. The report states that:

> "On the other hand, the Core Issues Trust points out that the three scientific papers referred to by the Royal College of Psychiatrists at this point actually refuse to attribute the causation of mental health issues among gay and lesbian people to societal factors. For example, one paper cited states, 'It may be that prejudice in society against gay men and lesbians leads to greater psychological distress... conversely, gay men and lesbians may have lifestyles that make them vulnerable to psychological disorder'."[32]

The extraordinary case law precedent set by the London Bus Appeal case acknowledged that "ex-gay" functions as a protected category in UK law. Together with the admission of the Royal College of Psychiatrists that sexual "orientation" is influenced by "post-natal" factors, and Pilling's admission that life-style choice, rather than societal homophobia, might be at the root of psychological distress, witness the discrepancy between the gay activists'

---

[32] House of Bishops Working Group on Human Sexuality 2013. Page 63, paragraph 206 https://inavukic.files.wordpress.com/2013/12/pilling-report-church-of-england.pdf

version and other understandings of these issues in the UK. Nevertheless, political trends follow the activists' version and suppress the findings that highlight discrepancies.

If it's not bad enough that the city of London court system won't protect the rights of ex-gays to advertise, perhaps a more coordinated plan to eliminate them will suffice? That's exactly what a 2018 campaign intended to do! Titled: "LGBT Action Plan: Improving the Lives of Lesbian, Gay, Bisexual, and Transgender People." The £4.5 million plan, announced in July 2018, set out to:

- Appoint a national LGBT advisor to provide leadership on reducing the health inequalities that LGBT people face;

- Extend the anti-homophobic, biphobic and transphobic bullying program in schools;

- Bring forward proposals to end the practice of conversion therapy in the UK; and

- Take further action on LGBT hate crime— improving the recording and reporting of, and police response to, hate crime.

As a part of the national survey of 108,000 UK LGBT-identified persons, two reported they had undergone "conversion therapy" in an attempt to "cure" them of being LGBT, and a further five had been offered it. Interestingly, the section of the government report "conversion therapy" fell under was "Safety"—yet, two and five respectively, don't seem to be astronomical numbers of people to keep safe. But if a safe space is what gay activists are looking for—eliminating all opposition, including those who might challenge the "born that way, cannot change myth" they are achieving it—and they are well on their way in countries like

England. The case study below on the work of Core Issues Trust demonstrates just how deep international persecution and discrimination of individuals with unwanted same-sex attractions, and the counselors who assist them, are in the UK.

Case Study of International Discrimination: Core Issues Trust

Core Issues Trust[33] was started in 2007 and is a registered charity in the UK, working with men and women coming out of unwanted homosexual feelings. The organization's strapline, "challenging gender confusion, upholding science and conscience," indicates that the intention is to be educative, supportive of those coming out of homosexual practices and feelings, and capable of critical engagement with the narrative of homosexual normalization.

In 2009, the organization's founder, Dr. Mike Davidson, had begun training as a psychodrama psycho-therapist. Davidson had had a success-ful career in academic staff development in three UK universities, but sought to formalize his interest in counselling and psychotherapy. In 2012, following a Core Issues Trust conference featuring American former attorney, preacher, and writer, Jim Reynolds and Davidson were invited onto a BBC talk show to discuss the event. He dismissed claims that the conference pathologized gays as "lepers" with mental health diseases that needed to be cured. The intention had been to encourage orthodox Christians to see how those with homosexual issues might well be ostracized as the lepers of the ancient world were by religious communities.

The conference flyer[34] was tackled prejudice against gay people in the church. During the program, Davidson was

---

[33] https://www.core-issues.org
[34] https://www.core-issues.org/UserFiles/File/Lepers_Among_Us/Leper_among_us_Conference_Belfast_flyer.pdf

asked to identify the professional body with whom he was registered—the British Psychodrama Association (BPA). Following the second part of a three-part program,[35] Davidson received an e-mail indicating that he was under investigation by the UKCP which accredited the BPA. The program had also featured Dr. Andrew Samuels, an LGBT psychotherapist activist from the Rainbow Project, a northern Irish pressure group and an LGBT psychotherapist. Although accom-panied by Reynolds, the talk show was unbalanced in terms of representative opinions.

Following a lengthy appeal with the BPA, Davidson was removed from the trainee register, and refused permission to continue training on public safety grounds. There was no complaint from any client, and no opportunity to defend his position scientifically was granted, nor was documentation submitted or acknowledged. The judgment indicated however, that should he desist from propagating his opinions (that autonomous individuals should have the right to access professional help) he could return to complete his studies. Neither the term "Counsellor" nor "Psycho-therapist" are protected terms in the UK, so Davidson has continued as a counsellor accountable to Core Issues Trust.

Core Issues Trust has sought to encourage the development of a "once gay" voice in the UK, and for that reason, produced a feature movie, *Voices of the Silenced: Experts, Evidences and Ideologies*[36] which was released in 2018. Full interviews of the 15 case studies and expert opinion are available on line at voicesofthesilenced.tv.

For the film's premier, the Trust booked a movie theatre in Piccadilly Circus, central London in February 2018. But following pressure from *PinkNews*, Vue Entertainment cancelled the booking, and the organizers had

---

[35] https://www.core-issues.org/UserFiles/File/Audio/Radio_
Ulster/ethics_ 20120108_1043b.mp3
[36] https://www.voicesofthesilenced.com/

to find a suitable venue elsewhere in the city.[37] Massive media attention nevertheless propelled interest in the film, and most recently, although unreported by the media, Vue Entertainment admitted that its action in banning the screening had been unlawful.[38]

More recently, the Trust has been highlighted as the UK government moves towards a total ban on "conversion therapy." In response to the UK government's LGBT Action Plan, based as it was on the National LGBT Survey, Core Issues Trust has lodged a paper[39] with the OSCE (Organization for Security and Cooperation in Europe)— Europe's largest human rights body. Working closely with an international partnership, the IFTCC (International Federation for Therapeutic and Counselling Choice) of which Davidson is chairman, the Trust supports the development of an alternative self-regulating body attracting international groups standing together on an agreed ethical framework and practice guidelines. The IFTCC is likely to represent groups wanting to stand together on a common ethical basis for both clinicians and pastoral care workers to help those who seek to overcome unwanted same-sex attractions.

International Therapy Bans as a Precursor to a Media Blackout of Ex-Gays

In October 2018, singer and vocal coach Matthew Grech, appeared on the country of Malta's version of the X Factor, a popular variety show that showcases talented singers, dancers, and entertainers. Grech, who formerly engaged in a homosexual lifestyle, com-mented in a video interview segment that played before his performance:

---

[37] https://www.christianconcern.com/our-issues/freedom/why-vue-cinemas-is-muddled-in-saying-ex-gay-film-contradicted-its-values
[38] https://www.core-issues.org/news/vue-cinemas-admits-it-was-unlawful-to-block-ex-gay-film
[39] https://www.osce.org/odihr/394403?download=true

I used to lead a homosexual lifestyle, and then I found God. For a long time, I stopped following my passions to follow Jesus. There can be love between two men and two women, yes—but only friendship love. Everything else is a sin.

Unsurprisingly, this drew a huge backlash from certain segments of the population, including the government of Malta. According to *The Christian Post*, the *Times of Malta* reported:

> ... the Maltese government felt compelled to release a statement assuring that sexual orientation and gender identity were protected by law on the Mediterranean archipelago. The government also condemned the practice of what it derisively called "conversion therapy" in which people with unwanted same-sex attraction seek counseling. "While the government condemns all such homophobic comments, broadcasting this message, without calling out the harm caused by conversion therapy is damaging," the government statement reads. "It puts at risk those youths who are vulnerable to such practices despite Malta's adoption of strict legislation in 2016."[ccxxxv]

In conclusion, my friend, and current president of Voice of the Voiceless, Daren Mehl, wrote an excellent commentary on how this type of media censorship of ex-gay stories represents a rising global suppression towards those who have left the LGBT lifestyle. Daren, like me, left homosexuality and is married, and together he and his wife have two children. Daren comments:

The whole fiasco around Matthew Grech's interview raises the question of whether the ex-gay movement is being suppressed in the western world. Malta was the first country to ban therapy for unwanted same-sex attraction and gender identity, and its law did not have a lower age limit. The law prohibited advertising of such therapy and offering it. The fact that the press report on Matthew Grech suggests he was not actually advertising any type of therapy shows how distorted the media treatment of this topic has become. It seems that the meaning of 'advertising' has been stretched to mean simply talking out loud about leaving homosexuality behind. In addition, the real coded meaning of the term 'conversion therapy' here appears to be 'choosing to leave homosexuality regardless of whether therapy is involved in the process!' Unfortunately for the censors it seems that individuals are still leaving the gay lifestyle. The fact is that not everybody who leaves the gay lifestyle chooses to see a counselor or a therapist as part of that journey. So, we have to ask, is it just therapy that gay activists want to ban, or is it evidence of people leaving the gay lifestyle? It seems the latter. Censoring the mere mention by someone that they themselves are ex-gay amounts to a total media blackout on the very existence of ex-gays. It is as if the powers that be really do not want people to be able to leave the gay lifestyle at all. It is fair to say that this is a deliberate attempt to push the ex-gay movement, including and especially Christian ex-gays, underground across the western world. Everybody is forced to pretend that the Emperor has new clothes and that ex-gays don't exist.

CHAPTER 10
THE WAR FROM WITHIN:
RELIGIOUS IDEOLOGY, EXTREMISM, AND
GAY−REVISIONIST THEOLOGY

If you talk to a man in a language he understands, that goes to his head. If you talk to him in his language, that goes to his heart.

~ Nelson Mandela

☙

Criticizing LGBT activists for what LGBT activists do, namely lying and deceiving, is relatively easy. I've often remarked to my supporters and clients over the years, when asked how I handle the criticism from the extreme, Godless left, that their attacks don't bother me so much because I know these people do not know the Lord. When you understand that Satan, the father of lies, operates on deception, you learn to accept that strategy of warfare. But when the assault comes from within the Body of Christ, that's much harder to swallow.

The former rejects the Bible's authority on sexuality, and lumps all efforts to heal, change, or reduce homoerotic activity as "conversion therapy." The latter is much more complicated, in that some reject psychology as offering any help or hope for those who struggle with unwanted sexual or gender identity conflicts. Jason Thompson, a counselor and former same-sex attracted man who is happily married to his wife (and the father of two children), distinguishes this well in his work, *Differing Views on Christian Doctrine, Identity, and Homosexuality* (see Figure 10.1). Thompson helpfully divides Christian views on homosexuality into four categories. The major distinction, as you can see in Figure 10.1, has to do with identity and labels.

The two groups on the left identify as LGBT Christians, though they differ in one key area: Members of the far-left group think they were born gay and that homosexuality is good and designed by God, while the second group believes in a Biblical sexual ethic, yet their views on identity and transformation are not Biblical and they do not believe their homosexuality can change. The two groups on the right do not identify people as LGBT, but have differences of opinion about transformation and change from homosexuality, often related to their Biblical views on healing and their understanding of psychology. Let's look at each group more closely to see the distinctions.

Christian Doctrine, Identity, and Homosexuality: Revelers

Revelers, the far-left column in Figure 10.1, embrace their homosexual or transgender feelings as an identity given and created by God. They believe they were born this way, and therefore, it is completely impossible to change or alter their sexual or gender identity. Transgender-identified persons take this one step further in that they believe they were born in the wrong body, and seek hormonal and surgical treatments to alter their bodies in order to feel more congruent. The biggest conflict that both gay and transgender revelers face is that neither the Bible nor science confirms their identity. The Bible clearly does not embrace homosexual unions, nor does it embrace a gnostic view of the body which would permit a spirit being poured into the wrong body. In addition, the Bible makes clear distinctions between men and women and includes "effeminate men" in its condemnation of homosexual behavior. Furthermore, psychology does not provide a scientific basis for the idea that someone can be physically born in the wrong sex. As

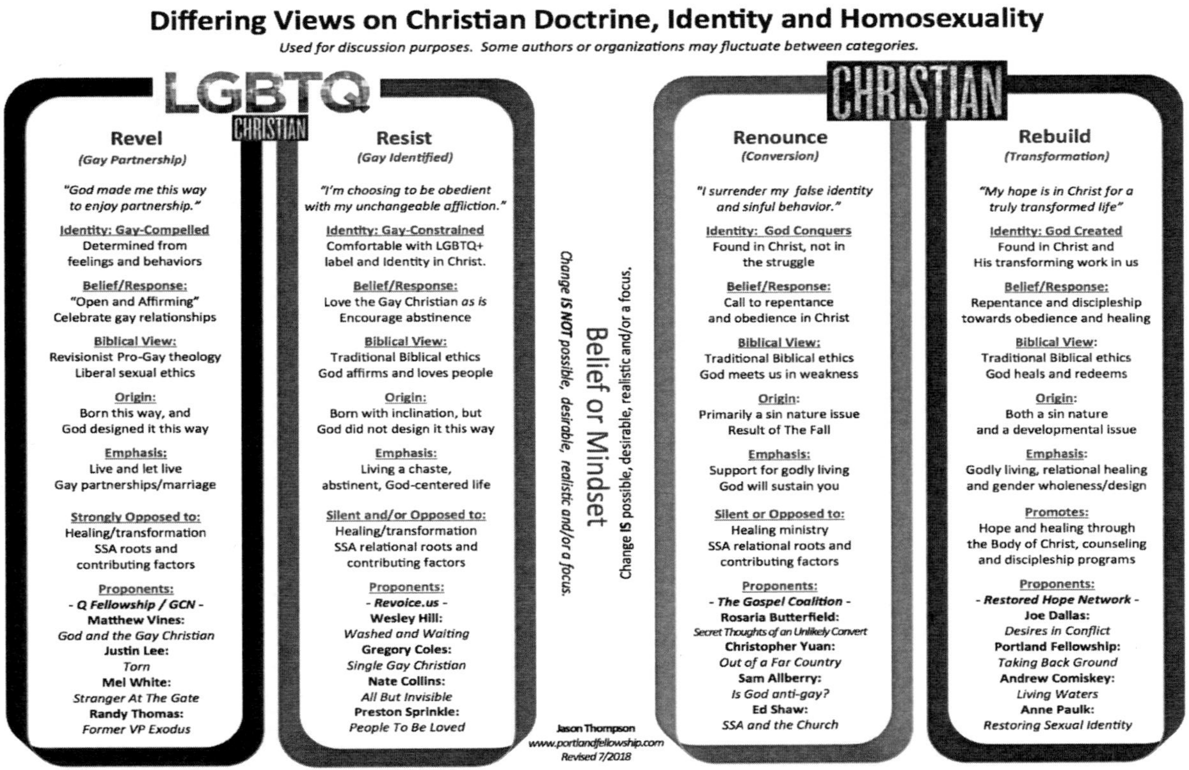

Differing Views on Christian Doctrine, Identity and Homosexuality

Used for discussion purposes. Some authors or organizations may fluctuate between categories.

LGBTQ CHRISTIAN

Revel
(Gay Partnership)

"God made me this way to enjoy partnership."

Identity: Gay-Compelled
Determined from feelings and behaviors

Belief/Response:
"Open and Affirming"
Celebrate gay relationships

Biblical View:
Revisionist Pro-Gay theology
Liberal sexual ethics

Origin:
Born this way, and
God designed it this way

Emphasis:
Live and let live
Gay partnership/marriage

Strongly Opposed to:
Healing/transformation
SSA roots and contributing factors

Proponents:
- Q Fellowship / GCN -
Matthew Vines:
God and the Gay Christian
Justin Lee:
Torn
Mel White:
Stranger At The Gate
Randy Thomas:
Former VP Exodus

Resist
(Gay Identified)

"I'm choosing to be obedient with my unchangeable affliction."

Identity: Gay-Constrained
Comfortable with LGBTQ+ label and identity in Christ.

Belief/Response:
Love the Gay Christian as is
Encourage abstinence

Biblical View:
Traditional Biblical ethics
God affirms and loves people

Origin:
Born with inclination, but
God did not design it this way

Emphasis:
Living a chaste,
abstinent, God-centered life

Silent and/or Opposed to:
SSA relational roots and contributing factors

Proponents:
- Revoice.us -
Washed and Waiting
Gregory Coles:
Single Gay Christian
Nate Collins:
All But Invisible
Preston Sprinkle:
People To Be Loved

Belief or Mindset

Change **IS** possible, desirable, realistic and/or a focus.

Change IS NOT possible, desirable, realistic and/or a focus.

Jason Thompson
www.portlandfellowship.com
Revised 7/2018

Renounce
(Conversion)

"I surrender my false identity and sinful behavior."

Identity: God Conquers
Found in Christ, not in the struggle

Belief/Response:
Call to repentance and obedience in Christ

Biblical View:
Traditional Biblical ethics
God meets us in weakness

Origin:
Primarily a sin nature issue
Result of The Fall

Emphasis:
Support for godly living
God will sustain you

Silent or Opposed to:
Healing ministry
SSA relational roots and contributing factors

Proponents:
- The Gospel Coalition -
Rosaria Butterfield:
Secret Thoughts of an Unlikely Convert
Christopher Yuan:
Out of a Far Country
Sam Allberry:
Is God anti-gay?
Ed Shaw:
SSA and the Church

CHRISTIAN

Rebuild
(Transformation)

"My hope is in Christ for a truly transformed life"

Identity: God Created
Found in Christ and
His transforming work in us

Belief/Response:
Repentance and discipleship towards obedience and healing

Biblical View:
Traditional Biblical ethics
God heals and redeems

Origin:
Both a sin nature
and a developmental issue

Emphasis:
Godly living, relational healing
and gender wholeness/design

Promotes:
Hope and healing through the Body of Christ, counseling and discipleship programs

Proponents:
- Restored Hope Network -
Joe Dallas:
Desires in Conflict
Portland Fellowship:
Taking Back Ground
Andrew Comiskey:
Living Waters
Anne Paulk:
Restoring Sexual Identity

Figure 10.1: Differing Views on Christian Doctrine, Identity, and Homosexuality

Source: Jason Thompson, Portland Fellowship

pediatrician Dr. Michelle Cretella, President of the American College of Pediatricians states: "Our bodies declare our sex, not our minds."

To justify their lifestyle, revelers must completely reinterpret the Bible's teachings on sexuality. A good example of the reveler is Matthew Vines, author of *God and the Gay Christian*. Revelers like Vines have a mission to change the church's sacred doctrines to normalize so-called "gay Christians" in the Body of Christ, and they do this by relying on what is often called "Gay-Revisionist Theology." Gay-revisionist theology is full of contradictions, bad logic, and questionable historical accuracy. It espouses the idea that the Bible condemned only casual homosexual encounters, not committed, loving same-sex relationships and gay marriage. It also makes wild claims that some of the Bible's most important figures, such as David and Jonathan, were actually secret gay lovers who were simply unable to "come out" during their time, due to societal prejudice and stigma (never mind the fact that David had hundreds of female concubines during his reign as king of Israel). Revelers also believe in psychology, but selectively choose to embrace only debunked studies that confirm their bias that they were "born LGBT" and therefore, cannot change.

Christian Doctrine, Identity, and Homosexuality: Resisters

Resisters, also sometimes known as "Side B Gay Christians" (while Revelers are known as Side A Gay Christians), espouse the Biblical view that sexual expression is reserved for marriage, view homosexual behavior as sin, but see their homosexuality as an unchangeable condition and refuse to allow themselves to undergo a redemptive or therapeutic healing process. Resisters claim an unbiblical "gay" identity, some calling themselves "gay celibate Christians." Some resisters actually view their same-sex attractions as having good, redeemable components. Unlike revelers, who openly embrace and practice homosexuality, resisters are some of the most frustrated and conflicted same-sex attracted persons I have come into contact with. They are tortured souls who choose to repress their sexual desires and emotional wounds and live chaste lives—or at least attempt to do so. In order to achieve this, resisters must completely reject what psychology has to say about the roots of homosexuality and gender confusion and simply accept that neither religion nor science has a solution for them.

Recently, two national networks of resisters have risen up to embrace their identity: Gay Christian Network (GCN) and Revoice. While GCN embraces revelers as well as resisters, Revoice appears to only embrace the chaste and abstinent "Gay Christian" and rejects the idea that gays should marry and celebrate homosexual partnerships. Rather than seeing themselves as male or female, resisters such as those identified with Revoice cling to the gay identity, refusing to fully enter the world of men and women, which is God's view as seen in creation. They also tend to view themselves as sexual minorities, as if they were a separate ethnic group of some sort, deserving special treatment based on their sexual minority status.

Revoice held its first ever national conference on July 26–28, 2018 at Memorial Presbyterian Church in St. Louis, Missouri with the stated objective:

> Supporting, encouraging, and empowering gay, lesbian, same-sex attracted, and other LGBT Christians so they can flourish while observing the historic, Christian doctrine of marriage and sexuality.[ccxxxvi]

One of the most troubling aspects of Revoice and "Side B Gay Christians" is their efforts to normalize LGBT culture while merging it with Christianity, as if these two

The War from Within

entities can really work together. It's contradictory and confusing: The Bible says He made me "male or female" but yet, I'm also a part of the "queer culture" at the same time and have access to "queer treasure"? Read just one of the many workshop descriptions at the Revoice conference below:

> Redeeming Queer Culture: An Adventure
> Presenter: Grant Hartley
>
> For the sexual minority seeking to submit his or her life fully to Christ and to the historic Christian sexual ethic, queer culture presents a bit of a dilemma; rather than combing through and analyzing to find which parts are to be rejected, to be redeemed, or to be received with joy (Acts 17:16–34), Christians have often discarded the virtues of queer culture along with the vices, which leaves culturally connected Christian sexual minorities torn between two cultures, two histories, and two communities. So questions that have until now been largely unanswered remain: What does queer culture (and specifically, queer literature and theory) have to offer us who follow Christ? What queer treasure, honor, and glory will be brought in to the New Jerusalem at the end of time (Revelation 21:24–26)?

In an article posted shortly after the Revoice conference, Dr. Michael L. Brown eloquently explains why this troubling aspect of the conference (embracing queer culture) goes against Christian teaching:

> "Queer" speaks of something contrary to God's order, something sinful and wrong, even

something perverse. So there are no virtues to be found in it. There will be no "queer treasure, honor, and glory" that "will be brought in to the New Jerusalem at the end of time." In fact, Revelation 21:27, the very next verse after the passage quoted on the Revoice website, reads, "No unclean thing shall ever enter it, nor shall anyone who commits abomination or falsehood, but only those whose names are written in the Lamb's Book of Life." There will be plenty of people redeemed *out of* queer culture who will enter the heavenly city. But nothing "queer" will enter there, for sure. And there's no way a follower of Jesus should identify as "queer." That is who some of us once were. Some would argue that those on the margins—including those in the "queer" community—learn to care for others who are marginalized. But this is not a virtue unique to queer culture. Rather, it's a virtue found in many communities, since within every culture and community, there are positive aspects to be found. Yet we don't speak about the "adventure" of redeeming aspects of the KKK culture, or the Satanist culture, or the terrorist culture, or the drug culture, or the greedy business culture, or the gambling culture.[ccxxxvii]

Revoice and Collins justify inclusion of terms and communities such as "queer" in their "Theological Big Tent" philosophy, which goes something like this: "We are all God's children, and we are all sinners—therefore, we should accept all viewpoints and embrace all sexual and gender identities–whether they are consistent with a right Biblical worldview, or not. After all, Jesus ate with the tax collectors and had compassion for the prostitutes and adulterers. So why shouldn't we also celebrate them?"

Yes, Jesus did eat with the sinners. But His message was not: "God celebrates your sin," but rather: "You are forgiven, now go and sin no more." By doing this, Revoice strongly identifies with the LGBT community, which is confusing and puts their focus on an unbiblical identity. Nevertheless, Revoice's Collins justifies inclusion for the sake of discussion:

> Personally, I think that while the language of queerness can point to real things that we experience and that we're trying to make sense of, I don't think it's the most helpful theologically. But, again, that's a conversation that I think needs to happen, and I want it to happen in the context of involving people who do use that language. I want there to be consensus about these matters. So that means trying to be a big tent for a certain group of people to participate and come together.[ccxxxviii]

Dr. Brown goes onto discuss the flaws of this "Theological Big Tent" when he comments about Collins' justification:

> In reality, that is the guaranteed way to fail. When you open the door this wide for respectful interaction, you give legitimacy to illegitimate viewpoints. In other words, Revoice was not a place for theological debate. It was billed as a place where people who identify as LGBTQ+ and Christian can share their viewpoints and find "consensus." This would be like welcoming Hindus, Muslims, and Buddhists into an interfaith dialogue with Christians, saying, "We want to move towards a consensus in our jointly held

beliefs." To do so is to make concessions and to validate invalid beliefs. [ccxxxix]

And while Collins and Revoice claimed to have had a "Big Tent" attitude for inclusion at the conference, vocal critics who wished to attend, including Stephen Black of the First Stone Ministries, and Peter LaBarbera, former columnist for *Life Site News* and founder of Americans for Truth About Homosexuality, were banned from attending. I only wish Nate would have included in his "Big Tent" a redemptive and transformational perspective, but he chose not to do so.

Christian Doctrine, Identity, and Homosexuality: Renouncers

The third view on homosexual identity and Christianity are those who renounce the LGBT identity, yet do not believe that authentic transformation can really occur through therapy or healing ministry. Renouncers are unlike resisters in that they completely reject the LGBT culture and refuse to advocate for its merging into the church. The two biggest ex-LGBT proponents for this view are Christopher Yuan and Rosario Butterfield, both of whom I have met and respect very much. However, I have disagreements with some of their philosophy.

Yuan and Butterfield once identified as gay and lesbian and engaged in same-sex sexual relationships, and according to their testimony, decided to embrace a Christ-led life and chose to stop engaging in homosexual behaviors. Instead, they now dedicate themselves to spreading the Gospel. I have seen both Yuan and Butterfield speak, on separate occasions, and their stories are inspirational. They appear to be authentic, compassionate persons who lovingly speak against homosexual practice.

Where I disagree with the views Yuan and Butterfield take is their adamant rejection of psychology.

Their approach is problematic because it offers very little developmental or psychological understanding of the roots of same-sex attraction, while at the same time, encouraging homosexual persons to leave their LGBT social networks and relationships and absorb themselves in the Bible alone without a healing community or professional therapy to help them. To be fair, Butterfield believes Biblical community and healthy relationships are very important, and she emphasizes many important spiritual tools for those struggling to overcome sexual sin, such as confession, repentance, forgiveness, worship, and scripture reading—and I agree with her that these practices have a transformational effect—but there are additional tools for healing, transformation, and change that can occur by integrating psychology into Christian practice, which she rejects.

Renouncers like Butterfield and Yuan believe pastoral care through Biblical (or *Nouthetic*) counseling may be helpful, but reject para-church ministries (sometimes known as ex-gay ministries) and adamantly oppose psychotherapy that includes secular psychological methods, even if that therapy is integrated with Christian values or scripture. Instead, they emphasize spiritual and religious practice for their sustenance and condemn organized ministry or therapy to help those struggling with sexual and gender identity. Many renouncers also have deep connections with The Gospel Coalition, a consortium of evangelical churches and pastors that embraces *Nouthetic* Biblical counseling. In my book *The Meaning of Sex: A New Christian Ethos*, I discuss the flaws of *Nouthetic* biblical counseling:

> Theoretical models such as the *Nouthetic* approach are built upon the assumption that counseling should be based solely on the Bible. *Nouthetic*, which comes from the Greek word *noutheteo* (to admonish) was originally con-

ceived by Jay Adams in the 1970s, who rejected the integration of science and theology in favor of a pure Biblical approach which aims to help Christians grow simply by pointing to the truths of scripture. The basic problem in the work of Adams ... is that it does not recognize God is the author of all truth, both in scripture and in science. Imagine if the medical community took this approach to the treatment of cancer. As frightening as it seems, try to envision a group of doctors that practice medicine only by using the wisdom and principles of the Bible, neglecting important evidence-based treatments such chemotherapy. These doctors would do nothing but read the Bible and pray over their patients, insisting that the patient's cure is measured by their faith in God's power to eradicate the cancer cells. Undoubtedly, this approach would cause great harm to thousands. Yet, *Nouthetic* counseling has continued under this paradigm in a movement now called "Biblical Counseling," which renamed itself in 1993 amidst a multitude of criticism ... for example, *Nouthetic* counselors believe that psychology can be used to illustrate and describe, but not to explain, which only scripture can do authoritatively.[ccxl]

In a recent article on The Gospel Coalition website, Dr. Bob Kellemen, a leading figure in the *Nouthetic* movement, describes how scripture alone is sufficient for counseling:

The Biblical counseling movement continues to flesh out robust and nuanced perspectives on the relevance, sufficiency, profundity, and authority of God's Word for Christian living. The same confidence that pastors take into the pulpit when preaching God's Word, Biblical counselors share in the personal/conversational ministry of the Word. Biblical counselors are convinced that the inspired and inerrant Scriptures, rightly interpreted and carefully applied, offer us God's comprehensive wisdom where we learn to understand who we are, the problems we face, how people change, and God's provision for that change in the gospel.[ccxli]

The Gospel Coalition also has deep ties with the Southern Baptist Convention (SBC) and its Ethics and Religious Liberty Commission (ERLC), and are very critical of integrated Christian psychological therapy for sexual and gender identity conflicts. In fact, at its 2014 National Conference, themed: "The Gospel, Homosexuality and the Future of Marriage," ERLC president Russell Moore held a press conference specifically to condemn the practice of reparative therapy and ex-gay ministry:

"The utopian idea if you come to Christ and if you go through our program, you're going to be immediately set free from attraction or anything you're struggling with, I don't think that's a Christian idea," he said. "Faithfulness to Christ means obedience to Christ. It does not necessarily mean that someone's attractions are going to change." Moore said evangelicals had an "inadequate view" of what same-sex attraction looks like. "The Bible doesn't promise us freedom from temptation. The Bible promises us the power of the Spirit to walk through temptation."[ccxlii]

Moore's statement, that spiritual programs or counseling, act as a panacea to any sin issue, sexual or otherwise, is an easy straw man to deconstruct. In fact, I don't know of any therapist or para-church ministry that would make such a statement. *The Christian Post* guest contributor and Christian journalist, Chelsen Vicari, reached out to interview me for an article she wrote about Moore and ERLC's position. Here is what I said:

> Moore's comments that the "idea that one is simply the sum of one's sexual identity is something that is psychologically harmful ultimately" is a statement I completely agree with. My clients come to me and my colleagues distressed about unwanted homosexual feelings, but it's not the sexual feelings we treat or seek to change. Homosexual feelings are often the result of underlying sexual trauma or emotional detachment from same-sex peers and parents. When individuals realize the source of their feelings and pursue healing in their lives, change happens. Change happens in the pews, and change happens in the counseling office. I don't think we should limit God's power to heal, transform, and change. After all, if God is the source of all truth, then why can't He use psychology to help us heal? This past Monday night, I worked with over 20 Christian men from all over the world who are conflicted about their unwanted same-sex attraction (SSA) in an online support group called Joel 2:25. These men are confronting their wounds, healing with other Christian men, and learning to form emotionally healthy relationships with other men. God is at the center of this therapy, because these men are surrendering their sexual desires for a higher pursuit—and that is not heterosexuality, it's

healing, and God is in that safe place. In my work ... so much of our ministry is dedicated to working with church leadership to help them better understand how to minister to those who experience SSA. We're helping them transform their pews from places of judgment and condemnation to hope and healing. This is not a "utopian idea" of changing people, but rather, loving them where they are at and helping them pursue healing. My desire is for Russell Moore to sit down with me and so many of these men that I know whose lives have been transformed because of Christian therapists who understand how to help those struggling with unwanted SSA so we can better help the church in its ministry towards those struggling with homosexuality.[ccxliii]

For the record, members of our therapeutic community reached out to Moore and ERLC to sit down and discuss his remarks and clarify our positions, but he declined. It's worth noting that at the 2014 ERLC conference, several para-church ministries offering support and healing for those conflicted about sexual and gender identity conflicts applied for booth space to exhibit at their conference, and were declined due to a "lack of space" in the exhibit hall. Some of these members ended up attending the conference anyway, only to find empty exhibit booth space in the hall.

Unfortunately, this is not the only time the SBC has shunned those who disagree with their positions or seek to advocate for individuals within the church that support therapy. At the very least, it appears that Russell Moore does not like to be challenged by those from within the SBC, and in some cases, has allegedly forced out and/or silenced people who wish to dialogue with or question him. At their 2018 national convention, Robert Oscar Lopez, himself a

Southern Baptist and former same-sex attracted man, wrote extensively about the questionable dealings of the SBC and Moore when it comes to LGBT politics:

> Thomas Littleton, a Southern Baptist reporter, was forced by Dallas Police to leave the Southern Baptist Convention's annual meeting after posing an uncomfortable question to Russell Moore about LGBT issues. Until we can investigate this matter more closely, we have enough evidence to infer that someone in Moore's circle *might have* lied to police to get Littleton thrown out and *might have* lied to the *Christian Post* to cover up this abusive act. Once Littleton was forcibly removed from the building, Moore came to the platform to deliver a public report on his ERLC. He gave a less than completely accurate answer to the messengers when someone else, tipped by Littleton, asked him the same question about Karen Swallow Prior and the Revoice conference.

Lopez then reports Moore's refusal to meet with him or discuss the harassment of LGBT activists toward him, while at the same, meeting with the Human Rights Campaign, the largest LGBT activist organization in the world:

> Russell Moore ... has never communicated with me about the many struggles I had with religious liberty, including my being blacklisted by the Human Rights Campaign, GLAAD, and the Southern Poverty Law Center. Russell Moore met with the Human Rights Campaign in October 2014 at the same time that the HRC ran stories and a video tagging me as an "exporter of hate"

for advocating for the right of every child to a mother and father. During that time, Russell Moore would not engage with me about my case, although I was a Southern Baptist who had written for many of his friends, including Robert George, Ryan Anderson, and the editors of *First Things*.

Finally, Lopez describes with some anguish the totalitarianism at the SBC Convention—a refusal to even hear or debate a resolution to condemn therapy bans:

> The law against ex-gay therapy in California had ramped up and alarmed most people in the Christian world. It was the most totalitarian "stay gay" bill to come forward yet and had no religious exemption. After about eight weeks of looking for someone to submit a resolution on this to the Southern Baptist Convention, I submitted "On Ministry and Counseling to Lead People from Homosexuality to Heterosexuality" under my own name. It turns out mine was the only resolution submitted to the SBC addressing the rash of bans against ex-gay therapy. Partly the SBC owed its silence to Russell Moore and the ERLC. Coming out of talks with the HRC in October 2014, Dr. Moore had denounced reparative therapy. The Nashville Statement, which came out in 2017, had avoided discussing sexual orientation change or reparative therapy. So the bans on ex-gay therapy could proliferate while SBC leaders lulled and placated Baptists by the constant claims that they supported marriage—an issue already moot because of *Obergefell* in 2015. In context, the gay movement's aims faced no obstacle in Baptist

support for marriage. The real need lay in clarifying the denomination's stance on sexual orientation change. By 2018, the ERLC's position aligned with the pro-LGBT people forcing California's law down the pipeline ... On June 12, the SBC announced that my resolution was declined in committee and would not be brought to the floor. Sixteen resolutions went to the floor, mostly with left-wing inflections. The same day, the judiciary committee of the California State Senate was moving to approve the California law banning any ex-gay counseling. The Southern Baptist Convention was deciding, it seemed, to give up on helping anyone in its churches leave homosexuality for heterosexuality. These people will play in what I will and would choose not only indifference, but rather supportive dialogue with gay groups that seek to punish people for trying to make such changes.[ccxliv]

Christian Doctrine, Identity, and Homosexuality: Rebuilders

The fourth and final category is rebuilders. Rebuilders believe both in Christian, integrated psychotherapy, as well as "Transformational Ministry" approaches of care for the same-sex attracted or gender identity struggling person. Rebuilders take a traditional, Biblical view of sexuality and marriage and believe non-heterosexual attractions and identity are the result of a sinful nature. But they also believe that homosexuality often has developmental and relational factors from early childhood and adolescence, which good therapy helps people sort through. After all, it's not just the individual that is sinful and broken; it's also our relationships, the world around us, and spiritual influences on these, as well.

Key figures in this category include counselors such as Joe Dallas (former chairman of the Board of Exodus International), Dr. Keith Vennum (licensed counselor and the current president of the Alliance for Therapeutic Choice and Scientific Integrity, formerly called NARTH), as well as prominent ministry leaders such as Anne Paulk, Andrew Comiskey, and Stephen Black. All of the individuals above are now involved in the Restored Hope Network (RHN), a coalition of nearly 60 para-church organizations, pastors, and counselors across the United States that provides healing ministries and Christian counseling for individuals struggling with sexual and gender identity conflicts. RHN was formed in 2012 during the collapse, and subsequent closure, of Exodus International under the leadership of Alan Chambers. Their stated mission is:

> ... restoring hope to those broken by sexual and relational sin especially those impacted by homosexuality. We proclaim that Jesus Christ has life-changing power for all who submit to Christ as Lord; we also seek to equip the church to impart that transformation.[ccxlv]

In their position paper on counseling, RHN articulately describes the role of integrated Christian counseling's need to identify and heal the wounds that lead to homosexuality:

> Especially important is the skill required to identify early relational wounds and to impart love there. "The goal for the client is to no longer act out his past hurts in the present but to experience authentic feelings about his past in the present. Given therapeutic encouragement, the client's identified conflict is redefined, trans-formed, and imbued with coherent meaning." Love liberates the possibility for persons to see

reality differently and to make choices for love that help to restore broken histories and lead to a more whole future.[ccxlvi]

The Demise of Exodus International and the Post-Ex-Gay Era

No conversation about the intersection of Christianity and psychotherapy would be complete without discussing Exodus International. Exodus was founded in 1976 by five men, including Frank Worthen, considered by many to be the "father of the ex-gay movement." Frank remained faithful to his wife, Anita, until his death in 2017. Unfor-tunately, not all of the Exodus co-founders remained faithful to its cause as did Worthen. Michael Bussee and Gary Cooper, two other co-founders, left their wives and became partners with each other until 1991, when Cooper died of AIDS.

At its pinnacle, Exodus had an operating budget of over $1,000,000 and employed some 25 people to oversee and provide resources to over 400-member ministries in 17 countries around the world. Originally formed to be a loose coalition of member ministries, the national Exodus leadership was supposed to provide support for a yearly gathering of those ministries, something that shifted under the leadership of Alan Chambers. As the largest Christian ex-gay organization, Exodus had a significant amount of influence in the evangelical church, but it also dealt with its share of controversy.

When Alan Chambers was hired to lead the organization in 2001, Exodus was recovering from a recent scandal. They had to oust John Paulk, then chairman of the board of directors, from leadership, after he was photographed in a Washington, D.C. gay bar. Paulk, who stepped down as chairman but remained on the board to receive counseling for the purpose of restoration, became a famous ex-gay after appearing on the cover of *Time* magazine with his then wife, Anne (also a former lesbian). Unfortunately, John appeared to be unable to withstand the publicity and pressure to remain faithful to Anne, who later went on to lead the aforementioned Restored Hope Network once Exodus shut down.

Recounting the decision to hire Chambers right after Paulk's removal in 2000, an article in *The Atlantic* summed up the tense atmosphere at Exodus:

> Being chosen to lead Exodus in 2001 was like becoming the ex-gay Pope following the Catholic sex-abuse scandals. The ministry's board knew it could not survive another public scandal, so it questioned Chambers rigorously before deciding to hire him. During the interview process, Chambers recalls a board member asking him what success would look like under his leadership. He replied, "It looks like Exodus going out of business because the church is doing its job." Chambers words would later seem prophetic, but he first needed to travel a long road.[ccxlvii]

That long road included a series of "political battles, both outside and within the organization." Among other perceived "anti-gay activities" he participated in during this tenure as president of Exodus, Chambers campaigned against Proposition 8 in California and lobbied for a Constitutional Amendment against gay marriage, all the while public acceptance for the LGBT community increased in the United States.[ccxlviii] During this time, Chambers was slowly driving the ex-gay umbrella organization into the ground with a series of poor decisions, unwise associations, and departure from biblical orthodoxy. When Alan and the board changed the leadership structure from a coalition of ministries to an autonomous, top-down ministry that tried to impose its ideas on members, bad philosophy and theology began to take hold, and former Exodus board members silently worried about the future of the organization with Alan in charge.

For example, Alan once publicly made a statement in a media interview that "99.9% of homosexuals do not change" without offering any documentation or statistic to back up his claim; and according to multiple eye-witness accounts during this time, Chambers was also disengaged from the board, preferring the council of the board's chairman, Clark Whitten, pastor and advocate of *pure grace*-theology[40] (Dr. Michael L. Brown actually calls this "hyper-grace") and Randy Thomas, vice president of Exodus, is now an openly gay man who is living with his partner and has met with the Southern Poverty Law Center and the Human Rights Campaign regarding their work to end "conversion therapy."

It is important to understand just how Chambers was able to change, and eventually, kill, Exodus with his terrible and unbiblical leadership. He did it by instituting a series of changes within the organization's bylaws that essentially shut out all those dissenters that may have put a stop to his divisive leadership, poor decision-making, and departure from Biblical orthodoxy. Stephen Black, former homosexual, executive director of First Stone Ministries in

---

[40] For example, Stephen Black recounted once to me that at a national Exodus conference in Ashville, NC, Clark Whitten taught a main morning session and said (and I paraphrase): God's grace was so good that if you all want to go out to town tonight and "lasciviousness" all over yourselves (essentially, have a night of sexual sin), you can; God's grace is that good! Whitten went on to joke about the word "lasciviousness" and said he would not recommend going out to "lasciviousness," but God's grace really is that good! Whitten was essentially telling a national conference delegation of several hundred ex-gays that it would be OK with God to practice "lasciviousness" because God's grace is that good!

Oklahoma City, OK, and author of the 2017 book *Freedom Realized: Finding Freedom From Homosexuality & Living a Life Free From Labels,* recalled the events leading up to the demise of Exodus. According to Black, Alan had to do three things in order to drastically change the course of Exodus, and eventually, cause its death:

1) Within one year of becoming president, Chambers sent out e-mails that started the idea that the board should be restructured, per Clark Whitten's leadership. Previously, the board of directors was comprised of ministry leaders that were voted in by the actual ministries. Once Chambers was able to convince Exodus to do away with this policy, he could essentially manipulate the board and its members to do what he wanted.

2) Once the organization was restructured, the bylaws of Exodus were effectively changed from a ministry-run organization to an autocratic regime that made organizational decisions at the top without having member ministry buy-in. While there were ministry councils with board member involvement, those councils had no real power, except to make recommendations, which would ultimately be ignored by Chambers and Whitten at the board level.

3) Finally, due to this horrible leadership structure, the board of directors became a revolving door of people that were brought in to affirm Whitten and Chambers' "pure grace" theology. Board members would be appointed and voted in, only to become disillusioned by Chambers' poor leadership, and eventually, leave when they sensed something was drastically wrong. If they stayed on, they were successfully indoctrinated into the

"pure grace" theology and essentially affirmed the way Chambers ran the organization into the ground.[41]

On June 19, 2013 the board of directors announced the closing of Exodus International at the organization's annual conference in Irvine, California. Of the closing, Chambers said the following:

> I am sorry for the pain and hurt many of you have experienced. I am sorry that some of you spent years working through the shame and guilt you felt when your attractions didn't change. I am sorry we promoted sexual orientation change efforts and reparative theories about sexual orientation that stigmatized parents.[ccxlix]

On its face, Exodus' closure may have appeared calculated, well-thought-out, and with broad consensus throughout the organization. But the previous year of "dialogue"—as Chambers described it—was actually a year of oppression and mass exodus. Due to Chambers' poor leadership and increasing lack of accountability to the board of directors and mission of the organization, current and former Exodus board members left leadership and key member ministries started to resign from the organization in large numbers. Stephen Black recounts some of the troubling

---

[41] For example, in the years 2011–2013, many directors were voted onto the board, only to shortly resign, leave, or have very little investment into the current leadership structure's decisions. In some ways, they were board members in name only. Before 2011, other former board members under Chambers' leadership became disillusioned by Alan's lack of engagement and leadership within the board, and eventually, resigned. For more information, see page xliv in Stephen Black's *Freedom Realized*.

years leading up to the closing of Exodus in his book, *Freedom Realized*:

> Some of the more mature leaders in the network of ministries of Exodus started seeing an erosion of theological soundness in 2009–2010 under the leadership of Clark Whitten, Alan's surrogate father and emotionally enmeshed pastor. A few ministries departed. Most raised quiet concerns. These two men have brought about untold damage spiritually to thousands of people in the Body of Christ. All who bring this to their attention are mocked as legalists. Anyone who does not agree with the Whitten and Chambers' message of "pure grace" (which is a perverted grace message of antinomianism) is mocked as a Pharisee. Sadly, they have become heretical teachers of grace in an attempt to assure a segue to "gay Christianity," and communicate to the world that sound teachers of orthodox Christianity are legalists. This is truly an oxymoron.[ccl]

This led Black and a small number of committed ministry leaders to become very concerned with the future of Exodus under Alan's leadership. Many others were also disillusioned by Chambers' poor communication and his rambling, unprepared messages at Exodus conferences, as well as his flip-flopping statements to the press, which constantly had to be explained and spun. But what happened shortly thereafter ignited a rebellion in Black's heart towards Chambers' disrespect and lack of accountability toward the majority of member ministry leaders who did not share his views on "gay Christianity." In June 2011, Black, then chairman of the ministry council, put together an agenda for a meeting with Chambers and other leaders of the council to discuss his concerns over Chambers' proclamation that one could be a practicing homosexual and still go to Heaven.

> Alan saw the last agenda item and stood up, looked right at me, and said he had another meeting to attend. He did this with complete disregard to me as Chairman of the Ministry Council. Such was Alan Chambers' leadership style ... It was a couple of months later, at the end of the Summer 2011, when I called Frank Worthen ... Frank was grieved over hearing what I told him, yet he was not surprised. He saw Chambers as a biblically illiterate, immature leader. In typical Frank Worthen kindness, he felt sorrowful for Alan. *"Poor Alan ..."* Frank said. He calmly, yet with great authority, told me, "Stephen, you have no other choice, you must put together a Truth Squad! You must get together leadership and confront the Exodus board and Alan."[ccli]

At that time, Black started the "Truth Squad" that eventually led many member ministries out of Exodus before and during its collapse in June 2013. Along the way, Black recounts how Chambers became more oppressive in the face of those like Black, who would confront him.

> It was two weeks later (after Chambers appeared on Lisa Ling's *Our America*, proclaiming that 99% of SSA [same-sex attracted] people do not change) that the Exodus Member Ministries had an annual leadership meeting in Orlando. It was the first time in Exodus history where all leadership was required to sign a confidentiality form. The agreement demanded that nothing from the leadership meetings be repeated to

anyone outside of the meetings. The atmosphere was controlling and oppressive, to say the least. It seemed that Chambers and Whitten were determined to "free" Exodus of directors, like myself, who confronted their unbiblical views. They had selected two board members, Clark Whitten and Mike Goeke, to sit at my table to "manage" me. Alan had preemptively sent me an e-mail to warn me to be quiet about my disagreements. He warned me that I had better not be disruptive to his plans for the meetings, or I would be asked to leave. I was in shock. His plan was to re-market Exodus in his new way of thinking or to shut it down altogether. I was sick with grief over what was happening to Exodus.[cclii]

Not long after that meeting, Black reunited with Frank and Anita Worthen, who helped him put together the shell of what eventually become the first board of directors of the Restored Hope Network, and in September of 2012, the first meeting of RHN took place in Irvine, California, with about 60 leaders and ministries attending. During that same year, more and more member ministries began to drop out before Chambers and the board of directors officially announced its closure in June of 2013. The writing was on the wall: Exodus was dead, but hope was alive!

Relevant, Redemptive, and Transformational Ministry

As I was thinking and praying about how to end this chapter, I was unsure how I would appropriately distinguish among ethical, licensed Christian mental health therapists, effective transformational ministries, misguided churches who adhere to "revisionist/pro-gay" theology, and fear-based religious bigots who encourage parents and families to shame their children in a desperate attempt to "cure" them of homosexuality or transgenderism. It is a tool of Satan and an effective strategy for LGBT activists to combine all of these groups into one, single group of religious zealots offering "conversion therapy." In the aftermath of Exodus International's closing, some churches and Christian denominations have even gone so far as to officially condemn "ex-gay ministry" or "reparative therapy" in their big tent theological efforts,[ccliii] while others offer tacit support for various forms of Christian counseling but refuse to take a stance on political attempts to ban licensed therapy.

As was discussed earlier in this chapter, for example, many (but not all) Southern Baptists support *Nouthetic*/ Bible-only counseling for homosexuals, but condemn any form of therapy that includes secular psychological methods, all the while remaining silent on therapy ban legislation. This is especially unwise on their part, since current legislative efforts to ban licensed therapy do not forbid certain methods of counseling (*Nouthetic*/Bible-only versus psychological/ integrated Christian therapy) but rather, the goal of the client (to reduce or eliminate unwanted sexual or gender conflicts). So, in practice, even if a teenager struggling with sexual orientation or gender identity attending a Southern Baptist church seeks therapy to overcome such conflicts, a licensed therapist, no matter the theoretical orientation of their counseling, could not legally help that minor in 14 states and over 45 cities/counties in the United States!

For all that I have written against misguided religious approaches to "cure" homosexuals and theologically incorrect networks like GCN and Revoice, a network of committed para-church organizations does exist that offers hope and healing for those struggling with sexual and gender identity. After bad leadership forced Exodus International to close in 2013, ministry approaches to help those struggling splintered in a few directions. The largest, and soundest of these networks, in my opinion, is the Restored Hope Network (RHN).

While many of its ministry directors are gifted counselors, published authors, and brilliant theologians, RHN member ministries operate largely as non-profit ministries, offering spiritually transformative groups and pastoral counseling. While the majority are not trained, mental health professionals, they provide one-on-one discipleship and supportive groups for those seeking sexual and relational wholeness. A very common approach for this type of ministry is a spiritual program developed by Andrew Comiskey, called *Living Waters*, which has now been used throughout the United States and in many countries internationally.

I went through this eight-month intensive program over a decade ago when I first started my healing journey, and it was very helpful! Member ministries in networks such as RHN may end up being "the last of the Mohicans," so to speak, if LGBT activists succeed in making licensed therapy illegal and prevail in branding it culturally unacceptable for the church at large to educate its parishioners on traditional biblical sexual ethics.

Over the last several years, I have become personally and professionally acquainted with some of the men and women who are what I consider to be the heart of these member ministries. Stephen Black, Anne Paulk, Andrew Comiskey, and Jason Thompson are just a few of dozens, if not hundreds, of leaders that understand the life-giving power of transformational ministry for those struggling with sexual and relational brokenness. LGBT activists love to describe the spiritual growth that results in ministries such as these as efforts to "pray away the gay" and conflate it with licensed, mental health therapy. But in my opinion, I can personally attest that nothing could be further from the truth. Yes, these folks pray, and they pray hard. But they know how to pray the right prayers, and they know how to form disciples of Jesus Christ.

When one peels away the layers of distorted facts and confusing narratives on psychotherapy, transformational ministry, and religious practice, it can clearly be seen that transformational ministry, as well as effective psychotherapy, does not offer "cures" or provide false or misleading hopes to those struggling. It empowers clients to get to the roots of their struggles, and encourages them to become disciples of Jesus Christ, who is the ultimate healer of the brokenhearted. My pastor recently offered a God-inspired sermon listing ten characteristics of a true disciple-maker, and these are clearly seen in the persons I mention above.

I list them here for your study.

An effective disciple-maker is:

1. Intentional;
2. Has eternal values (and is willing to sacrifice in order to invest those values to the next generation);
3. Loves people;
4. Has a personal, vibrant devotional life;
5. Works to find the right students;
6. Can communicate basic ideas that are not necessarily exceptional, but sound;
7. Lives a life to be imitated;
8. Can inspire and motivate;
9. Is able to reprove another (in relationship); and
10. Will persevere.[ccliv]

I have come to understand in my 13 years of personal healing and professional work in the behavioral and mental health field, that science, psychology, and even the Bible, cannot fully explain the complexities of our sexuality and gender identity or the depths of our capacity, as humans, to experience brokenness. But what I do know is that God heals and redeems us, even when we cannot fully fathom or grasp how He does it. He doesn't ask us to understand or know how all of His plans work. Rather, he instructs us to be faithful and persevere as He slowly reveals His plans for our hearts and lives. I know this, because He tells us this in Jeremiah 33:2–3:

> "This what the Lord says, he made the earth, the Lord who formed it and established it—the Lord is his name: 'Call to me and I will answer you and tell you great and unsearchable things you do not know'."

CHAPTER 11
A CALL TO LAY DOWN ARMS: GOOD FENCES MAKE GOOD NEIGHBORS

The greatest teacher, failure is.

This is how we win. Not by defeating what we hate, but by keeping what we love.

~ The Last Jedi

&

In October of 2017 at the annual meeting of the Alliance for Therapeutic Choice and Scientific Integrity (formerly known as NARTH) in Salt Lake City, Utah, one of the key authors of the 2009 American Psychological Association (APA) task force report, Dr. A. Lee Beckstead, admitted, regrettably, that he and his fellow authors at the APA made a great mistake by failing to include pro-change therapy clinicians and researchers in the task force report. "By doing this," said Beckstead, "we missed an opportunity to learn from those who held a different perspective...who saw the elephant from a different view than ours."[cclv]

Not only that, Beckstead admitted that many of the laws banning "conversion therapy" have done very little to curb harmful practice for those seeking therapy. Instead, practitioners, by and large, continued to do the same work, using different names for their therapy, and possibly with stricter informed consent policies to protect themselves from increased liability. Unfortunately, neither the *Los Angeles Times* nor the *Washington Post* wrote stories or editorials about Beckstead's change of heart, as they previously did when the APA Governing Body voted 121−4 at its 2009 annual meeting in Toronto, Canada, to accept the task force report's recommendations.

Figure 11.1: Members of the Reconciliation and Growth Project (from left to right): Jerry Buie, Jim Struve, Justin McPheters, Marybeth Raynes, David Pruden, David Matheson, Lee Beckstead, and Shirley Cox

Why did this former Mormon and gay-identified psychologist have a change of heart? According to Beckstead, by sitting down and meeting with his enemies. Much like me, Beckstead had engaged in an "us vs. them" war for two decades—*gay-affirming therapy vs. change therapy*. He would debate and argue his side, but as he describes, never really listen to those he disagreed with.

That changed when an attorney from the Southern Poverty Law Center, Sam Wolfe, advised him and his colleague, Jim Struve, a social worker (pictured on the left) to meet informally first with the providers against whom they were ready to file ethical complaints. Mr. Wolfe reminded Beckstead and Struve that their professional ethics state that providers first attempt to bring to the attention of the provider which ethical concerns they have about the provider's practice, for the purpose of finding an appropriate resolution. Following this advice, Beckstead and Struve created a day-long workshop where they and others across the divide sat down with their enemies and engaged in a meaningful conversation about their differences. What came out of that workshop was a group of eight professionals in Utah on either side of the issue, listening and finding common ground, with each other. Beckstead writes:

> From the very start of engaging respectfully with my enemies, I have felt *surprise* at how wrong I was about them. I kept being shocked about the positive things they were saying and how much we had in common regarding our intentions, desires, and needs. I have really come to like each one of them. They have been so kind and often hilarious. This surprise allowed me to listen more to them and they to listen to me. Above all else, I have learned that sexual and religious conflicts are not just a religious issue or a psychological issue, but a relational issue. *How* we respond to these conflicts and to others will influence what happens. Our communities, our leaders, and we ourselves have been acting aggressively, passively, compartmentally, and passive-aggressively in dealing with these issues. And this has kept us in a stuck and fragmented place. If we are ever to resolve these conflicts, we need to approach each other with more skills, more openness, more compassion, respect, and more curiosity.
>
> ... I have felt *compassion from* them and compassion toward them as we've talked about some of the hurt we've experienced being part of all this. I learned how they felt dismissed and excluded from the APA task force and therefore, *realistically* dismissed our recommendations. Our exclusion of them on the task force shut

313

down the process of change. As I heard their reactions to this process, I needed to quiet my own defensiveness so that I could really listen to them and therefore understand the problem better. I learned how they were not surprised about being dismissed because it was par for the course. For the first time, I understood their rejection and realized how wrong it was to leave them out, especially people like Shirley Cox and David Pruden who have such a long history of earnest desire, wisdom, and caring dedication to these issues. We on the task force missed out on co-creating a plan that we all could agree on. But, when I had expressed feeling excluded *from them* when I had requested to present at an Evergreen conference, David Pruden expressed regret and he was tearful. Seeing his tears, compassion, and sorrow for leaving me out really changed me and of course changed my perception of him and them. This happened during our first meeting. Throughout our subsequent meetings, they have been willing to hear more about my pain and the pain of the others in this group and the hurt of other LGBTQ individuals and families who have been rejected. These four have expressed true compassion for our suffering. This change reflects what the writer Iyanla Vanzant expressed, "A wound needs a witness."

Finally, Beckstead gives us much wisdom when he quotes one of his former teachers, Dr. Lorna Benjamin:

... she taught me the proverb, "Good fences make good neighbors." This means that we each are responsible to know our own boundaries, limits, and needs while we also respect and

314

protect our neighbor's boundaries, limits, and needs. When two neighbors build a fence between them, it can allow for positive communication between them. As we strengthen our own identity and our neighbors' identity, it allows for more peace and thriving in the neighborhood. Good fences make good neighbors.[cclvi]

Good Fences Make Good Neighbors

What eventually grew out of these meetings was the Reconciliation and Growth Project, which produced a document titled: "Resolving Distress Between Faith-Based Values & Sexual Diversity and Gender Diversity: A Guide for Mental Health Professionals." Lee spoke about this guide at the Alliance conference in Salt Lake City, and after hearing him discuss this, I approached him after his presentation and began a dialogue. I must admit, several of us sort of formed a mob around him and aggressively asked him some questions. If you're an outsider to this movement, you have to understand that this sort of opportunity—mental health professionals working in the sexual and gender identity field that have, in many ways, diametrically opposed views to treatment—is an unusual and unique experience. So, I wanted to take advantage of the opportunity.

I'll admit, our group was angry! We viewed Lee as the enemy, spearheading these bans against therapy that were beginning to really affect our practice, so while our questions were professional, our tone was not as inviting. We confronted him about some of the consequences that his task report was having, namely, that therapy for adults (not only minors) was now being banned in some cities, and that in other instances, activists were committing fraud and making us out to be torturers! To his credit, he listened. He didn't defend himself. He acknowledged our frustration. Then I said: "What can we do to work together?" To my surprise, he invited me to be a part of a book project he was putting together to reduce harm for sexual and gender minorities. I was very excited at the prospect of bridge-building, even though I had my own wounds and mistrust around the APA and gay-affirming practitioners.

Subsequently, I began to dialogue with him over e-mail about this book project, called "No Boxes." (I must admit that he and I had one prior phone call, years ago when I first started to investigate the "conversion therapy torture" issue during which he admitted that he had never worked with a client who had undergone torture to change sexual orientation, although he had met two individuals who claimed they had, one in the late 90s and the other in the early 2000s. He had also interviewed several who had undergone aversion therapy in the 70s and provided psychotherapy to several who had undergone aversion therapy in the 70s).

As we began to dialogue, I grew optimistic that our "two sides" could come together and possibly lay down arms. I must admit that a part of me didn't want to write the book you are now reading, because I felt that perhaps, it would further anger LGBT-identified psychologists, like Beckstead, and this might push them away from working with me. Perhaps my harsh condemnation of LGBT activism and some aspects of the LGBT lifestyle may cause dissension towards those who have different viewpoints than I?

However, after much contemplation and prayer, I accepted the fact that this may happen. I know full well that many LGBT-identified persons who read this book will feel attacked. I also recognize that these same people need to understand my (our) perspective on how the last six years has affected our clinical practice with the clients we love and wish to help. Personally—and I'll be vulnerable here—I have lost nights of sleep worrying about the future of my clients, my practice, and my family. I have worked very hard to establish a reputation of excellence among my com-munity, and the clients and families we serve, and I do not wish to have that all taken away by what I consider to be senseless politics.

Therefore, what I am about to say is my attempt to make sense out of the senseless. I fully expect that ideologues and culture warriors, some of whom may endorse this book, may not like or agree with all of what I have to say below. That is OK with me. After working with over 200 clients (and many dozen families) struggling with sexual and gender identity over the last ten years, my compassion and empathy for their struggles has caused me to become less ideological, more compassionate, and far more accepting of their diverse experiences. Let me be clear: I still retain the same values for sex and sexuality. But my values do not dictate my therapeutic ethics.

Overarching Principles

The guide for mental health clinicians (*Resolving Distress Between Faith-Based Values & Sexual Diversity and Gender Diversity: A Guide for Mental Health Professionals*) provides some very wise principles to follow. While it would be too long to effectively summarize this guide, I will offer a brief commentary on its valuable aspects. The guide seeks to define a set of standards and practices that are ethical and fair in order to:

1. Provide guidance for individual mental-health providers;

2. Provide a framework of ethical practices to guide professional and licensing boards in regulating the work of mental health providers; and

3. De-escalate the polarized battles around legislation and litigation regarding these matters.

Without even listing the many principles of the guide, the rationale for producing such a document is, in my opinion, in the best interests of both practitioner and client, in that it does not seek to eliminate one viewpoint in favor of another, realizing that the opposing sides have each positioned themselves in such a way that the other will not simply go away because of political oppression, societal rejection, or cultural shifts:

> We believe that legislation without an ethical practice framework informed by ideologically diverse perspectives increases divisiveness and polarization within our communities. This may have the unintended consequence of forcing unethical providers underground, thereby creating a "prohibition-like" environment, contributing to fewer appropriately trained providers, and leaving consumers at the risk of seeking services from untrained or fraudulent providers. Therefore, we propose this booklet as a working document of principles and practices based upon our collective understanding of the current research, clinical literature, and our various professional codes of ethics. We are aware that more work is needed to make this document comprehensive and inclusive. For example, we realize that the term "same-sex" leaves out individuals who do not identify with a binary sex, such as individuals who fall within the intersex and transgender spectrums. Also, avoiding harm requires a broader acknowledgment and inclusion of people and experiences that exist outside narrow constructions of sex, gender, sexuality, religiosity, and spirituality.

The group addresses, and rejects, certain labels historically used to describe therapeutic processes that contain ideological overtones:

> The continued use of terminologies such as "reparative," "conversion," "sexual orientation change efforts," and "affirmative" therapies fuels adversarial tensions among people with different perspectives about sexual orientation and gender identity. This obscures the substantial common ground among diverse perspectives. We advocate leaving such language behind in favor of language that focuses on resolving the individual's distress with their sexual attractions and/or gender identity and fosters their ability to thrive. The authors of this document began to discover our common ground when our diverse group moved beyond these historical labels. This allowed us to create a Peacemaking Dialogue Skills protocol to help therapists assist families and others in resolving their interpersonal conflicts regarding these issues.

The guide describes many principles that concentrate on respecting diverse spiritual, faith, and religious values while recognizing the diverse experiences of clients who have sexual and gender identity conflicts, and how clinicians may navigate among these conflicts. Sections are devoted to: 1) self-determination and avoiding harm; 2) reducing assumptions and practices that may increase harm and/or client distress; 3) therapeutic practices that support client self-determination; 4) consideration for partners (of clients); and 5) consideration for parents and families (of clients).

While I do not support every single principle in this document, I largely agree with the spirit and heart behind it, especially those principles promoting client self-determination and compassion, empathy, and respect for parents, families, and partners of clients who experience distress over sexual and gender identity conflicts. In addition to the guidelines set forth by the Reconciliation and Growth Project, I have suggested below some ethical principles that I believe are essential in practice with clients that experience sexual and gender identity conflicts.

Ethics for Working with Clients Open to Change

This list is formally titled Ethics for Licensed Practitioners Working with Clients Distressed by Sexual Orientation/Gender Identity Conflicts Open to Change or Sexual Fluidity. While it by no means constitutes an extensive or exhaustive list of ethics or principles, I have composed these principles as a solution to some common problems I have seen in my therapeutic community, as well as some accusations LGBT-affirming practitioners and activists have made concerning "change therapy" over the years.

1. First and foremost, treat each client as an individual—a beloved man or women of a loving God and respect his or her self-determination and autonomy to make his own choices regarding sexual and gender identity based on personal values.

2. Refrain from offering "one size fits all" therapeutic approaches, despite how similar client experiences may be. Conduct thorough assessments with each client and offer individualized treatment plans to fit their specific needs.

3. Do not overstate therapeutic outcomes or promise dramatic changes in orientation (for example, using phrases such as "gay" to "straight"), arousal, or behavior. Explain the differences among behavior change, attraction change, arousal change, and identity change. To the best of your

knowledge, offer statistics based on current, scientific studies and inform clients on likely outcomes without offering false hope.

- For example, research demonstrates (and my clinical practice shows) that individuals experience sexual attraction on a continuum and rarely identify or present with binary (gay or straight) attractions/behavior/identity. When the client begins therapy, assess his or her sexuality on the Klein Grid (or similar scale) and inform the client of possible outcomes, not understating or overstating what may be possible (see Figure 11.2).
- In this sense, inform a client who presents on the far end of the spectrum (7) of homosexuality that he/she will likely not experience a categorical shift, to complete heterosexuality (1), and instead, may fall somewhere in the range of 3–5 (4 being equal same-sex and opposite-sex attraction). Likewise, it is important to never offer a promise or guarantee that a client will not experience complete change (1), just as you should educate them that they may not experience any change at all (meaning, they may remain at a 7).

4. Refrain from judgement and condemnation over client sexual behaviors you may find objectionable. In my experience, this only further shames the client and is clinically counterproductive. Most clients already feel a tremendous sense of guilt when they "act out" unwanted sexual impulses or behaviors. Take time to understand the intention and need of their sexual behaviors. Does the client feel they are unhealthy? If so, what would be healthier behaviors to experience these sexual impulses? What makes the behaviors/attractions "unwanted"? Fear, shame, anxiety, anger, etc.? Focus more on exploring how they feel, think,

and act on these impulses rather than judging them. If the client has spiritual/religious conflicts over his behavior, explore how he can seek forgiveness and/or reconciliation in a supportive, non-judgmental manner.

The Klein Sexuality Grid

	Variable	Past	Present	Ideal
A	Sexual Attraction			
B	Sexual Behavior			
C	Sexual Fantasies			
D	Emotional Preference			
E	Social Preference			
F	Heterosexual/Homosexual Lifestyle			
G	Self Identification			

For Variables A to E:	For Variables F and G:
1 = Other sex only	1 = Heterosexual only
2 = Other sex mostly	2 = Heterosexual mostly
3 = Other sex somewhat more	3 = Heterosexual somewhat more
4 = Both sexes	4 = Hetero/Gay-Lesbian equally
5 = Same sex somewhat more	5 = Gay/Lesbian somewhat more
6 = Same sex mostly	6 = Gay/Lesbian mostly
7 = Same sex only	7 = Gay/Lesbian only

Figure 11.2: The Klein Sexuality Grid

5. Never coerce a client, subject him/her to counseling against his or her will, or use shame, blame, or subtle pressure to achieve compliance. Work with parents and families to help them better love and accept their child or loved one unconditionally, and design therapeutic interventions that produce relational healing among family members.

- It is a requirement at my practice that if parents wish for me to counsel their underage teenager, that they also undergo family therapy and parent coaching/

therapy with me. I have actually refused to work with many families who were not willing to do this, sincerely telling them that they could potentially harm their LGBT-identified child if they do not take part in a therapeutic process with their child that promotes relational healing, healthy bonding, attachment, intimacy, and communication.

- It is important to also help clients to understand their family members' perspectives, avoiding a victim mentality that is unproductive. Sometimes it is helpful for clients to understand that love allows room for disagreement. If parents have concerns about relational decisions their children make, voicing those concerns may be the most loving thing a parent can do. Therefore, part of the therapy for both the individual and the family might include helping them to understand the other members' perspectives, learning to respect the differences, and maintaining appropriate boundaries while continuing to love unconditionally.

6. Reassure clients that you will support them no matter their therapeutic outcome. In my experience, clients often transfer authority wounds (from parents and important adults) onto the therapist and may seek to people-please. If they do not achieve their desired outcome, they may actually feel like they are disappointing the therapist. Assure clients that their process is about them, not (you) the therapist, and show the client unconditional positive regard. Some self-reports indicate that clients felt the need to lie to their therapists about changes because they didn't want to look bad in the therapist's eyes or admit to themselves they had not changed or made as much progress as they would have liked.

7. Practice only within the confines of your professional training. It is unethical for therapists to work with clients if

they have insufficient training. Not all clients are created equally, and not all therapists have the skills to help them. For example, some clients struggling with sexual and gender identity conflicts present with complex post-traumatic stress disorder (PTSD) or other personality disorders that may make treatment difficult. Personally, I am skilled at helping clients with PTSD, but do not work well with clients who have some personality disorders. If you are like me, you need to understand your limits and be able to make appropriate referrals if this occurs. Additionally, providing therapy for those who are questioning, confused, and/or distressed with their gender identity requires a separate set of skills than providing therapy for sexual identity distress. Competent clinicians seek appropriate training and continuing education to work with clients who experience these diverse struggles.

8. Separate therapeutic and advocacy roles. Licensed therapists should feel free to voice their opinions on a range of social issues, but they must be careful not to do so in their formal, therapeutic roles, unless their advocacy is directly related to mental health.

- For example, I have never publicly taken a stance, for or against, same-sex marriage, as it would diminish my role as a therapist helping a wide variety of clients on the sexual orientation spectrum. However, when clients ask me my opinion, I honestly express my values and ask them why my opinion is important to them, carefully listening to their views and offering respect.
- This is not to say that all therapists should refrain from taking public stances in any circumstance. However, they should be careful not do this in the therapy office with their clients, unless asked by the client, as discussed above. In addition, when

speaking publicly on therapeutic issues that may affect clients, therapists should consider the impact their opinions may have on the mental health of those in treatment. What may seem right for one may be offensive for another client. Sensitivity to diversity and compassion for those struggling should guide the therapist in these circumstances.

9. Be honest. When clients ask your opinion on socio-political issues, be honest with them, and ask them why this is important to them. Most clients want their therapist to be sincere, but will not require them to agree on every issue that may come up in the helping context. At the same time, it's not important for therapists to self-disclose unless requested by the client, or if they feel their lack of disclosure may act as an impediment to the therapeutic process.

- Let me provide an example: If I have a conscientious objection for a transgender client who wants to transition to another sex, and this client is seeking objective, scientific information from me on how to proceed, I had better disclose to the client if I am philosophically opposed to these procedures, while at the same time assure the client, that I will seek to present them comprehensive information so they can make an informed choice on if and how they should proceed.

10. Recognize that your therapeutic treatment is not the "be all, end all" for the client, and that diverse experiences in the client's life impact their sexuality, orientation, gender identity, behavior, and choices. Respect the client's sincerely held spiritual/religious beliefs, and appreciate that God has a

heavy hand in their outcome. As a mentor once told me: "Christopher, there is a God. You are not He!"[42]

For a more comprehensive list of ethical practices for LGBTQU clients, seek out your professional guild or association's code of ethics.

Ethics for LGBT−Affirming Practitioners

This list is formally titled Ethics for LGBT-Affirming Licensed Practitioners Working with Clients Who Experience Sexual Orientation/Gender Identity Conflicts

First, many of the ethics listed above are applicable and relevant to LGBT-affirming clinicians. Please review the ten points above and decide which apply to you. The ethics listed below are specifically tailored towards mental health clinicians that practice LGBT-affirming therapy; I suggest several ways these professionals can be more accepting and inclusive of clients that may be open sexual orientation change, may wish to explore sexual fluidity, or are conflicted about their sexual or gender identity.

1. Recognize that a client's sexual and gender identification constitutes only one part of his being, and that his spiritual/religious values may actually be more important to him than his sexual orientation and/or gender identity or attractions. For example, in the last 20 years, the American Psychological Association has increasingly recognized the importance and role of faith in a client's therapeutic process. Cultural competence and sensitivity in this area is important to increase success and the potential of reducing harm.

2. Refrain from discouraging clients or providing insufficient information regarding sexual fluidity and change in

---

[42] As clinicians, we must also recognize that some clients do not have a belief in God or practice a particular religion and/or are not spiritual, and respect their experiences in that regard.

orientation/identity/behavior. If you hold deep biases in this area, seek out trusted clinicians, even if you disagree with them, that you believe are ethical practitioners, and engage in professional consultation and/or make appropriate referrals, when necessary.

3. Distinguish among sexual minority populations. Even though a client may experience same-sex attractions and/or gender dysphoria does not mean he or she identifies as LGBT. Distinguish between experience and identity and respect the client's right to self-determination. Do not push a socio-political identity on a client; allow the client to make that choice. Offer appropriate information when necessary and allow clients to explore their options without insisting on a label.

4. When working with minors, and their families, encourage teenagers and adult children to develop healthy avenues of communication and discourage parental alienation. While parents may sometimes reject or disapprove of a non-heterosexual identity, competent clinicians work with clients, and their families, to build bridges of healthy communication and intimacy. If the client is open to sharing his or her sexual/gender conflicts with the family, establish trust with parents and work towards relational healing, if possible. Clinicians should remain mindful of the fact that parents may reject behaviors, or sexual identity labels, and yet, that does not mean they are rejecting the child altogether. There may be some cases of outright parental rejection of a child, but in many cases, parents love their children unconditionally while rejecting behaviors or sexual identity labels. Therapists can help parents to convey their concerns in ways that are more loving and less hurtful.

5. Practice only within the confines of your professional training. It is unethical for therapists to work with clients if

they have insufficient training. Not all clients are created equally, and not all therapists have the skills to help them. For example, if a client has a strong desire to explore sexual orientation change or fluidity and you lack sufficient training or reject theoretical foundations that contribute to therapeutic techniques that may assist the client, be honest, seek consultation with other professionals, and make appropriate referrals, if necessary.

For a more comprehensive list of ethical practices for LGBTQU clients, seek out your professional guild or association's code of ethics.

Ethics for Advocates, Media, and Concerned Citizens
This list is formally titled Ethics for Advocates, Media, and Concerned Citizens Speaking about Clients with Sexual and Gender Identity Conflicts.

Psychotherapy for clients that experience sexual and gender identity conflicts is complex. Client experiences, both positive and negative, are often used as weapons in the broader culture war between secular and religious views on sexual and gender identity. The following guidance is meant to be broad so that individuals and organizations on either side of the debate can come together in civil conversation and attempt to build avenues of productive dialogue. Unfortunately, some may reject these points altogether due to ideological positions; such reactions are understandable, yet necessary for those engaged in political battles that seek victory on either side, rather than peaceful co-existence.

1. When speaking about research among clients undergoing any type of therapeutic intervention around sexual and gender identity, do not generalize the outcomes for all populations and make broad, sweeping conclusions. Client populations are diverse, and certain populations respond differently to various therapeutic interventions.

2. Recognize that clients who speak about their past therapeutic experiences may perceive their counseling in ways that others may not understand or relate. Clients with negative experiences may exaggerate harm, while clients with positive experiences may over-inflate success. Scientific data, as well as anecdotal evidence, is subject to biased interpretations and has limitations. Self-reported experience in social science research is common, yet has limitations.

3. When reporting or describing therapeutic outcomes, make sure to verify key dates, names of clinicians, licensing status, and pertinent details. Unfortunately, some clients may embellish stories for various reasons. Public reporting of therapy harm or helpfulness is problematic when unverified claims are made.

4. Avoid making judgments and assumptions about client motivations for seeking therapeutic interventions. Individuals have the right to make choices regarding their sexual and gender identity, and their decisions to do so often involve a variety of factors. Simplistic explanations for why a client may seek a particular type of therapy or therapist disregard the multi-faceted nature of human psychology.

5. Admit your biases openly and honestly, and listen to the stories of clients and therapists while reporting only the facts. Bias permeates our culture, and influences the media, advocates, and concerned citizens equally. Simply repeating or relying on talking points with socio-political overtones dilutes the conversation and does not contribute to effective dialogue with or education of the general public.

A Call to Lay Down Arms

A Blessing in Disguise: Conversion

In the 1950s, the term Mutually Assured Destruction (MAD) was coined to describe the feared outcome in the race between capitalists and communists to build their nuclear arsenals. Each side engaged in an aggressive arms race in order to fuel and protect itself and both recognized that either could essentially annihilate each another if worse came to worst. Today, liberals and conservatives are still operating in this mode when it comes to sexual and gender identity; and as long as we refuse to talk with each other and seek reconciliation, this MAD war will continue.

When I began to practice psychotherapy ten years ago, I entered a mental health field that I would describe as a MAD war zone. Politics has influenced our trade now more than any time in our history, and the carnage that has ensued is palpable. At the end of the day, mental health clinicians have an obligation to provide quality, ethical, and professional care to the clients we serve. However, our personal biases often get in the way of the best interest of our clients.

In my opinion, both conservatives and liberals are responsible for the war being waged to ban "conversion therapy" in the last six years. We have failed to listen to each other and have separated ourselves into divisive communities that take an "us vs. them" approach to the sociopolitical issues that divide us. Indeed, there is wrong-doing on both sides of the spectrum, and we all need to take responsibility for our behavior and seek to serve each other better. Sadly, there are ideologues on both sides that are far more invested in warfare than peace, and will continue to throw grenades at each other.

In 2013, I co-founded a coalition of clinicians, psychiatrists, medical doctors, and public policy professionals called the National Task Force for Therapy Equality to fight against the activism that was seeking to ban therapy for the clients my colleagues and I serve. For the first three years, I engaged in an aggressive lobbying campaign, both on the federal and state level. I met with dozens of politicians and policy organizations to advocate for legislation to stop the current war. We were successful in stopping the majority of bills on the state level. In our first year, we defeated 16 out of 17 bills. But ultimately, we were not successful.

The reason we began to fail was not because of poor effort or lack of passion. No, it was mostly because politicians were not genuinely interested in the truth. In the face of overwhelming lobbying, bullying, and well-funded strategic plans by LGBT activists, the facts no longer mattered. They began to get adept at convincing the "mainstream" institutions of their narrative, that "conversion therapy" is actually torture, and that it should be banned. Despite evidence to the contrary, including 100 years of data showing therapy could help some individuals experience change, and in the face of hundreds of testimonies of change.

The problem was that no politician, liberal or conservative, was or is interested in laying down arms. They are too invested in the "us vs. them" war to find effective solutions. In hindsight, I now realize it really wasn't that politicians *would not* solve this problem; in reality, they *could not* solve it. This problem must be solved from within our community. While the courts may ultimately decide the legality of banning therapy, that will not stop this war. When it comes down to it, mental health clinicians will continue to work with clients in such a way that allows them to operate legally and ethically, and ideologues will use their clients' outcomes, for better or worse, as ammunition in the greater culture war of sexual and gender identity.

That being said, in the last two years, I have stopped engaging in lobbying and advocacy as I once did. After investing so much time and energy, I realized that the facts no longer mattered to politicians, the media, and ideologues. Each side tends to exaggerate research and stories that strengthen their position, and therefore, I chose to invest my time and energy in documenting this war from a historical and political perspective. After all, I needed to somehow justify those bachelor's degrees in history and political science!

I believe I have written an accurate account of what is occurring, being fair to those real victims of abuse and coercion, while calling out the activists I believe are committing fraud and deceiving the public. But when all is said and done, most people will believe what is convenient and complementary to their world view. If that is you, this book probably didn't surprise you all that much. However, if your view has somehow changed after reading these pages, I would like to congratulate you for having an open mind!

One thing I can tell you for certain is that this war has changed me for the better. It has caused me to examine myself, my motivations, and the way I practice psycho-therapy. In the face of many allegations of abuse, I took an honest inventory of my informed consent, therapeutic practices, and approach to working with clients across the sexual and gender identity spectrum, and I improved my practice to be more ethical and effective. My values haven't changed, but my heart has. Whereas I once held contempt for the LGBT community, that has completely transformed to love and compassion.

So, I wish to express my gratitude for the many gay activist organizations out there spreading misinformation and committing mass fraud. You have sharpened my clinical practice and have helped me become more conscientious and compassionate to the clients I serve. And your movement has kept my colleagues on their toes as well. They have heard these stories of harm, including the many fabricated ones, and our professional guilds understand the need for con-scientious, compassionate care. But your job is now over, and I hope you can take a break. I have been changed and converted!

CHAPTER 12
A DAY IN THE LIFE OF A POLITICALLY INCORRECT (P.I.) PSYCHOTHERAPY OFFICE

DR. SWITZER: Just have a seat and let me tell you a bit about our billing. I charge five dollars for the first five minutes and then absolutely nothing after that. How does that sound?
KATHERINE: That sounds great. Too good to be true, as a matter of fact.
DR. SWITZER: Well, I can almost guarantee you that our session won't last the full five minutes. Now, we don't do any insurance billing, so you would either have to pay in cash or by check.
KATHERINE: Wow. Okay.
DR. SWITZER: And I don't make change.

~ Bob Newhart, *Stop It!* (MAD TV)

ରେ

Six years later...

Dr. P.I.: "Good morning, my name is Dr. P.I."

Client: "Yes, we've met before, don't you remember?"

Dr. P.I.: "Why yes, I do recall now. That was a long time ago. Things have changed a lot since that time..."

Client: "Including your name. The last time I saw you, it was Dr. P.C."

A Day in the Life of a Politically Incorrect (P.I.) Psychotherapy Office

Dr. P.I.: "Ha-ha, yes, it did change. Well, times have changed. I don't need to be *P.C.* any longer…"

Client: "Really? Why is that?"

Dr. P.I.: "Well, for one, I completely got out of the insurance business. Doing so allows me to see clients without having to diagnose them with something that is 'acceptable' to insurance companies."

Client: "What do you mean, 'acceptable'?"

Dr. P.I.: "Insurance companies will only reimburse clinicians for certain diagnosable mental disorders that are listed in the *Diagnostic and Statistical Manual (DSM)*, but in my experience, many clients seek out therapy for a variety of issues not found in the *DSM*. So, this essentially causes clinicians to label their clients with a condition that may not even be completely appropriate in order to be paid for their services."

Client: "I see. Isn't that dishonest?"

Dr. P.I.: "It can be, but don't worry. For the insurance companies, the facts don't really matter. They're only interested in profit; so as long as you play their game, everyone wins. Except for the client, that is."

Client: "How does the client lose?

Dr. P.I.: "By being placed in a box with a label and having an insurance company manage their care, which essentially means that the insurance company tells the clinician how many sessions their client needs until they are cured."

A Day in the Life of a Politically Incorrect (P.I.) Psychotherapy Office

Client: "What if I don't get cured? What if there is no cure? What if I don't want to be cured?"

Dr. P.I.: "That doesn't matter to the insurance companies. All they care about is that you get 8–10 sessions and get 'cured'."

Client: "That's absurd!"

Dr. P.I.: "I agree, so that's why I got out of the insurance game."

Client: "I see, so what shall we do now?"

Dr. P.I.: "Let's talk about why you're here."

Client: "Ok, well, I'm still struggling with this homosexual issue."

Dr. P.I.: "Really? It's been six years since you've walked out of my office. You still haven't gotten over this? You're a hopeless case, aren't you? Why don't you just be gay?"

Client: "That's kind of, politically incorrect, don't you think?"

Dr. P.I.: "Exactly! This is the new me! Do you want to keep on talking?"

Client: "Yeah, sure…at least you're being honest now!"

Dr. P.I.: "Ok, now…tell me about your mother…"

Client: "Oh my, this is gonna take a while…"

AFTERWORD
THE WAR IN THE FAMILY

Fathers hug your sons, or else another man will.

~ Joseph Nicolosi, Ph.D. (1947 – 2017)
Founder of Reparative Therapy
Co-Founder, National Association for
Research and Therapy of Homosexuality

ༀ

It's only fitting that I end this book with a quote from the late Dr. Joseph Nicolosi, or Joe, as we called him. I remember very well the morning of March 9, 2017 when a colleague texted me that Joe had died from complications of the flu. It was surreal, and completely unexpected. I know what you're thinking: Death is almost always unexpected. But if you knew Joe personally, as I did, his exit from this world was nothing less than anti-climactic. I say this because Joe was a fighter. He was a giant in our field. I would almost go as far as to describe him as a living legend during his time on earth.

The first time I met Joe was in Denver, Colorado in 2008 at the annual convention of the National Association for Research and Therapy of Homosexuality (NARTH). Joe was standing on the second floor of the hotel's atrium, talking with some colleagues, when I approached him and introduced myself. I have to admit, I was a bit star-struck. I had read Joe's book and studied much of his work on the development and treatment of male homosexuality. To say that Joe had a huge reputation in our relatively small community of therapists, was, well, an understatement. If anyone's reputation preceded him, Joe's was it!

As I introduced myself, Joe was very engaging and welcoming. He was especially interested in the fact that I was just finishing graduate school and wanted to learn about therapy for unwanted same-sex attractions. As *the* pioneer in the Reparative Therapy movement, Joe was eager to teach younger therapists and pass along his work. In fact, he was so enthusiastic about passing on his craft to the next generation, that he actually gave his working copy (full of all his personal notes) of his final book, *Shame and Attachment Loss: The Practical Work of Reparative Therapy*, to a young man in the audience of one of his lectures. I later became the first recipient of the Dr. Joseph Nicolosi award and scholarship for early career excellence.

You see, Joe knew something, and he was eager to pass it along to anyone who was willing to listen and consider what he had to say. He loved a good debate, but even more than that, he loved a good glass of wine. Some of the fondest memories in my career include sitting across from Joe at a hotel restaurant, listening to him tell stories over a glass or two of red wine while my colleagues and I howled in laughter! Joe's stories almost always had political overtones, and while other professionals shied away from the controversy of homosexuality and therapy, Joe embraced it.

Having treated over 1,000 male homosexuals in his career,[43] Joe butted heads with the leading professionals at the American Psychological Association over the etiology and development of same-sex attractions. Right around the time Joe began to specialize in the treatment of male homosexuality in the 1980s, millions of dollars of funding was being poured into researching the "born gay" myth. In 1993, just a couple of years after Joe's first book, *Reparative Therapy of Homosexuality: A New Clinical Approach,* was published, gay-identified researcher Dean Hamer published his infamous "gay gene" study. Hamer's research was the first of many "born gay" studies, largely published by

---

[43] Joe's son, Joseph Jr., also a psychologist, once remarked that his father treated the most male homosexuals in the history of the world, which is unverifiable, but I believe to be true.

LGBT-identified researchers, in the effort to prove that homosexuality was inborn, and therefore, unchangeable.

Joe's work was a huge contradiction to the growing body of "born gay" research (which the mainstream media adored), and despite the "mainstream" professional guild's and liberal media's promotion of the "born gay" junk science, Nicolosi continued to advocate for the client's right of self-determination to move away from homosexuality through professional psychotherapy. I contracted the same fever, if you will, as Joe had 20 years before me. He discovered, as I later did, through personal and professional experience, that homosexuality is essentially caused by childhood trauma; most often, this trauma occurs in the family of origin.

The Red Pill or the Blue Pill: Choose One Only

As a clinician, once you see a very similar (if not identical) psychosocial pattern in your clients, you begin to get quite adept at diagnosing it, and eventually, treating it. Joe rightly discovered that homosexuality was essentially an emotionally based, maladaptive condition caused by various forms of childhood trauma. If you successfully treat the trauma, the homosexual impulses lessen, and in some cases, completely dissipate. I know this because I have experienced it in my own life, personally, and professionally, by working with hundreds (mostly men) of clients who experienced unwanted same-sex attractions, for ten years. When you witness this pattern and understand how to treat it, you are forced to choose between the red pill and the blue pill.

In the 1999 film, *The Matrix*, Morpheus (Laurence Fishburne) gives Neo (Keanu Reeves) the choice to take the red pill, which leads to knowledge and freedom, as well as the brutal truth of reality, or the blue pill, which would keep him feeling secure and happy, but completely ignorant. Like Neo, Joe chose the red pill. I also chose the red pill; and as the story goes, once you take the red pill, you can never go back. You must live in the reality of truth, despite the harsh realities this choice may entail. The harsh reality is that the war on psychotherapy (as it pertains to homosexuality) often starts in the family.[44] Indeed, this is a very tough pill for many families to swallow.

In my clinical work, the population I have come to work with the most is the conservative, Christian family. In recent years, it has become even more specific in that many of my clients come from small, tight-knit religious communities where it is common for the families to home-school their children. If the family does not home-school, it is very likely they will send their child to a small Christian or Catholic school; or, if the family is Orthodox Jewish, a Yeshiva school. It is these families that I have worked with the most, and I have come to understand some very familiar patterns. These patterns are perfectly illustrated in a documentary film I took part in about five years ago.

In January of 2014, Maryland Delegate Jon Cardin was one of the first politicians to introduce a "conversion therapy" ban in the country, following lawmakers in California and New Jersey. In response, I organized a small group of colleagues and concerned citizens to talk with Annapolis legislators and discourage them from supporting the legislation. Shortly after our two visits to the state capital, the legislation was withdrawn, never receiving a committee hearing. Our community was thrilled! Since I am a licensed clinical professional counselor in Maryland affected by the ban, I decided to sue the state, represented by Liberty Counsel, a non-profit religious liberty law firm. Thereafter, Baltimore-native film maker Richard Yeagley read a story in *The Baltimore Sun* about my clinical and advocacy work

---

[44] While it is important to note that sexual abuse and/or other sexual trauma may be associated with the development of homosexuality, in my clinical experience, most clients with sexual and/or gender identity conflicts experience problems with attachment and other forms of emotional trauma.

and became intrigued. He wanted to film a documentary about my work. I was very skeptical. I explained to Yeagley that even if I agreed to go on camera, I was 99.9% certain that none of my clients would want to expose themselves to what would almost certainly be a hostile general public. After our initial conversation, I dismissed the idea and went on with my work. But Richard was persistent. He contacted me again a few weeks later and we had a longer conversation. He explained to me that he didn't have a position on the subject, and that he merely wanted to show the public what this therapy was really about.

After much prayer and consideration, I decided to tell all of my clients about the opportunity, fully expecting to get a 100% "No." To my surprise, one client said "Yes." That client was Nathan.

The Baltimore Sun

Figure A.1. Christopher Doyle and client, Nathan, talking with *The Baltimore Sun*

At first, I tried to talk Nathan out of doing the film. I informed him of the risks. I told him he might not like the outcome, and that it would certainly invade his privacy. But Nathan persisted. A year and one-half prior, this same young man—who was raised in a devout Catholic family—had come to me in crisis. He had just ended a homosexual relationship and was experiencing a crisis of conscience. His parents had heard about my work and referred him to me for counseling. At first, Nathan, who was in his mid-twenties, was very skeptical about the possibility of moving away from homosexuality. But after a few sessions, I had learned enough about Nathan to describe to him his childhood and the subsequent causes of his homosexuality. At that point, Nathan took the red pill and there was no turning back.

For the first time in his life, Nathan expressed to his father in one of his therapy sessions how much pain their emotional disconnection had caused him. As Nathan grieved for what seemed like an eternity, his father held him in his arms on my therapy couch and apologized for his years of emotional neglect. Months after that pivotal session between Nathan and his father, he was making steady progress in therapy and wanted to tell the world of this work that had helped him heal the wounds he experienced in his family during his formative years.

The documentary was tough. It was heart-wrenching and emotionally taxing. We filmed one session per month for nearly 18 months. At the end of Nathan's journey with me, his therapy culminated in a two-day-long family therapy intensive at his parents' home with his sisters. Like many Christian families that I have worked with over the years, Nathan's parents were unaware of their contributions to Nathan's wounding, and subsequent same-sex attractions. During the first morning of family therapy, Nathan's younger sister cried for three hours straight. Later that day, one of his older sisters described the deep wounds she also experienced in the family. Much like Nathan, she was faithful to the Catholic Church's teachings and the family's faith values, but the emotional dysfunction that permeated their household caused her to be detached and disconnected.

What became very clear to the family after the therapy was that Nathan's homosexuality was not really the problem; it was the emotionally dysfunctional patterns that originated from the parents' unhealed and unresolved issues. It wasn't genetic, it was hereditary. It wasn't the evil world, it was the wounded family! So often in my clinical work with families like Nathan's, Mom and Dad are so frightened of, and overprotective against, the world's influence on their children's health and formation, they neglect to see the war happening in their own family. The sad irony is that we can try to protect our children from the demons of this world, but we are powerless to protect them from the demons inside of us we if fail to recognize them.

This is precisely what the vast majority of religious families and parents fail to understand—our children's wounds are, in large part, a manifestation of our own emotional brokenness. Once Nathan's parents were able to clearly see this, their eyes were open. Unfortunately, it appears that filmmaker Richard Yeagley was either unable, or unwilling, to recognize this in his own documentary. This winter (2019), *The Sunday Sessions* will finally be released to the public. Despite his self-described objectivity, Yeagley tried his hardest to paint the film as proof of the horrors of "conversion therapy."

He marketed and promoted the film to the LGBT community and reached out to gay activists trying to sell the product. There was really only one problem. The therapy Nathan underwent wasn't harmful. It was emotionally challenging, and, at some points, caused him distress. But at the end of his suffering, Nathan remained true to his Catholic values. His relationships with his family are stronger and healthier, and he has moved onto bigger and better things in his life. Make no mistake, the world will not celebrate Nathan when they watch his story, and they will probably not understand him. Many will mock him. But such is the war we are engaged in.

The War Is Being Waged All Around Us

In conclusion, I wish to leave you with these words. A successful war is fought on many fronts and from many angles. This war we are engaged in is largely spiritual, but the battles are being fought in many areas (emotional, psychological, physical, and more) and the assaults that hurt us the most are often experienced by those who are the closest to us. That is why we need to be on guard and search deep within ourselves; in our relationships; in our communities; and in our families, for the healing of our hearts, minds, bodies, and souls. The most precious gift the Lord has given us—outside of Himself and His sacrifice on the Cross—is our marriage, children, and family. That is why the war begins in the family and is waged most powerfully in this unit. While the enemy can inflict great damage from the outside, the hurts from within are the most painful and take the longest to heal. Fathers and mothers, take great care of your marriage and your relationships with your children.

May the Lord's blessings be upon you and your house.

RESOURCES

Legal

Alliance Defending Freedom (Arizona)
www.adflegal.org

Freedom X (Washington, D.C.)
www.freedomxlaw.com

Liberty Counsel (Florida, Virginia, Washington, D.C.)
www.lc.org

Pacific Justice Institute (California)
www.pacificjustice.org

Public Policy

American Family Association (Mississippi)
www.afa.net

Concerned Women for America (Washington, D.C.)
www.concernedwomen.org

Eagle Forum (Illinois, Washington, D.C.)
www.eagleforum.org

Focus on the Family (Colorado)
www.focusonthefamily.com

Family Research Council (Washington, D.C.)
www.frc.org

Heritage Foundation (Washington, D.C.)
www.heritage.org

Resources

Ruth Institute (Louisiana)
www.ruthinstitute.org

The American Conservative Union (Washington, D.C.)
www.conservative.org

Young America's Foundation (Virginia)
www.yaf.org

Therapeutic

Alliance for Therapeutic Choice and Scientific Integrity (Utah)
www.TherapeuticChoice.com

Core Issues Trust (United Kingdom)
www.core-issues.org

Desert Hope (Colorado)
www.deserthope.com

Family Strategies (Arizona)
www.familystrategies.org

Institute for Healthy Families (Virginia)
www.InstituteforHealthyFamilies.org

International Federation for Therapeutic and Counselling Choice (International)
www.iftcc.org

Reconciliation and Growth Project (Utah)
www.reconciliationandgrowth.org

The American Association of Christian Counselors (Virginia)
www.aacc.net

Medical

American College of Pediatricians (Florida)
www.acpeds.org

American Association of Physician and Surgeons (Arizona)
www.aapsonline.org

Catholic Medical Association (Pennsylvania)
www.cathmed.org

Christian Medical and Dental Associations (Washington, D.C.)
www.cmda.org

Freedom 2 Care (Washington, D.C.)
www.freedom2care.org

Medical Institute for Sexual Health (Texas)
www.medinstitute.org

The International Network of Orthodox Mental Health Providers (New York)
www.nefesh.org

Political/Advocacy

Center for Family and Human Rights/C–FAM (New York, Washington, D.C.)
www.c–fam.org

Equality And Justice For All (Virginia)
www.equalityandjusticeforall.org

Ex–Gay Calling (International)
www.exgaycalling.org

Family Watch International (Utah)
www.familywatch.org

Jewish Institute for Global Awareness (JIGFA) (New Jersey)
www.jifga.org

National Task Force for Therapy Equality (Washington, D.C.)
www.therapyequality.org

Parents and Friends of Ex-Gays and Gays (PFOX) (Virginia)
www.pfox.org

Voice of the Voiceless (Virginia)
www.voiceofthevoiceless.info

Ministry

Brothers on a Road Less Traveled (Virginia)
www.brothersroad.org

Campus Crusade for Christ/Cru (Florida)
www.cru.org

Celebrate Recovery (International Affiliates)
www.celebraterecovery.org

Courage (Connecticut)
www.couragec.org

Desert Stream Ministries/Living Waters (Missouri)
www.DesertStream.org

Exodus Global Alliance (International Affiliates)
www.exodusglobalalliance.org

First Stone Ministries (Oklahoma)
www.firststone.org

Hope for Wholeness (South Carolina)
www.hopeforwholeness.org

Restored Hope Network (Colorado)
www.restoredhopenetwork.org

Media

American Family Association/Radio (Mississippi)
www.afa.net

Dr. Michael Brown and the Line of Fire Radio (North Carolina)
www.thelineoffire.org

Dr. James Dobson's Family Talk (Colorado)
www.drjamesdobson.org

Janet Mefferd Today (Texas)
www.janetmefferd.com

The Dacus Report (California)
https://www.pacificjustice.org/the-dacus-report

APPENDIX A: SUPPLEMENTAL JONAH DEFENSE

On June 25, 2015, in the first ever trial of therapy for unwanted same-sex attractions (SSA), a New Jersey (NJ) jury found JONAH (and several individuals associated with the organization) guilty of consumer fraud. Our crime? Providing resources to help a person change their sexual orientation. Six months later, on December 18, 2015, NJ Superior Court Judge Peter Bariso ordered a permanent shutdown of JONAH and prohibited myself and a counselor from engaging in "any form of conversion therapy in New Jersey."

The lawsuit was initiated by the Southern Poverty Law Center (SPLC), a radical legal advocacy organization notorious for classifying traditional values organizations as "hate groups." In our case, they actually advertised for clients, had over a dozen activist lawyers on the case, and use part of their approximately $280 million war chest to pursue us. In their pre-trial publicity, they made clear that this case was the "opening salvo" in their nationwide campaign to shut down what is misleadingly called "conversion therapy" and listed approximately 70 other groups and individuals on their website which they targeted for future lawsuits. After our loss, they filed an action at the Federal Trade Commission against People Can Change, an organization that runs experiential weekends for those with unwanted SSA and whose director was a witness in our case.

Simply stated, we were victims of the culture war against religious freedom. SPLC sought to eliminate, to intimidate, and to silence us, but we will be neither silenced nor intimidated! Below are some examples of several of the court decisions, which illustrate how absurd the "guilty" ruling was, and how these issues during the trial caused the jury to decide wrongly in this case.

1. Whether the Consumer Fraud Act applies to a duly constituted not-for-profit organization. No case has been found prior to ours which applied the law to a legally constituted non-profit. This reasoning makes sense because consumer fraud is intended to curtail unfair business practices where people are cheated out of their money (used cars, refrigerators, etc.). The Judge's denial of our motion for summary judgment was a misuse of these laws, promoted a political agenda, and had nothing to do with protecting consumers: JONAH did not charge for its services and its two co-directors were volunteers for 15 years who never received personal compensation.

2. The Court permitted evidence—over the objection of our attorneys—that a weekend program called "Journey Beyond" run by People Can Change, an entirely different entity which was not a defendant in this litigation, could be used against us even though none of the plaintiffs ever attended those programs. Nevertheless, several of our fact witnesses testified that the controversial processes in those programs worked for them.

3. The Court excluded our expert witnesses on the grounds that the American Psychiatric Association (APA) delisted homosexuality as a mental disorder from the *Diagnostic and Statistical Manual of Mental Disorders (DSM)* and the Judge improperly believed that all our experts said it was a mental disorder. The opinion that homosexuality was a mental disorder was not found in their expert reports presented to the Court and did not form the basis of their opinion on Sexual Orientation Change Efforts (SOCE). Instead their opinions were based on their own first-hand experience. To make matters worse, the Judge chose to analogize our experts to those who believe that the Earth is flat. "The theory that

homosexuality is disordered is not novel but like the notion that the Earth is flat and the Sun revolves around it—instead is outdated and refuted." Of course, it was the seafarers who actually navigated the seas who understood the reality that the Earth was a sphere just like the reality of change has been observed by several honest mental health professionals as well as "ex-gays" who testify to the reality of change in their own lives. But the Judge chose to make a false analogy which made a great sound-bite for the press.

4. The Court ruled that it was a per se violation of the Consumer Fraud Act (CFA) if we ever said homosexuality was a mental disorder or disease "or the equivalent thereof." The only exception would be if it was said from a religious liberty [perspective] to the jury. A real fraud here was the Court permitting the CFA to be applied to a religious organization for the first time.

5. While the Court denied the plaintiffs' motion to strike our First Amendment religious liberty defense, it refused to instruct the jury on that defense and prohibited defense counsel from mentioning our First Amendment right in our closing argument.

6. While permitting their openly identified lesbian expert to testify that we used scare tactics in citing medical statistics relevant to homosexual behavior, the Court refused to allow us to present evidence supporting those statistics or to call our medical expert (Dr. John Diggs) to show the accuracy of the information for those engaged in such high-risk behavior.

7. Each plaintiff signed documents, submitted into evidence, that no guarantees as to success were provided by defendants. Nevertheless, these were ignored by the Court and the Jury.

8. The judge also made derogatory comments about several fact witnesses who explained how they overcame SSA. For example, after a man who overcome not only his SSA but also sadistic and masochistic sexual behaviors, alcohol, and drug addiction (DeJiacomo) testified via video, the judge commented that he did not "understand what the accomplishment was there" and went on to observe, "I'm not even sure how it's a success story witness, based upon his testimony."

9. There were a host of other technical issues, such as: 1) Numerous faulty jury instructions to which we objected; 2) Permitting the plaintiffs to claim alleged emotional distress even though no other New Jersey case permitted recovery for noneconomic damages (in fact, there is case law that specifically forbids collecting money for noneconomic damages); 3) Introduction of numerous e-mails to third parties that the plaintiffs neither saw nor relied upon. Nevertheless, they were improperly used by the plaintiffs to show how they were supposedly induced to enter into a commercial transaction; 4) The Court's improper exclusion of us offering testimony about, or entering into evidence, client surveys showing success rates of those who were helped by fact witnesses Thaddeus Heffner, Alan Downing, and PCC director Rich Wyler, and; 5) The Court's refusal to rely upon a New Jersey Supreme Court case (*Acuna*) that the courts should not decide controversial issues that are subject to intense public debate such as abortion or homosexuality.

In a perceptive article in *World Net Daily*, Dr. Laura Haynes and Charles LiMandri (JONAH's defense attorney) concluded that questions concerning therapy for unwanted SSA must be taken out of the hands of the judiciary. They further stated: "When the JONAH case is examined closely, it becomes clear that JONAH was a model example of a small, religious organization serving the most helpless and defenseless, and that it was only taken down due to a concerted effort to undermine its ability to defend itself." And LiMandri said after the decision: "I view the trial in hindsight as nothing short of a charade and legal travesty" and cited several of the overtly biased rulings and attitude of the trial court judge set forth above.

APPENDIX B: JAMES MADISON UNIVERSITY CASE STUDY

James Madison University[45] is located in Harrisonburg, VA and has a total enrollment of just under 20,000 students. Their LGBTQ resource center is co-coordinated by Dr. Tammy.[cclvii] JMU has a history of anti-ex-sentiment within its faculty and LGBT advocacy programs,[cclviii, cclix] and in the past has refused to display educational brochures offered by Parents and Friends of Ex-Gays & Gays (PFOX) in their LGBTQ resource center. A FOIA request from 2009 obtained from PFOX indicated that faculty members of JMU were conspiring with other university LGBT activists and anti-ex-gay organizations including Truth Wins Out and Lambda Legal to keep ex-gay information out of their LGBTQ resource center.

Figure B.1: The Logo of JMU's LGBTQ Resource Center

On September 12, 2013, I met with a representative of the JMU Safe Zone, presenting as a graduate student with conflicts over his unwanted same-sex attraction due to his Christian beliefs. The representative did not offer any referrals for SOCE therapy during the session, nor did the LGBTQ resource center make them available among the many gay-affirming pamphlets and magazines offered. As a result, Liberty Counsel

---

[45] To view all seven university case studies carried out by VOV, please visit: www.VoiceoftheVoiceless.info and download the entire "Campus Climate Report."

determined there was evidence to suggest that the actions of JMU's LGBTQ resource center constituted viewpoint discrimination. During the session, the representative also made a number of troubling statements, described in detail below.

To view videos of nine segments of the interview, visit:https://www.youtube.com/results?search_query=Voice+of+the+Voiceless+James+Madison+University

Summaries of the interchange follow here.

The question: "Information-wise, what do you think would help you?" was appropriate. However, she quickly suggests a campus support group called "Queer to Questioning" that may not be acceptable for a student who is QU. It would have been more appropriate for her to explore the student's values around sexuality and then determine a suitable referral.

The statement: "New Jersey is one of the first states to outlaw that, what they call conversion therapy. Because in a lot of ways it can be very traumatic and very psychologically detrimental to people. A lot of times parents will put their children in conversion therapy at young ages. If that's something that people do as adults on their own accord, that's one thing. When parents do that to children who really are essentially born that way, and acting that way, 2–3 years old. There are a lot of different opinions."

The facts: She misstates that SOCE is outlawed in New Jersey, rather than distinguishing the fact that a law was just passed to prohibit the therapy for minors only. She also incorrectly asserts that SOCE therapy (which she pejoratively calls "conversion therapy") is traumatic and detrimental, which is scientifically incorrect. Additionally, her claims that many parents put their children in SOCE therapy against their will is impossible to verify, yet is stated as a fact. Finally, she suggests that children who exhibit homosexual tendencies at young ages are born with same-sex attraction, which is an oversimplification and is scientifically incorrect.[cclx]

The statement: "It would be difficult (to have same-sex attractions) and be married to a woman, because you would be living a lie, and that's why you see it happen in the media, with certain politicians who, like, have affairs on the side with men, because they weren't truly being themselves" assumes that no one can live a heterosexual life while having unwanted same-sex attraction, and that doing so is not being true to oneself.

The facts: This statement is offensive to individuals who may experience unwanted same-sex attractions and desire to remain true to their religious convictions and engage only in heterosexual behavior. It also ignores the fact that some individuals can and do experience change in sexual orientation through SOCE therapy.[cclxi] For such individuals, SOCE therapy and ex-gay organizations provide important guidance, support, and assistance.

The statement: "A lot of people who choose to live that way, like I said (living a heterosexual life with same-sex attractions) but they're fundamentally unhappy. Think about the partner that you choose and how you're lying to them for most of your life."

Analysis: The student then goes on to share about his fear of emotional intimacy with women, to which the representative seems unable to provide any insight. Never does she consider that perhaps this is may be the result of emotional trauma from women, or suggest to the student that he might want to explore the origins of these feelings. Further, to make a statement that people with unwanted SSA that live heterosexual lives are "fundamentally unhappy" is offensive, impossible to verify, and assumes that acting on same-sex attractions and not staying faithful to one's deeply held religious convictions will make a person happy.

The response to the question: "What would it be like if I were to 'come out' to my church?" was discouraging. Rather than encouraging the student to seek help from his religious community, which plays a very important role in his life, the representative encourages the student to come out in other, more accepting places first and build support before attempting to tell people in the church.

Analysis: This response is disrespectful to the student's faith and values in the sense that it may be more important that he seek guidance from clergy and leaders in the church rather than develop a gay identity in secret and not integrate his sexuality with his faith. It also suggests that no one in the church can provide guidance, assistance, or support to those struggling with sexual orientation.

The statements about SOCE therapy: "That it comes from the perspective that having homosexual feelings is wrong and that the therapy is essentially brainwashing ... some of them are way more intense than others. I think a lot of times when they are a lot more religious, when they talk about those feelings not being natural, and not feelings, but the devil. They used to (use electroshock therapy) but I don't know if they do now ... yeah, yeah, can you believe that someone would shock your brain into like, being straight ... and a lot of them are very isolating, because sometimes they, like, take you away, isolate you for weeks or like months, like a camp, not all of them, but some of them are like that, yeah. So that's why, especially the ones with the kids, the parents would ship their kids away for like, a month. Yeah, that in and of itself is like 'hey I'm gonna ship you away and you're gonna come back straight' ... so you know, it's not really something that advocates in the LGBT (community) support, for sure, and it's not something that's healthy really anyway. It does a lot of stigmatizing and treating it as a disease that can be cured."

The facts: There are a number of statements made in this dialogue that are inaccurate and are based on stereotypes, including the assertion that religious SOCE programs suggest that homosexual feelings are from the devil. The counselor also cites a myth that kids are shipped away to "conversion therapy camps" to become straight.[cclxii] It is also incorrect to say that SOCE therapy is stigmatizing. For individuals that have unwanted SSA, SOCE therapy and ex-gay organizations provide support, guidance, and assistance to help clients meet their goals. Competent SOCE therapists respect the dignity of all clients, do not shame or stigmatize clients, nor do they treat their client's homosexual feelings as a disease.[cclxiii]

The statements: "There are health risks within (all) sexual activity ... you always want to have protected sexual activity (wear a condom), and beyond that it's not really any more risky (gay sex) than sexual activity with a female. I mean, if this were the 80s then maybe I'd say, 'yes, the risk of HIV is higher' unless you have a partner that you know is engaged in other risky behaviors, just like if you had a female partner that you knew was in other risky behaviors. I guess you can say the risk is a little bit higher, because, I guess sometimes people will say it's easier for males to transmit things than it is necessarily for a female to give something to a male, because essentially males are always, like, depositing things as opposed to a female who is not ever really depositing something in a male, but really as long as you're using a condom and you're not with somebody who's an IV drug user ... alcohol always is a risk, because when people are drunk and they're having sex than they're usually less careful about using a condom and asking for consent. But yeah, you're not like 'Oh my God you're having gay sex you're super risky'."

The facts: These statements are medically inaccurate. Data from the Centers for Disease Control and Prevention found that in 2011, 94.9% of HIV diagnoses among young men ages 13–19 were linked to men that have sex with men (MSM) and 94.1% of the HIV cases among young men ages 20–24 were from MSM.[cclxiv] While condoms may reduce the risk of contracting and spreading HIV through anal sex, the Food and Drug Administration has advised the following on their website: "Condoms provide some protection, but anal intercourse is simply too dangerous to practice ... condoms may be more likely to break during anal intercourse than during other types of sex because of the greater amount of friction and other stresses involved. Even if the condom doesn't break, anal intercourse is very risky because it can cause tissue in the rectum to tear and bleed. These tears allow disease germs to pass more easily from one partner to the other."[cclxv]

The statements: "There is not a lot of research that shows (sexual orientation) change. The research leads to being born that way, and also that there is a genetic component. I just saw something, I forgot, oh crap, I just saw it. There was a study that just came out saying that an older brother who's gay, obviously it wasn't like causation, but something about an older brother who's gay raises the risk of a sibling, not a risk, but chances that a younger brother being gay ... I don't know, it's a genetic link as well. But yeah, it's really interesting the genetic component ... yeah it's biological. It would be nice if we could just like prove it, it would be great. Look it's just genetic, but that would also kind of be bad, because then there would be somebody who's like, 'let's take care of that gene' and like, you know erase it or something."

The facts: While no one simply chooses to experience homosexual feelings, they are not hard-wired and research indicates that some individuals may experience change or fluidity.[cclxvi] A recent study indicated that while heterosexual feelings are more stable in both genders, women might have even more fluidity in their same-sex attractions than men.[cclxvii] Similarly, previous research has found that heterosexual attractions are 17 times more stable in men and 30 times more stable in women than homosexual attractions.[cclxviii] While there have been many studies attempting to find genetic and/or biological causes to same-sex attractions, the APA has stated that scientists cannot conclude that people are born homo-sexual.[cclxix] Further, researchers have reviewed the many biological theories surrounding homosexuality and have concluded that the evidence is not strong enough to support genetic, hormonal, or otherwise biological associations.[cclxx]

Recommendations for JMU Policy Reforms

In order to make JMU's LGBTQ Resource Center a more welcoming and safe for QU students, we recommend a number of policy reforms that will help to rectify the viewpoint discrimination that has occurred and the troubling statements that were made by the representative on September 12, 2013. It would be appropriate for JMU to set aside a reasonable amount of funding from their LGBTQ Resource Center budget for the following:

1. Tolerance and sensitivity training for LGBTQ resource center, CAPS, and other professional coun-seling staff to better understand the needs of QU students.

2. Professional development training for LGBTQ resource center, CAPS, and other professional counseling staff in order to provide competent counseling and/or referrals for QU students.
3. Medical accuracy training for LGBTQ resource center, CAPS, and other professional counseling staff, especially as it relates to contraception failure rates and the increased risk of HIV for men who have sex with men.
4. Production and distribution of educational resources for QU students in LGBTQ Resource and counseling centers. The university should work with Voice of the Voiceless and Parents and Friends of Ex-Gay and Gays to ensure that resources do not contain anti-ex-gay bias and include appropriate information, including a list of referrals that are sensitive to the needs of QU students.
5. A list of online resources and referrals on the JMU & Community LGBTQIQA Resources/safe zone web-site that provide counseling, support, and legal assistance for former homosexuals and students with unwanted same-sex attractions.
6. Periodic compliance checks from neutral university administrators to ensure that resources for QU students are prominently and properly displayed in LGBTQ Resource Centers and counseling centers on campus.

APPENDIX C: MEASURES OF HARM

Peer-Reviewed Journal Articles and Academic Books on "Conversion Therapy" Outcomes that Include Measures of Harm

Arthur, E. (2014). Playing it straight: Framing strategies among reparative therapists. *Sociological Inquiry, 84* (1), 16.

Beckstead, A.L. (2001). Cures versus choices: Agendas in sexual reorientation therapy. *Journal of Gay and Lesbian Psychotherapy, 5*(3/4), 87−115.

Beckstead, A.L. (2003). Understanding the self-reports of reparative therapy "successes." *Archives of Sexual Behavior, 32,* 421−423.

Beckstead, A.L. (2012). Can we change sexual orientation? [Special issue on What is sexual orientation?]. *Archives of Sexual Behavior, (41)*121−134. doi:10.1007/s10508−012−9922−x

Beckstead, A.L., & Morrow, S.L. (2004). Mormon clients' experiences of conversion therapy: The need for a new treatment approach. *The Counseling Psychologist, (32)* 651−690.

Borowich, A. (2008). Failed reparative therapy of Orthodox Jewish homosexuals. *Journal of Gay and Lesbian Mental Health, 12*(3), 167−177.

Bradshaw, K., Dehlin, J.P., Crowell, K A., Galliher, R.V., & Bradshaw, W.S. (2015). Sexual orientation change efforts through psychotherapy for LGBQ individuals affiliated with the Church of Jesus Christ of Latter-Day Saints. *Journal of Sex & Marital Therapy, 41*(4), 391−412.

Bright, C. (2004). Deconstructing reparative therapy: An examination of the processes involved when attempting to change sexual orientation. *Clinical Social Work Journal, 32*(4), 471−481.

365

Burack, C. (2015). From heterosexuality to holiness: Psychoanalysis and ex-gay ministries. *Journal for the Psychoanalysis of Culture and Society, 20*(3), 220–227.

Cramer, R.J., Golom, F.D., LoPresto, C. & Shalene, M.K. (2008). Weighing the evidence: Empirical assessment and ethical implications of conversion therapy. *Ethics & Behavior, 18* (1)93–114.

Dehlin J.P., Galliher, R.V., Bradshaw, W.S., Hyde, D. & Crowell, K.A. (2014). Sexual Orientation Change Efforts among Current or Former LDS Church Members. *Journal of Counseling Psychology.* doi:10.1037/cou0000011

Davison, G.C. (1978). Not can but ought: The treatment of homosexuality. *Journal of Consulting and Clinical Psychology (46)*170–172.

Diamond, L.M., & Rosky, C.J. (2017). Scrutinizing immutability: Research on sexual orientation and U.S. Legal advocacy for sexual minorities. *Journal of Sex Research, 53*(4–5), 363–391.

Dickinson, T., Cook, M., Playle, J., Hallett, C. (2012). 'Queer' treatments: Giving a voice to former patients who received treatments for their 'sexual deviations'. *Journal of Clinical Nursing, 21*(9–10), 1345–1354.

Drescher, J. (1998). I'm your handyman: A history of reparative therapies. *Journal of Homosexuality, 36*(1), 19–42.

Drescher, J. (2001). Ethical concerns raised when patients seek to change same-sex attractions. *Journal of Gay & Lesbian Psychotherapy*, 5(3/4), 181–1210.

Drescher, J. (2003). The Spitzer study and the culture wars. *Archives of Sexual Behavior, (32)*431–432.

Drescher, J. (2009). When politics distort science: What mental health professionals can do. *Journal of Gay & Lesbian Mental Health (13)*213–226.

Fetner, T. (2005). Ex-gay rhetoric and the politics of sexuality: The Christian anti-gay/pro-family movement's "truth in love" ad campaign. *Journal of Homosexuality, 50* (1): 71–95.

Fischer, A.R., & Good, G.E. (1997). Men and psychotherapy: An investigation of alexithymia, intimacy, and masculine gender roles. *Psychotherapy: Theory, Research, Practice, Training (43)*160–170.

Fjelstrom, J. (2013) Sexual orientation change efforts and the search for authenticity.
Journal of Homosexuality, 60 (6) 801–827.

Flentje, A., Heck, N.C., & Cochran, B.N. (2013). Sexual reorientation therapy interventions: Perspectives of ex-ex-gay individuals. *Journal of Gay & Lesbian Mental Health, 17* (3) 256–277.

Flentje, A., Heck, N.C., & Cochran, B.N. (2014). Experiences of ex-ex-gay individuals in sexual reorientation therapy: Reasons for seeking treatment, perceived helpfulness and harmfulness of treatment, and post-treatment identification. *Journal of Homosexuality (61)*1242–1268. http://doi.org/10.1080/00918369.2014.926763

Ford, J. G., Healing homosexuals: A psychologist's journey through the ex-gay movement and the pseudo-science of reparative therapy. *Journal of Gay and Lesbian Psychotherapy*, 5 (3–4), 69–86. Reprinted in A. Shidlo, M. Schroeder, & J. Drescher (Eds.), *Sexual conversion therapy: Ethical, clinical, and research perspectives* (New York: Haworth Medical Press, 2001), 69–86.

Forstein, M., Overview of ethical and research issues in sexual orientation therapy. In A. Shidlo, M. Schroeder, & J. Drescher (Eds.), *Sexual conversion therapy*, ibid., 167–179.

Friedman, R.C. (2003). Sexual orientation change: A study of atypical cases. *Archives of Sexual Behavior, 32*(5), 432–434.

Freund, K. (1960). Some problems in the treatment of homosexuality. In H.J. Eysenck (ed.), *Behavior therapy and the neuroses.* Oxford University Press.

Freund, K. (1977). Psychophysiological assessment of change in erotic preferences. *Behaviour Research and Therapy, 15*(31977. 297–301.

Freund, K. (1977). Should homosexuality arouse therapeutic concern. *Journal of Homosexuality 2*(3), 235–240.

Gonsiorek, J.C. (2004). Reflections from the conversion therapy battlefield. *The Counseling Psychologist, (32)*5, 750–759.

Grace, A. (2008). The charisma and deception of reparative therapies: When medical science beds religion. *Journal of Homosexuality,* 55(4) 545–580.

Green, R. (2017). Banning therapy to change sexual orientation or gender identity in patients under 18. *Journal of the American Academy of Psychiatry and the Law, 45* (1) 7–11.

Green, R.J. (2003). When therapists do not want their clients to be homosexual: A response to Rosik's article. *Journal of Marital and Family Therapy, 29,* 29–38.

Haldeman, D.C. (1994). The practice and ethics of sexual orientation conversion therapy. *Journal of Consulting and Clinical Psychology, 62,* 221–227.

Haldeman, D.C. (2001). Therapeutic antidotes: Helping gay and bisexual men recover from conversion therapies. *Journal of Gay and Lesbian Psychotherapy, 5(3–4),* 117–130.

Haldeman, D.C. (2004). When sexual and religious orientation collide: Considerations in working with conflicted same-sex attracted male clients. *The Counseling Psychologist, 32(5),* 691–715.

Haldeman, D.C. (2012). Sexual orientation conversion therapy: Fact, fiction, and fraud. In S. H. Dworkin & M. Pope (Eds.), *Casebook for counseling lesbian, gay, bisexual, and transgendered persons and their families*, 297–306. American Counseling Association.

Halpert, S.C. (2000). "If it ain't broke, don't fix it": Ethical considerations regarding conversion therapies. *International Journal of Sexuality and Gender Studies, 5*(1), 19–35.

Hein, L.C., & Matthews, A.K. (2010). Reparative therapy: The adolescent, the psych nurse, and the issues. *Journal of Child and Adolescent Psychiatric Nursing, 23*(1), 29–35. doi: 10.1111/j.1744–6171.2009.00214.x

Herek, G. M. (2003). Evaluating interventions to alter sexual orientation: Methodological and ethical considerations. *Archives of Sexual Behavior, 32,* 438–440.

Hill, C.A., & DiClementi, J. D. (2003). Methodological limitations do not justify the claim that same-sex attraction changed through "reparative therapy." *Archives of Sexual Behavior, 32,* 440–442.

Hoffmann, H. (2012). Considering the role of conditioning in sexual orientation. *Archives of Sexual Behavior, 41,* 63–71. doi: 10.1007/s10508–012–9915–9.

Jacobsen, J. & Wright, R. (2014). Mental health implications in Mormon women's experiences with same-sex attraction: A qualitative study. *The Counseling Psychologist, 42*(5), 664–696.

Jenkins, D., & Johnston, L.B. (2004). Unethical treatment of gay and lesbian people with conversion therapy. *Families in Society: The Journal of Contemporary Social Sciences, 85*(4) 557–561.

Johnson, W.B. (2004). Rational emotive behavior therapy for disturbance about sexual orientation. In P.S. Richards & A.E. Bergin (eds.), *Casebook for a spiritual strategy in counseling and psychotherapy* (247−265). Washington, D.C.: American Psychological Association.

Johnston, L.B., & Jenkins, D. (2006). Lesbians and gay men embrace their sexual orientation after conversion therapy and ex-gay ministries: A qualitative study. *Social Work in Mental Health, 4,* 61−82.

Jones, S.L., & Yarhouse, M.A. (2007). Ex-gays?:A Longitudinal Study of Religiously *Mediated Change in Sexual Orientation.* IVP Academic.

Jones, S.L., & Yarhouse, M.A. (2011): A longitudinal study of attempted religiously mediated sexual orientation change. *Journal of Sex & Marital Therapy, 37*(5), 404−427. doi.org/10.1080/0092623X.2011.607052

King, M., Smith, G., & Bartlett, A. (2004). Treatments of homosexuality in Britain since the 1950s—an oral history: The experience of professionals. *British Medical Journal, 328,* 429−432.

Krajeski, J.P. (1984). Masters and Johnson article "seriously flawed." *American Journal of Psychiatry, 141,* 1131.

Krajeski, J. P., Myers, M. F., Valgemae, A., & Pattison, E.M. (1981). "Ex-gays": Religious abuse of psychiatry? *American Journal of Psychiatry, 138,* 852−853.

Lasser, J.S., & Gottlieb, M.C. (2004). Treating patients distressed regarding their sexual orientation: Clinical and ethical alternatives. *Professional Psychology: Research and Practice, 35*(2), 194−200.

Maccio, E.M. (2010). Influence of family, religion, and social conformity on client participation in sexual reorientation therapy. *Journal of Homosexuality, 57*(3), 441−458.

Maccio, E. (2011). Self−reported sexual orientation and identity before and after sexual reorientation therapy. *Journal of Gay & Lesbian Mental Health, 15*(3), 242−259.

McGeorge, C.R., Carlson, T.S., & Toomey, R.B. (2015). An exploration of family therapists' beliefs about the ethics of conversion therapy: The influence of negative beliefs and clinical competence with lesbian, gay, and bisexual clients. *Journal of Marital and Family Therapy, 41* (1), 42–56 doi: 10.1111/jmft.12040

Miville, M.L., & Ferguson, A.D. (2004). Impossible "choices": Identity and values at a crossroads. *The Counseling Psychologist, 32,* 760–770.

Moor, P. (2001). The view from Irving Bieber's couch: "Heads I win, tails you lose." *Journal of Gay and Lesbian Psychotherapy, 5*(3/4), 25–36.

Moran, M.E. (2007). An examination of women's sexuality and spirituality: The effects of *conversion therapy: A mixed study.* Unpublished doctoral dissertation, University of Utah, Salt Lake City.

Morrow, S.L., & Beckstead, A.L. (2004). Conversion therapies for same-sex attracted clients in religious conflict: Context, predisposing factors, experiences, and implications for therapy. *The Counseling Psychologist, 32,* 641– 650.

O'Donohue, W., & Plaud, J.J. (1994). The conditioning of human sexual arousal. *Archives of Sexual Behavior, 23,* 321–344.

Pfaus, J.G., Kippin, T.E., Coria-Avila, G.A., Gelez, H., Afonso, V.M., Ismail, N., & Parada, M. (2012). Who, What, Where, When (and Maybe Even Why)? How the experience of sexual reward connects sexual desire, preference, and performance. *Archives of Sexual Behavior, 41*(1), 31–62.

Ponticelli, C.M. (1999). Crafting stories of sexual identity reconstruction. *Social Psychology Quarterly, 62*(2), 157–172.

Reamer, F. (2014). Ethical issues and challenges: Managing moral dilemmas. In A. Dessel, A.B. & Bolen, R.

(eds.), *Conservative Christian beliefs and sexual orientation in social work: Privilege, oppression, and the pursuit of human rights* (233–256). Alexandria, VA: CSWE Press.

Ryan, C., Toomey, R.B., Diaz, R.M., & Russell, S.T.(2018). Parent-Initiated Sexual Orientation Change Efforts With LGBT Adolescents: Implications for Young Adult Mental Health and Adjustment. *Journal of Homosexuality.* Retrieved online at: https://www.tandfonline.com/doi/full/10.1080/0091 8369.2018.1538407?scroll=top&needAccess=true&

Santero, P.L., Whitehead, N.E., & Ballesteros, D. (2018). Effects of therapy on religious men who have unwanted same-sex attraction. *The Linacre Quarterly*, 1−7.

Savin-Williams, R.C. (2016). Sexual orientation: Categories or continuum? Commentary on Bailey et al. (2016). *Psychological Science in the Public Interest, 17*(2), 37−44. doi.org.ezproxy.lib.utah.edu/10.1177/15291006166 37618

Schneider, M.S., Glassgold, J.M., & Brown, L.S. (2002). Implementing the resolution on Appropriate Therapeutic Responses to Sexual Orientation: A guide for the perplexed. *Professional Psychology: Research and Practice, 33,* 265-276.

Schreier, B.A. (1998). Of shoes, ships and sealing wax: The faulty and specious assumptions of sexual reorientation therapies. *Journal of Mental Health Counseling, 20,* 305–314.

Schrimshaw, E.W., Siegel, K., Downing Jr., M.J., & Parsons, J.T. (2013). Disclosure and concealment of sexual orientation and the mental health of non-gay-identified, behaviorally bisexual men. *Journal of Consulting and Clinical Psychology, 81(1),* 141–153.

Schroeder, M., & Shidlo, A. (2001). Ethical issues in sexual orientation conversion therapies: An empirical study of consumers. *Journal of Gay & Lesbian Psychotherapy, 5*(3/4), 131–166.

Serovich, J.M., Craft, S., Toviessi, P., Gangamma, R., McDowell, T., & Grafsky, E.L. (2008). A systematic review of the research base on sexual reorientation therapies. *Journal of Marital and Family Therapy, 34*(2), 227–238.

Shidlo, A., & Schroeder, M. (2002). Changing sexual orientation: A consumers' report. *Professional Psychology: Research and Practice, 33,* 249–259.

Silverstein, C. (2003). The religious conversion of homosexuals: Subject selection is the *voir dire* of psychological research. *Journal of Gay & Lesbian Psychotherapy, 7*(3), 31–53.

Smith, G., Bartlett, A. & King, M. (2004). Treatments of homosexuality in Britain since 1950—an oral history: The experience of patients. *British Medical Journal, 328*(7437), 427–429.

Steigerwald, F., & Janson, G.R. (2003). Conversion therapy: Ethical considerations in family counseling. *The Family Journal: Counseling and Therapy for Couples and Families, 11*(1), 55–59.

Tozer, E.E., & Hayes, J.A. (2004). The role of religiosity, internalized homonegativity, and identity develop-ment: Why do individuals seek conversion therapy? *The Counseling Psychologist, 32,* 716–740.

Tozer, E.E., & McClanahan, M.K. (1999). Treating the purple menace: Ethical considerations of conversion therapy and affirmative alternatives. *The Counseling Psychologist, 27,* 722–742.

Wakefield, J.C. (2003). Sexual reorientation therapy: Is it ever ethical? Can it ever change sexual orientation? *Archives of Sexual Behavior, 32,* 457–460.

Walker, M.D. (2013). When clients want your help to "pray away the gay": Implications for couple and family therapists. *Journal of Feminist Family Therapy: An International Forum, 25*(2), 112–134.

Weiss, E., Morehouse, J., Yeager, T., & Berry, T. (2010). A qualitative study of ex–gay and ex-ex-gay experiences. *Journal of Gay & Lesbian Mental Health, 14*(4), 291–319.

INDEX

Index

[This book is] a study in how the ideological extremism of the Sexual Revolution has not only permeated into the mainstream of our culture but has distorted our learned professions, curtailed our civil liberties, and corrupted our common sense. With moderation, but also with depth and nuance, Doyle describes the power of an ideology that makes us lie to one another and even to ourselves. Even people who do not share his faith or his views on homosexuality itself will find this account enlightening and should be truly disturbed by the power of political doctrines to inhibit our freedom of thought and to abrogate our civil freedoms.

—Stephen K. Baskerville, Ph.D., Professor of Government, Patrick Henry College

***

The War on Psychotherapy *is a must-read for anyone who cares about truth in caregiving to the souls of hurting people, especially people with unwanted same-sex attractions... [E]very student desiring to go into counseling or therapy and every school leader and minister in the church should read this book. ...Its message is too important to keep to yourself.*

—Stephen Black, executive director, First Stone Ministries

***

With remarkable insight and precision, Christopher Doyle documents how counseling is being weaponized as an instrument of far-left sexual politics. How many adolescents are now barred from effective treatment for confusing homosexual inclinations, or gender confusion, as an outcome of being molested? Unless thoughtful, freedom-

cherishing Americans see 'LGBT' politics for what it is—the attempt to dismantle one's core human identity—our culture will continue down the road of abandoning Judeo-Christian morality and rush toward primitive sexual self-destruction.

—Linda Harvey, Mission America, www.missionamerica.com, host, WRFD ,http://thewordcolumbus.com

***

Christopher Doyle has done an excellent job of detailing how a movement aimed at stopping oppression has become oppressive to those who hold a dissenting opinion. ...This book is a must-read resource for understanding what is happening both in the field of psychotherapy and the culture at large. Not only does Doyle describe the problem, but he also offers a solution and path forward.

—Julie Harren Hamilton, Ph.D., licensed marriage and family therapist, co-editor of *The Handbook of Therapy for Unwanted Homosexual Attractions*

***

With the art of a story teller, Doyle chronicles the lies, deception, fraud, bullying, and intimidation that have characterized the war on therapy and religious freedom. The recounting of his mutually reconciliatory dialogue with Dr. Lee Beckstead, an author of the APA Task Force Report that activists still use to fuel so much misinformed animus against therapy that is open to sexual orientation change, is worth the price of admission. As a psychologist and activist defending the right to therapy, I am pleased he includes ground-breaking acknowledgements in the American Psychological Association's Handbook of Sexuality and Psychology (2014). *Specifically, that there's no gay gene, sexual attraction and childhood gender distress are not simply inborn and always have psychological causes, they shift or change for many through life experience....*

—Laura Haynes, Ph.D., California licensed psychologist, chair of research and legislative policy, National Task Force for Therapy Equality

***

The War on Psychotherapy *deconstructs the one-sided LGBT- affirming therapy narrative which has metastasized into choice limiting, must-choose-gay doctrines which themselves are based on belief and ideology, not sound science. ... This is a must read for those who are questioning their sexuality and have a hunch there is more to the issue than what is being presented by the LGBT elites.*

—Daren Mehl, president, Voice of the Voiceless
www.VoiceoftheVoiceless.info

***

Christopher Doyle's The War on Psychotherapy *presents a fearless, evidence-based expose of the truth about the efforts of LGBT activists to change the very nature of the United States culture.... Mr. Doyle demonstrates how the Constitutional right of free speech, religious rights for licensed therapists who are employees of churches, and the right of all clients to receive the kind of professional therapy that works for them has been betrayed.*

—David Pickup, MA, LMFT, co-founder, National Task Force for Therapy Equality

***

The War on Psychotherapy *is an outstanding resource addressing a complicated subject: a detailed history of the successful efforts of LGBTQ+ activists to culturally establish and weaponize their ideology as the "new normal" in halls of law, courts, media, academia, professionals, and religion. Doyle draws on his considerable experience as studied author, compassionate professional, and seasoned street fighter with expertise as a psychotherapist, author, media resource, and political science-trained once-gay turned husband and father. Doyle exposes popularly believed falsehoods of the movement and provides counterbalancing reality along with guidance for response, and achieves this with calm clarity and clear reason. This book is exceptional.*

—Andre Van Mol, MD, Board-certified family physician, co-chair, Committee on Adolescent Sexuality, American College of Pediatricians, blogger for the Christian Medical & Dental Associations

***

The War on Psychotherapy *details how politically correct ideas have been used to politicize social science and psychotherapy with respect to sexual and gender identity. While there is considerable scientific evidence that sexual attractions can change both with and without therapeutic interventions, efforts are being made to legally dictate terms to psychotherapists on what is a valid goal for clients. Christopher Doyle argues ably for the independence of the trained psychotherapist from empirically unjustified interference from the state.*

—Walter Schumm, Ph.D., Professor of Applied Family Science, School of Family Studies and Human Services, College of Health and Human Sciences, Kansas State University

***

The War on Psychotherapy *is a must read for everyone, not just psychotherapists. The war is real—this book's title describes one of the targets of the politically-motivated LGBT agenda. Having litigated against laws prohibiting counselors from providing or clients from receiving any counsel to change or reduce their unwanted same-sex attractions, behavior, or gender confusion, I know firsthand that there is no scientific and demonstrable evidence for these bans. This war is not based on science or objective fact. It is based on a destructive and coercive agenda to not only prohibit difference of options but also to force people to accept and promote LGBT sexual politics. Having represented counselors and clients who benefit from such counsel, I have seen how government intrusion into the private counseling relationship has hurt people.*

—Mathew D. Staver, Esq., B.C.S., founder and chairman, Liberty Counsel

***

Christopher Doyle, a traveler from homosexual to heterosexual who counsels others on that journey, describes in frightening detail the weaponization of psychotherapy ... It is a riveting story of malicious professional and governmental authorities who manipulate science, demean religious motivation, and ignore genuine successes to hide evidence that contradicts their cherished notion that homosexual orientation is immutable. He documents them in action—in our courts, in the media, in our schools, in our legislatures, within our borders and beyond.

Doyle reveals a war on humans in their most intimate personhood. The real tragedy is the collateral damage for persons banned from finding relief for their suffering. From turning spouses against each other, then mothers against

Praise for *The War on Psychotherapy*

their children, the legal elites of the sexual revolution have come to turn persons against themselves

—Dr. Paul Sullins, Professor of Sociology (retired),
The Catholic University of America
Senior research associate, Ruth Institute

ABOUT THE AUTHOR

Christopher Doyle, MA, LPC, LCPC is a licensed psychotherapist and the executive director of the Institute for Healthy Families, a non-profit Judeo-Christian therapeutic organization in the Washington, D.C. area. He is also the founder and clinical director of Northern Virginia Christian Counseling, specializing in the integration of psychology and theology in counseling. Christopher also serves as a therapist at Patrick Henry College, where he provides mental health counseling for their students.

A leader in the #TherapyEquality movement, Christopher is the co-founder of the National Task Force for Therapy Equality and the plaintiff in *Doyle v. Hogan,* challenging the unconstitutional ban on licensed therapy for minors struggling with sexual and gender identity conflicts in the state of Maryland. In 2013, he founded Voice of the Voiceless, a non-profit organization advocating for individuals and families struggling with unwanted same-sex attraction and gender identity conflicts.

Christopher is the author of several books on sexuality, including: *The Meaning of Sex: A New Christian Ethos, Benefits of Delaying Sexual Debut,* and *Acception: Bullying Solutions and Prevention Health Education Curriculum.* He frequently writes on sexual health and has been published in *Issues in Law & Medicine* and the *Journal of Human Sexuality,* along with many print and online outlets, including *Townhall, World Net Daily,* and *The Christian Post.*

As an advocate for sexual health, Christopher has been featured in six documentaries, including *Voices of the Silenced* (Core Issues Trust), *The Third Way: Homosexuality and the Catholic Church* (Blackstone Films), *Inside Out* (Adam Perez), and *The Sunday Sessions* (Dickie Bruce Productions), a 2019 documentary on his work as a sexual identity psychotherapist. He has been interviewed in hundreds of media outlets, including *The Dr. Oz Show,* Fox News Radio, National Public Radio, American Family Radio, and the Christian Broadcasting Network. His work has been featured in *USA Today,* NBC News, CNN, Associated Press, ABC/Fusion, AOL, BuzzFeed, *The Washington Post, World Magazine, Atlantic Magazine, National Catholic Register, Citizen Magazine,* and many more.

Christopher and his wife, Sherry, have five children. They make their home in Purcellville, Virginia.

ENDNOTES

[i] Personal confidential communication with a concerned public-school, middle-school nurse (fall 2010) after she attended a continuing education lecture by adolescent pediatrician Dr. Michelle Forcier of Brown University. Dr. Forcier is the current director of the Gender and Sexual Health Program at Hasbro Children's Hospital and Brown University Medical School in Providence, RI.

[ii] J. Van Maren, "In their own words – What transgender activists have in store for your children," *Life Site News*, July 12, 2018, https://www.lifesitenews.com/blogs/in-their-own-words-what-transgender-activists-have-in-store-for-your-children, accessed January 7, 2019.

[iii] Ryan Anderson, "The Philosophical Contradictions of the Transgender Worldview," *The Public Discourse*, February 2018, https://www.thepublicdiscourse.com/2018/02/20971/, accessed January 7, 2019.

[iv] C. Daly King, "The Meaning of Normal," *Yale Journal of Biology and Medicine* 17, no. 3 (January 1945): 493–501, https://www.ncbi.nlm.nih.gov/pmc/articles/PMC2601549/

[v] Van Maren, Op.cit.

[vi] James Risdon, (2018). WATCH: Drag queen admits he's 'grooming' children at story hour events." *Life Site News.* November 27, 2018. Accessed January 8, 2019 at https://www.lifesitenews.com/news/watch-drag-queen-admits-hes-grooming-children-at-story-hour-events.

[vii] Corin Hoggard. "Shelter forced women to shower with person who identified as a transgender woman and sexually harassed them, lawsuit says." ABC 30 Action News, Fresno, CA, May 23, 2018; Accessed January 9, 2019 at: https://abc30.com/homeless-women-harassed-in-showe....

389

Endnotes

[viii] Sam Pazzano, "Predator who claimed to be little round things I least be transgender declared dangerous offender," *Toronto Sun*, February 26, 2014; online at: http://www.torontosun.com/2014/02/26/predator-who-claimed-to-be-transgender-declared-dangerous-offender.

[ix] Janet Fife-Yeomans, "Sex change killer Maddison Hall to be free as a bird," *Daily Telegraph*, April 2, 2010; online at: https://www.dailytelegraph.com.au/news/nsw/sex-change-killer-to-be-free-as-a-bird/news-story/b1fecc9a9a4717607de6e980980e0ba5?sv=e95663cd723e2f8ffa0caa3329e03203.

[x] Hudak, Amy. "Transgender track stars win state championship, ignites debate over rules". June 12, 2018. Available at https://www.wtnh.com/news/connecticut/transgender-track-stars-win-state-championship-ignite-debate-over-rules/1235044455. Accessed 1/8/19.

[xi] Shilton, A.C. "Transgender Track World Champion Defends Her Human Right—To Race". Bicycling. January 4, 2019. Available at https://www.bicycling.com/culture/a25736012/transgender-world-champion-track-cycling-race/ Accessed 1/8/19.

[xii] Alliance Defending Freedom, "US opens investigation into sexual assault of minor child in Georgia, violation of Title IX," Press Release (October 3, 2018). Available at: http://www.adfmedia.org/News/PRDetail/99205?search=1. Accessed 1/9/19.

[xiii] Rafferty, Jason. "Ensuring Comprehensive Care and Support for Transgender and Gender-Diverse Children and Adolescents." Pediatrics. October 2018, Vol. 142. Issue 4. Available at http://pediatrics.aappublications.org/content/142/4/e20182162. Accessed 1/8/19.

[xiv] Cantor, James. "American Academy of Pediatrics policy and trans-kids: Fact-checking." Sexology Today. October 17, 2018. Available at http://www.sexologytoday.org/2018/10/american-academy-of-pediatrics-policy.html. Accessed 1/8/19.

[xv] Ibid.

Endnotes

[xvi] Kearns, Madeleine. "Dr. Zucker Defied Trans Orthodoxy. Now He's Vindicated." National Review. October 25,2019. Available at https://www.nationalreview.com/2018/10/transgender-orthodoxy-kenneth-zucker-vindicated/. Accessed 1/8/19.

[xvii] Zucker KJ, Spitzer RL. Was the Gender Identity Disorder of Childhood Diagnosis Introduced into DSM-III as a Backdoor Maneurver to Replace Homosexuality? *Journal of Sex and Marital Therapy.* 2005;31:31-42.

[xviii] Bailey, J. Michael and Triea, Kiira. What many transgender activists don't want you to know: and why you should know it anyway. Perspect Biol Med. 2007 Autumn;50(4):521-34. Available at https://www.researchgate.net/publication/5893630_What_Many_Transgender_Activists_Don%27t_Want_You_to_Know_and_why_you_should_know_it_anyway. Accessed 1/8/19.

[xix] Gu J, Kanai R. "What contributes to individual differences in brain structure?" *Front Hum Neurosci* 2014;8:262.

[xx] Bavolek, Stephen J. "Hardwired to Connect: The New Scientific Case for Authoritative Community." (2003). YMCA of USA, Dartmouth Medical School, Institute for American Values. Available at https://www.nurturingparenting.com/images/cmsfiles/hardwired_to_connect.pdf. Accessed 1/9/19.

[xxi] Khandan S., Hedyeh R., et al. "Adaptation to maternal role and infant development: a cross sectional study". Journal of Reproductive and Infant Psychology, 2018, 36:3, pages 289-301.

[xxii] Davy, Zowie. The DSM-5 and the Politics of Diagnosing Transpeople. *Arch Sex Behav* (2015) 44:1165–1176. Available at https://www.sexrightsafrica.net/wp-content/uploads/2016/04/Davy-ASB2015.pdf. Accessed 1/8/19.

[xxiii] Raskin, Jonathan. "What's New in the International Classification of Diseases? When it comes to mental disorders, a lot has changed in the new ICD-11." *Psychology Today.* July 25, 2018. Available at https://www.psychologytoday.com/us/blog/making-meaning/201807/what-s-new-in-the-international-classification-diseases. Accessed 1/8/19.

[xxiv] Ibid.

Endnotes

[xxv] Op.cit, Davy 1165–1176.

[xxvi] Centers for Medicare & Medicaid Services, Proposed Decision Memo for Gender Dysphoria and Gender Reassignment Surgery (June 2, 2016), Available at http://www.transgendermandate.org/research#_ftn10. Accessed 1/8/19.

[xxvii] Hembree WC, et al. "Endocrine Treatment of Gender-Dysphoric/Gender-Incongruent Persons: An Endocrine Society Clinical Practice Guideline." *The Journal of Clinical Endocrinology & Metabolism*, Volume 102, Issue 11, 1 November 2017, Pages 3869–3903. Available at https://academic.oup.com/jcem/article/102/11/3869/4157558. Accessed 1/9/19.

[xxviii] Robbins, Jane. "U.S. Doctors Are Performing Double Mastectomies On Healthy 13-Year-Old Girls." *The Federalist*. September 12, 2018. Available at http://thefederalist.com/2018/09/12/u-s-doctors-performing-double-mastectomies-healthy-13-year-old-girls/. Accessed 1/8/19.

[xxix] Milrod, Christine & Karasic, Dan H. "Age is Just a Number: WPATH-Affiliated Surgeons' Experiences and Attitudes Toward Vaginoplasty in Transgender Females Under 18 Years of Age in the United States." J Sex Med. 2017 Apr;14(4):624-634. Abstract available at https://www.ncbi.nlm.nih.gov/pubmed/28325535. Accessed 1/8/19.

[xxx] The American College of Pediatricians https://www.acpeds.org/

[xxxi] The Alliance for Therapeutic Choice and Scientific Integrity https://www.therapeuticchoice.com/

[xxxii] The Association of American Physicians and Surgeons https://aapsonline.org/

[xxxiii] The Christian Medical and Dental Associations https://cmda.org/

[xxxiv] The Catholic Medical Association https://www.cathmed.org/

[xxxv] The Pediatric and Adolescent Gender Dysphoria Working Group: An International Discussion Space for Clinicians and Researchers

Endnotes

http://gdworkinggroup.org/. Accessed 1/8/19 from their homepage: In the past decade, the affirmative model of care has quickly become the standard when treating gender dysphoric or gender nonconforming (GNC) children and youth. This shift in treatment approach has coincided with a significant rise in the number of children and teens presenting with gender dysphoria. At the same time, the political nature of gender dysphoria has led to an increasingly polarized view of the diagnosis, making rigorous debate difficult. This site has been established as a space where clinicians and researchers can explore the evidence for different models or treatment. Our knowledge about gender dysphoria in children, adolescents, and young adults is still very incomplete. The affirmative model has become standard of care before there is enough evidence to determine the long-term risks and benefits of this approach. Our aim is to share a wide range of informed views on the key research findings so that clinicians are empowered to evaluate these critically. In this way, we hope to widen the dialogue in this important field of health care.

[xxxvi] Diamond, Milton. "Transsexuality Among Twins: Identity Concordance, Transition, Rearing, and Orientation." *International Journal of Transgenderism*, 2013, 14:1, 24-38.

[xxxvii] Cretella, Michelle. "Gender Dysphoria in Children and Suppression of Debate." *Journal of American Physicians and Surgeons*, 2016, 21:2, 50-54.

[xxxviii] Ibid.

[xxxix] Mayer, Lawrence S. and McHugh, Paul R. "Sexuality and Gender: Findings from the Biological, Psychological and Social Sciences." *The New Atlantis*. Fall 2016. Available at https://www.thenewatlantis.com/publications/executive-summary-sexuality-and-gender. Accessed 1/9/19.

[xl] Cretella, "Gender Dysphoria in Children", 2016, 50.

[xli] Bavolek. "Hardwired to Connect" (2003).

[xlii] Khandan. "Adaptation to Maternal Role" *Journal of Reproductive* and *Infant Psychology,* 2018.

Endnotes

xliii Tolman D and Diamond L. [Eds.] *American Psychological Association's Handbook of Sexuality and Psychology,* 2014, Vol. 1, 744.

xliv Turner, Camilla. "Number of Children Referred to Gender Identity Clinics Has Quadrupled in Five Years." *The Telegraph.* July 8, 2018. Available at https://www.telegraph.co.uk/news/2017/07/08/number-children-referred-gender-identity-clinics-has-quadrupled/. Accessed 1/9/19.

xlv PA Dad. "Letter to a gender clinic: A parent's call to action." 4thwavenow blog posted April 8, 2018. Available at https://4thwavenow.com/tag/increase-in-females-presenting-to-gender-clinics/. Accessed 1/9/19.

xlvi Hruz PW, Mayer LS and McHugh PR. "Growing Pains: Problems with Puberty Suppression in Treating Gender Dysphoria". *The New Atlantis.* Spring 2017. Available at https://www.thenewatlantis.com/publications/growing-pains. Accessed 1/9/19.

xlvii Grigorova M. , et al. "Effects of treatment with leuprolide acetate depot on working memory and executive functions in young premenopausal women." Psychoneuroendocrinology 31(8):935-47 October 2006. Available at https://www.researchgate.net/publication/6953204_Effects_of_treatment_with_leuprolide_acetate_depot_on_working_memory_and_executive_functions_in_young_premenopausal_women. Accessed 1/9/19.

xlviii Craig M, et al. "Gonadotropin hormone releasing hormone agonists alter prefrontal function during verbal encoding in young women." *Psychoneuroendocrinology* 32(8-10):1116-27 September 2007. https://www.researchgate.net/publication/5865155_Gonadotropin_hormone_releasing_hormone_agonists_alter_prefrontal_function_during_verbal_encoding_in_young_women

xlix Nelson CJ, et al. "Cognitive Effects of Hormone Therapy in Men With Prostate Cancer." *Cancer.* 2008 Sep 1; 113(5): 1097–1106. Available at https://www.ncbi.nlm.nih.gov/pmc/articles/PMC4333639/. Accessed 1/9/19.

Endnotes

[l] De Vries ALC, Steensma TD, Doreleijers TAH, Cohen-Kettenis, PT. Puberty suppression in adolescents with gender identity disorder: a prospective follow-up study. *J Sex Med* 2011;8:2276-2283.

[li] Eyler AE, Pang SC, Clark A. LGBT assisted reproduction: current practice and future possibilities. *LGBT Health* 2014;1(3):151-156.

[lii] Feldman J, Brown GR, Deutsch MB, et al. Priorities for transgender medical and healthcare research. *Curr Opin Endocrinol Diabetes Obes* 2016;23:180-187.

[liii] Johnson SB, Blum RW, Giedd JN. Adolescent maturity and the brain: the promise and pitfalls of neuroscience research in adolescent health policy. *J Adolesc Health* 2009;45(3):216-221.

[liv] Burgess D, Lee R, Tran A, van Ryn M. Effects of Perceived Discrimination on Mental Health and Mental Health Services Utilization Among Gay, Lesbian, Bisexual and Transgender Persons. Journal of LGBT Health Research 2008;3(4): 1-14.

[lv] Bertolote JM, Fleischmann A. Suicide and psychiatric diagnosis: a worldwide perspective. World Psychiatry 2002;1(3):181–185.

[lvi] Dhejne, C, et.al. "Long-Term Follow-Up of Transsexual Persons Undergoing Sex Reassignment Surgery: Cohort Study in Sweden." PLoS ONE, 2011; 6(2). Available at http://journals.plos.org/plosone/article?id=10.1371/journal.pone.00168 85. Accessed 1/9/19.

[lvii] Paglia, C (1/14/2014). *Lesbian Feminist Camille Paglia: "Sexual Orientation is Fluid and Can Change."* Summary and recording found online at: http://www.voiceofthevoiceless.info/lesbian-feminist-camille-paglia-sexual-orientation-is-fluid-and-can-change/

[lviii] Doyle v. Hogan (10/2018). Verified Complaint for Declaration, Preliminary, and Injunctive Relief, and Damages in the United States District Court for the District of Maryland, pp. 1-2.

[lix] https://leginfo.legislature.ca.gov/faces/billNavClient.xhtml?b ill_id=201120120SB1172

[lx] Phelan, J., Goldberg, A., & Doyle, C.J. (2012). A Critical Evaluation of the Report of the Task Force on Appropriate Therapeutic Responses

to Sexual Orientation, Resolutions, and Press Release. *Journal of Human Sexuality, 4,* 4–69.

[lxi] St. John, P. (August 10, 2015). *In a first, California agrees to pay for transgender inmate's sex reassignment.* Retrieved online at: http://www.latimes.com/local/california/la-me-inmate-transgender-20150810-story.html

[lxii] Sex Reassignment Surgery Cost. *How Much Does Sex Reassignment Surgery Cost?* Retrieved online at: http://health.costhelper.com/sex-reassignment-surgery.html

[lxiii] McHugh, P. (June 10, 2015). *Transgenderism: A Pathogenic Meme.* Retrieved online at: http://www.thepublicdiscourse.com/2015/06/15145/

[lxiv] CBS News. (August 12, 2013). *California law allows transgender students to pick bathrooms, sports teams they identify with.* Retrieved online at: http://www.cbsnews.com/news/california-law-allows-transgender-students-to-pick-bathrooms-sports-teams-they-identify-with/

[lxv] Baylor, G.S. (June 14, 2016). *New California Bill Threatens Religious Colleges.* Retrieved online at: http://www.fed-soc.org/blog/detail/new-california-bill-threatens-religious-colleges

[lxvi] McGreevy, P. (September 1, 2016). *State senator drops proposal that angered religious universities in California.* Retrieved online at: http://www.latimes.com/politics/essential/la-pol-sac-essential-politics-updates-senator-drops-proposal-that-had-angered-1470853912-htmlstory.html

[lxvii] Wheeler, D.R. (July 14, 2015). *Gay Marriage and the Future of Evangelical Colleges.* Retrieved online at: https://www.theatlantic.com/education/archive/2015/07/evangelical-colleges-struggle-gay-marriage-ruling/398306/?fb_ref=Default

[lxviii] Ibid.

[lxix] Williams, R. (November 6, 2013). *Pickup v. Brown (consolidated with Welch v. Brown)—Ninth Circuit.* Retrieved online at: https://apps.americanbar.org/ababoards/blog/blogpost.cfm?threadid=29364&catid=14923

Endnotes

[lxx] Carpenter, D. (June 29, 2014). *A constitutional right to "cure" gays? No way, says the Ninth Circuit.* Retrieved online at: https://www.washingtonpost.com/news/volokh-conspiracy/wp/2014/01/29/the-ninth-circuit-again-upholds-californias-ban-on-gay-conversion-therapy/?utm_term=.58bc97b31671

[lxxi] Williams, R. (November 6, 2013). *Pickup v. Brown (consolidated with Welch v. Brown)—Ninth Circuit.* Retrieved online at: https://apps.americanbar.org/ababoards/blog/blogpost.cfm?threadid=29364&catid=14923

[lxxii] Wyatt, F. (2014). *A Joyful Heart Is Good Medicine: Sexuality Conversion Bans in the Courts,* 21 Mich. J. Gender & L. 311, 320. Available at: http://repository.law.umich.edu/mjgl/vol21/iss2/3

[lxxiii] Ibid, pp. 320-321.

[lxxiv] *King v. Christie,* 767 F.3d 216, 227–28 (3d Cir. 2014) (citations and footnote omitted), *abrogated by Nat'l Inst. of Family & Life Advocates v. Becerra,* 138 S. Ct. 2361 (2018).

[lxxv] Wyatt Fore, *A Joyful Heart Is Good Medicine: Sexuality Conversion Bans in the Courts,* 21 Mich. J. Gender & L. 311, 324 (2014)

[lxxvi] Unruh, B. (January 12, 2017). *Supremes face bombshell: Law censoring Christian counselors.* Retrieved online at: http://www.wnd.com/2017/01/supremes-face-bombshell-law-censoring-christian-counselors/#Fsuae9eFU0UZ4YHA.99

[lxxvii] "Pride Marches and Parades", in *Encyclopedia of Lesbian, Gay, Bisexual, and Transgender History in America,* Marc Stein, ed. (2004), Charles Scribner's Sons.

[lxxviii] Nakamura, D. & Eilperin, J. (June 24, 2016). "With Stonewall, Obama designates first national monument to gay rights movement." *Washington Post.* Retrieved online at: https://www.washingtonpost.com/news/post-politics/wp/2016/06/24/with-stonewall-obama-designates-first-national-momument-to-gay-rights-movement/?utm_term=.897e1b3daaca

[lxxix] Kengor, P. (2016). "Harry Hay: Pioneering Gay Communist, Former Catholic." *Crisis.* Retrieved at https://www.crisismagazine.com/2016/harry-hay-pioneering-gay-communist-former-catholic.

[lxxx] Skousen, C. (2017). *The Naked Communist.* Salt Lake City: Izzard Publishing.

[lxxxi] Carter, D. (2004). *Stonewall:* The *Riots That Sparked The Gay Revolution.* New York: St. Martin's Press, 15-16.

[lxxxii] Ibid., 42.

[lxxxiii] Ibid., 42.

[lxxxiv] Ocamb, K. (2009). "Stonewall Remembered: Timeline: Why Should We Be Talking About Stonewall 40 Years After The Fact. What Does Stonewall Mean To You?" *Frontiers In LA*, Vol. 28, Issue 3.

[lxxxv] Ibid., 17.

[lxxxvi] Ibid., 17-18.

[lxxxvii] Ocamb, K. (2009). "Stonewall Remembered: Timeline: Why Should We Be Talking About Stonewall 40 Years After the Fact. What Does Stonewall Mean to You?" *Frontiers In LA*, Vol. 28, Issue 3.

[lxxxviii] Ibid, 143.

[lxxxix] Hevesi, D. (9/7/2010). "Seymour Pine Dies at 91; Led Raid on Stonewall Inn." Retrieved online at: https://www.nytimes.com/2010/09/08/nyregion/08pine.html

[xc] Marcus, E. (1993). Making History: The Struggle for Gay and Lesbian Equal Rights, 1945–1990: an Oral History. *Perennial.* 221.

[xci] Satinover, J. (1996). *Homosexuality and the Politics of Truth.* Grand Rapids, MI: Hamewith Books, 31.

[xcii] Madsen, H. & Kirk, M. (1991). *After the Ball: How America Will Conquer Its Fear and Hatred of Gays in the 90's.* Plume, *184.*

^{xciii} Drescher, J. (2015). Out of DSM: Depathologizing Homosexuality, *Behavioral Science. 2015, 5,* 570.

^{xciv} Thompson, M. & Shilts, R. (1994). *Long Road to Freedom: The Advocate History of the Gay and Lesbian Movement (Stonewall Inn Editions)*. St. Martin's Press, 1st Ed., 105–106.

^{xcv} Satinover, J. (1996). *Homosexuality and the Politics of Truth*. Grand Rapids, MI: Hamewith Books, 34.

^{xcvi} Bayer, R. (1981). *Homosexuality and American Psychiatry: The Politics of Diagnosis*. New York: Basic Books, 146.

^{xcvii} Carter, D. (2004). *Stonewall: The Riots That Sparked the Gay Revolution*. New York: St. Martin's Press.

^{xcviii} J. Phelan, N. Whitehead, & P.M. Sutton (2009). *What research shows: NARTH's response to the APA claims on homosexuality: A report of the scientific advisory committee of the National Association for Research and Therapy of Homosexuality*. Journal of Human Sexuality, 1: *1–121*. Available at https://media.wix.com/ugd/ec16e9_04d4fd-5fb7e044289cc8e47dbaf13632.pdf

^{xcix} Cummings, N. *Destructive Trends in Mental Health: The Well-Intentioned Path to Harm*. (2005). New York: Taylor and Francis.

^c *New York Times*. (December 23, 1973). *"The A.P.A. Ruling on Homosexuality: The Issues Is Subtle, The Debate Still On."* Retrieved online at: http://www.nytimes.com/1973/12/23/archives/the-issue-is-subtle-the-debate-still-on-the-apa-ruling-on.html?_r=0

^{ci} Bayer, R. (1981). *Homosexuality and American Psychiatry: The Politics of Diagnosis*. New York: Basic Books, 3–4.

^{cii} Teal, D. (1971). *The Gay Militants*. Stein and Day, 272–280.

^{ciii} http://www.psychiatricnews.org/pnews/00-09-01/recalling.html

^{civ} Drescher, J. (2015). Out of DSM: Depathologizing Homosexuality, *Behavioral Science. 2015, 5,* 570–571.

Endnotes

^{cv} Argetsinger, A. (12/28/2015). *Robert L. Spitzer. Washington Post.* Retrieved online at: http://www.pressreader.com/usa/the-washington-post/20151228/281556584794889

^{cvi} Spitzer, R. (2003). Can Some Gay Men and Lesbians Change Their Sexual Orientation? 200 Participants Reporting a Change from Homosexual to Heterosexual Orientation, *Archives of Sexual Behavior, Vol. 32, No. 5*, 412-413.

^{cvii} Dregor, A. (4/12/12). *How to Ex an "Ex-Gay" Study. Psychology Today.* Retrieved online at: https://www.psychologytoday.com/blog/fetishes-i-dont-get/201204/how-ex-ex-gay-study

^{cviii} Argetsinger, A. (2015).

^{cix} Carey, B. (5/18/2012). *Psychiatry Giant Sorry for Backing Gay 'Cure'. New York Times.* Retrieved online at: http://www.nytimes.com/2012/05/19/health/dr-robert-l-spitzer-noted-psychiatrist-apologizes-for-study-on-gay-cure.html

^{cx} Mercatornet. (5/31/2017). *Frail and aged, a giant apologizes: A leading figure in the study of homosexuality recently recanted his belief that some gays can change. There was no need to apologize, says a Dutch psychologist.* Retrieved online at: https://www.mercatornet.com/articles/view/frail_and_aged_a_giant_ap ologizes

^{cxi} Nicolosi, J. *APA Task Force Report —A Mockery of Science.* Retrieved online at: http://www.josephnicolosi.com/apa-task-force/

^{cxii} APA Task Force on Appropriate Therapeutic Responses to Sexual Orientation. (2009). *Report of the Task Force on Appropriate Therapeutic Responses to Sexual Orientation.* Washington, DC: American Psychological Association.

^{cxiii} Phelan, J.E., Goldberg, A. & Doyle, C. (2012). A Critical Evaluation of the Report of the Task Force on Appropriate Therapeutic Responses to Sexual Orientation, Resolutions, and Press Release. *Journal of Human Sexuality, (4)41-69*

^{cxiv} Ibid, 55.

Endnotes

[cxv] Maugh, T.H.II. (8/5/2009). "Psychologists say sexual orientation can't be changed through therapy." *Los Angeles Times*. Retrieved from http:// latimesblogs.latimes.com/.../2009/.../psychologists-sexual-orientation-cant-be -changed-through-therapy.html

[cxvi] Angier, N. (7/16/1993). "Report Suggests Homosexuality Is Linked to Genes." *New York Times*. Retrieved online at: http://www.nytimes.com/1993/07/16/us/report-suggests-homosexuality-is-linked-to-genes.html?pagewanted=all

[cxvii] Ryan, C., Toomey, R.B., Diaz, R.M., & Russell, S.T. (2018) Parent-Initiated Sexual Orientation Change Efforts With LGBT Adolescents: Implications for Young Adult Mental Health and Adjustment. *Journal of Homosexuality*. Retrieved online at: https://www.tandfonline.com/doi/full/10.1080/00918369.2018.1538407?scroll=top&needAccess=true&

[cxviii] Rosik, C.H. (11/18/2018). Letter to the Editor regarding research published by Ryan et al. (2018). *Journal of Homosexuality*. In Press.

[cxix] Ross, B. & Epstein, B. (March 6, 2017). *Gay conversion therapy advocates heartened by Republican electoral victories*. Retrieved online at: http://abcnews.go.com/US/gay-conversion-therapy-advocates-heartened-pence-republican-electoral/story?id=45940488

[cxx] Ibid.

[cxxi] Doyle, C. (March 2017). *ABC '20/20' contacted me for gay conversion therapy story, but didn't report what I told them*. Retrieved online at: http://www.christianpost.com/news/abcs-20-20-contacted-me-for-gay-conversion-therapy-story-but-ignored-what-i-told-them-177802/

[cxxii] Perkins, T. (3/17/2017). "*20/20's* Blurred Vision of Sexual Reorientation Therapy." Retrieved online at: https://www.frc.org/updatearticle/20170313/blurred-vision

[cxxiii] Murphy, T. (May 12, 2017). *How to survive a summer at gay conversion camp*. Retrieved online at: https://www.washingtonpost.com/entertainment/books/how-to-survive-a-summer-at-gay-conversion-camp/2017/05/12/034d0e6e-3740-11e7-b412-62beef8121f7_story.html?utm_term=.5a6e2d62e58e

401

Endnotes

cxxiv Doyle, C. (March 21, 2013). *'Transgender Woman' Lies About Therapy Torture.* Retrieved online at: http://www.wnd.com/2013/03/transgendered-woman-lies-about-therapy-torture/#cI8IQj4HEhFRIc46.99

cxxv Kutner, B. (January 26, 2016). *Virginia legislator compares being gay to cancer as ex-gay therapy bill voted down in Senate subcommittee.* Retrieved online at: http://www.gayrva.com/news-views/senator-compares-being- gay-to-cancer-as-ex-gay-therapy-bill-voted-down-in-ga-subcommittee/

cxxvi *GLAAD Media Reference Guide - In Focus: "Conversion therapy."* Retrieved online at: https://www.glaad.org/reference/exgays

cxxvii January, B. (February 12, 2018). "How journalists can avoid spreading misinformation about anti-LGBTQ conversion therapy." Retrieved online at: https://www.mediamatters.org/blog/2018/02/12/how-journalists-can-avoid-spreading-misinformation-about-anti-lgbtq-conversion-therapy/219278

cxxviii Diamond, L. (2014). "Chapter 20: Gender and same-sex sexuality," in Tolman, D. & Diamond, L. Co-Editors-in-Chief, *APA Handbook of Sexuality and Psychology.* Washington D.C.: American Psychological Association, *1: 636.*

cxxix Melzer, E. J. (7/22/2005). "Gay teen to be released from Tenn. ex-gay facility". *Washington Blade.* Archive retrieved online at: https://web.archive.org/web/20060331174447/http://www.washblade.com/2005/7-22/news/national/gayteen.cfm

cxxx United States District Court, Western District of Tennessee, Memphis Division. (10/27/2006). "Agreed order of dismissal." Archived and retrieved from: https://web.archive.org/web/20070927012629/http://www.loveinaction.org/media/documents/Dismissal.pdf

cxxxi Akhavan, D. (2017). "The Miseducation of Cameron Post." Retrieved online at: https://www.sundance.org/projects/the-miseducation-of-cameron-post

cxxxii Sims, D. (8/1/2018). "The Miseducation of Cameron Post Is a Graceful Coming-of-Age Tale." Retrieved online at:

https://www.theatlantic.com/entertainment/archive/2018/08/the-miseducation-of-cameron-post/566366/

cxxxiii Fleming, M. (6/21/2017). "Focus Lands Joel Edgerton's 'Boy Erased'; Lucas Hedger, Russell Crowe, Nicole Kidman Star." Retrieved online at: http://deadline.com/2017/06/boy-erased-focus-features-joel-edgerton-lucas-hedges-russell-crowe-nicole-kidman-1202117734/

cxxxiv *Star Observer.* (3/30/2010). "Ex-gay leader apologises." Retrieved online from: http://www.starobserver.com.au/news/national-news/new-south-wales-news/ex-gay-leader-apologises/23288

cxxxv See https://ew.com/movies/2018/05/21/boy-erased-joel-edgerton-gay-conversion-drama-photos/

cxxxvi Melzer, E. J. (7/22/2005). "Gay teen to be released from Tenn. ex-gay facility". *Washington Blade.* Archive retrieved online at: https://web.archive.org/web/20060331174447/http://www.washblade.com/2005/7-22/news/national/gayteen.cfm

cxxxvii Sprigg, P. (11/19/18). *'Boy Erased' film misrepresents sexual orientation counseling.* Retrieved online at: https://www.christianpost.com/voice/boy-erased-film-misrepresents-sexual-orientation-counseling.html

cxxxviii Smid, J. (11/1/2018). *Boy Erased Will Release Nov. 2.* Retrieved online at: http://www.gracerivers.com/my-role/

cxxxix https://www.cnn.com/profiles/jen-christensen#about

cxl Doyle, C. (9/9/2018). Personal correspondence with Jen Christensen, president of NLGJA.

cxli Balkholm, J. (February 14, 2014). "House Passes Ban on Life Change Therapy 94−4." Retrieved online at: http://www.fpiw.org/blog/2014/02/14/house-passes-ban-on-life-change-therapy-94-4/

cxlii Balkholm, J. (March 25, 2015). "Who Doesn't Oppose Child Abuse?" Retrieved online at: http://www.fpiw.org/blog/2015/03/25/doesnt-oppose-child-abuse/

Endnotes

cxliii La Corte, R. (3/28/18). "Washington governor signs ban on sexual-orientation conversion therapy." Retrieved online at:
https://www.seattletimes.com/seattle-news/politics/gov-jay-inslee-signs-ban-on-sexual-orientation-conversion-therapy/

cxliv Southern Poverty Law Center (May, 2016). "Quacks: 'Conversion Therapists,' the Anti-BGBT Right, and the Demonization of Homosexuality." Retrieved online at:
https://www.splcenter.org/20160525/quacks-conversion-therapists-anti-lgbt-right-and-demonization-homosexuality

cxlv Cratty, C & Pearson, M. (February 7, 2013). DC shooter wanted to kill as many as possible, prosecutors say. Retrieved online at:
http://www.cnn.com/2013/02/06/justice/dc-family-research-council-shooting/possible, prosecutors-say

cxlvi Southern Poverty Law Center (May 2016). "Quacks: 'Conversion Therapists,' the Anti-BGBT Right, and the Demonization of Homosexuality." Montgomery, AL, 35.

cxlvii Ibid, 9.

cxlviii This section was quoted extensively from: National Task Force for Therapy Equality (May 2, 2017). "Lies, Deception, and Fraud: Southern Poverty Law Center, Human Rights Campaign, and the National Center for Lesbian Rights' Hate Campaign to Ban Psychotherapy for Individuals with Sexual and Gender Identity Conflicts." Retrieved online at:
http://www.therapyequality.org/national-task-force-therapy-equality-complaint-ftc-report

cxlix Nicolosi, Jr., J. (February 14, 2018). Testimony delivered in front of the Maine State Legislature. Retrieved online at:
http://www.therapyequality.org/testimony-dr-joseph-nicolosi-jr

cl Mallory, C., Brown, T.N.T., & Conron, K.J. (January, 2018). *Conversion Therapy and LGBT Youth*. The Williams Institute, UCLA School of Law. Retrieved online at:
https://williamsinstitute.law.ucla.edu/demographics/conversion-therapy-and-lgbt-youth/

cli Farrell, P. (December 31, 2014). "Leelah Alcorn: 5 Fast Facts You Need to Know."Retrieved online at:

https://heavy.com/news/2014/12/leelah-alcorn-joshua-alcorn-dead-suicide-rip-ohio-tumblr-suicide-note/

clii McCabe, V.F. (2016). "Saving Alex: When I Was Fifteen I Told My Mormon Parents I Was Gay, and That's When My Nightmare Began." Retrieved online at: https://www.nyjournalofbooks.com/book-review/saving-alex

cliii Peters, S. (May 16, 2018). HRC Releases Powerful New Video Featuring Survivor of "Conversion Therapy". Retrieved online at: https://www.hrc.org/blog/hrc-releases-powerful-video-featuring-survivor-of-conversion-therapy

cliv Hodges, M. (2/28/2018). "LGBT advocates threaten to kill pastor over Bible workshop for sexually confused girls." Retrieved online at: https://www.lifesitenews.com/news/lgbt-advocates-threaten-to-kill-pastor-over-bible-workshop-for-sexually-con

clv Brinton, S. (June 26, 2014). Making "conversion therapy" culturally unacceptable. Presentation delivered at Google corporation. Retrieved online at: https://youtu.be/WN3_eFIbZkU

clvi Sowell, T. (8/1/2000). The 'gravitas' game. Retrieved online at: https://townhall.com/columnists/thomassowell/2000/08/01/the-gravitas-game-n739482

clvii Angier, N. (7/16/1993). "Report Suggests Homosexuality Is Linked to Genes." New York Times. Retrieved online at: http://www.nytimes.com/1993/07/16/us/report-suggests-homosexuality-is-linked-to-genes.html?pagewanted=all

clviii American Psychological Association. (2008). Answers to your questions: For a better understanding of sexual orientation and homosexuality. Washington, DC: Author. Retrieved online from: http://www.apa.org/topics/lgbt/orientation.pdf

clix Haynes, L. (9/27/2016). The American Psychological Association Says Born-That-Way-Can't Change Is Not True of Sexual Orientation and Gender Identity. Retrieved online at: https://www.acpeds.org/wordpress/wp-content/uploads/8.21.17-APA-Handbook-Born-That-Way-Not-True-16-9-21-Haynes-Update.pdf

Endnotes

clx Causley Court Reporting. (4/11/2014). Deposition of Wayne Besen, *Ferguson et al. v.* JONAH et al. Cook County Law Division, IL, 27–30.

clxi Superior Court of New Jersey, Hudson County Law Division. (11/27/2012). Civil Action Complaint and Jury Demand, Ferguson et al. v. JONAH et al. Hudson County, New Jersey, 15.

clxii Doyle, C. (6/23/2015). Courageous ex-gay witness fights back against SPLC's mischaracterization of JONAH in dramatic trial. Retrieved online at: http://www.christianpost.com/news/courageous-ex-gay-witness-fights-back-against-splcs-mischaracterization-of-jonah-in-dramatic-trial-140717/

clxiii Doyle, C. (9/25/14). Expert Report, Ferguson et al. v. JONAH et al., based on the deposition of Chaim Levin, 3/27/14, 803-804. Superior Court of New Jersey Law Division, Hudson County.

clxiv de Freitas, P., M.D. (2006). The Use of Nudity in Therapy with Gay Men, The Fallen Veil. Ph.D. dissertation submitted to the Faculty of Maimonides University.

clxv Nicholson, I. (2007). Baring the Soul: Paul Bindrim, Abraham Maslow and Nude Psychotherapy. Journal of the History of Behavioral Sciences, 43, p. 341.

clxvi Goodson, A. (1991). Therapy, Nudity, & Joy: The Therapeutic Use of Nudity Through the Ages from Ancient Ritual to Modern Psychology. Los Angeles: Elysium.

clxvii Howard, J. (1970). Please touch: A guided tour of the human potential movement (1st ed.). New York: McGraw-Hill, 95.

clxviii Woodall, E. (2002). The American nudist movement: From cooperative to capital, the song remains the same. Journal of Popular Culture, 36, 264–268.

clxix Mankind Project. (n.d.). What about Gay Men? Retrieved online 9/18/2014 from: http://mankindproject.org/frequently-asked-questions#gay

Endnotes

clxx Mankind Project (n.d.). Phearing the Phallus—Sexuality and Nudity on the NWTA. Retrieved online 9/18/2014 from: http://mankindproject.org/phearing-phallus-sexuality-and-nudity-nwta

clxxi Downing, A. (n.d.). *My history with therapeutic interventions involving nudity.* Supplemental defense document, *Ferguson et al. v. JONAH et al.*, 1–2.

clxxii Ibid. 3–4.

clxxiii Timmerman, T. (2012). A Bigger World Yet; Faith, Brotherhood, and Same-Sex Needs. Newberg, OR: Bird Dog Press, 198–200.

clxxiv Doyle, C. (6/10/2015). Trial of the Century: Media has already pronounced judgment against JONAH for helping gays go straight. Retrieved online at: http://www.christianpost.com/news/trial-of-the-century-media-has-already-pronounced-judgment-against-jonah-for-helping-gays-go-straight-140202/

clxxv Ibid.

clxxvi Doyle, J. (6/17/18). JONAH Trial Expert Witness for SPLC concedes sexual orientation is fluid and can change. Retrieved online at: http://www.christianpost.com/news/jonah-trial-expert-witness-for-splc-concedes-sexual-orientation-is-fluid-and-can-change-140490/

clxxvii Doyle, J. (7/6/2015). Judicial liberal bias forces jury to convict JONAH with deep ramifications. (July 6, 2015). Retrieved online at: http://www.christianpost.com/news/judicial-liberal-bias-forces-jury-to-convict-jonah-in-trial-with-deep-ramifications-141221/

clxxviii Southern Poverty Law Center, Human Rights Campaign, and National Center for Lesbian Rights (2/24/2016). "Complaint For Action To Stop False, Deceptive, Advertising And Other Business Practices." Complaint to the Federal Trade Commission. Retrieved online at: https://www.splcenter.org/sites/default/files/ftc_conversion_therapy_complaint_-_final.pdf

clxxix National Task Force for Therapy Equality. (5/2/2017). "In Their Own Words — Lies, Deception, and Fraud: The Southern Poverty Law Center, Human Rights Campaign, and National Center for Lesbian Rights' Hate Campaign to Ban Psychotherapy for Individuals with

Endnotes

Sexual and Gender Identity Conflicts." Complaint to the Federal Trade Commission. Retrieved online at: http://www.therapyequality.org

[clxxx] National Center for Lesbian Rights and The Trevor Project (n.d.). Sample Legislation and Advocacy Toolkit to Protect Youth from "Conversion Therapy." For a copy of this document, please e-mail: nationaltaskforce@therapyequality.org

[clxxxi] Brown. M. (4/20/18). "Will California go from banning religious books to burning them?" Retrieved online at: https://onenewsnow.com/perspectives/michael-brown/2018/04/20/will-california-go-from-banning-religious-books-to-burning-them

[clxxxii] Over 350 oppose AB 2943 During June 12 Sen. Judiciary Hearing. Retrieved online at: https://www.youtube.com/watch?v=S78rgepocJw

[clxxxiii] Doyle, C. (7/2/2018). *Pro-Life Supreme Court Decision Is Good for Religious Liberty, Sexual Freedom, and 'Gay Conversion Therapy' Bans.* Retrieved online at: https://www.christianpost.com/voice/pro-life-supreme-court-decision-is-good-news-for-religious-liberty-sexual-freedom-and-gay-conversion-therapy-bans.html

[clxxxiv] http://lc.org/013019TampaPIOrder.pdf

[clxxxv] Schmidt, S. (2/1/2019). Judge says Tampa conversion therapy ban violates First Amendment free-speech rights. Retrieved online at: https://www.washingtonpost.com/religion/2019/02/02/judge-says-tampa-conversion-therapy-ban-violates-first-amendment-free-speech-rights/?noredirect=on&utm_term=.600241bf41c6

[clxxxvi] http://lc.org/013019TampaPIOrder.pdf

[clxxxvii] Just the Facts Coalition. (2008). *Just the facts about sexual orientation and youth: A primer for principals, educators, and school personnel.* Washington, DC: American Psychological Association. Retrieved from www.apa.org/pi/lgbc/publications/justthefacts.html

[clxxxviii] American College of Pediatricians (2008). "What You Should Know as a School Official". Retrieved online at: http://factsaboutyouth.com/posts/what-you-should-know-about-sexual-orientation-of-youth-as-a-school-official/

408

clxxxix AFL-CIO. "NEA Partnerships". Retrieved online at:
https://aflcio.org/about/our-unions-and-allies/nea-partnerships

cxc Superior Court for the District of Columbia (6/26/2009). *Parents and Friends of Ex-Gays, Inc. v. Government of the District Office of Human Rights*, 8. Retrieved online at:
http://pfox.org/Judge_Ross'_Memorandum_Opinion.pdf

cxci Ibid., 7.

cxcii Halvorson, S. (10/17/10). "NEA Representative Assembly in New Orleans – 2010". Retrieved online at: https://nea-exgay.org/2010/10/17/49/

cxciii Halvorson, S. (7/9/18). "Do Facts Really Matter? The 2017 NEA Representative Assembly Caucus Report". Retrieved online at:
https://nea-exgay.org/author/shalvors/

cxciv Deely, K. (July 2018). *Resolution to condemn 'conversion therapy'*. 2018 National Education Association. Minneapolis, MN.

cxcv Harvey, L. (7/19/18). "America's largest teachers union is run by radical, pro-gay extremists. Here's proof." Retrieved online at:
https://www.lifesitenews.com/opinion/a-ray-of-hope-for-public-education

cxcvi AFT Resolution. (2016). "School Safety and Educational Opportunity for Lesbian, Gay, Bisexual, Transgender, Queer and Questioning (LGBTQ) Students." Retrieved online at:
https://www.aft.org/resolution/school-safety-and-educational-opportunity-lesbian-gay-bisexual-transgender

cxcvii Erikson's Psychosocial Stages Summary Chart. Retrieved 10/31/13 online from:
http://psychology.about.com/library/bl_psychosocial_summary.htm

cxcviii http://commonground.richmond.edu/programs/safe-zone/index.html

cxcix http://www.vtlgbtcaucus.org/docs/safe_zone_resource_manual_2006.pdf

cc http://www.virginia.edu/studenthealth/internCAPSdescr.html

Endnotes

[cci] http://pfox.org/Judge_Ross%27_Memorandum_Opinion.pdf

[ccii] *Rosenberger v. Rector and Visitors of the University of Virginia*, 515 U.S. 819, 828–29 (1995)

[cciii] *Good News Club v. Milford Central School District*, 533 U.S. 98 (2001)

[cciv] APA Task Force on Appropriate Therapeutic Responses to Sexual Orientation. (2009). *Report of the Task Force on Appropriate Therapeutic Responses to Sexual Orientation*. Washington, DC: American Psychological Association, 83–89.

[ccv] Phelan, J.E., Goldberg, A. & Doyle, C. (2012). A Critical Evaluation of the Report of the Task Force on Appropriate Therapeutic Responses to Sexual Orientation, Resolutions, and Press Release. *Journal of Human Sexuality, 4,* 41–69.

[ccvi] Phelan, J.E., Whitehead, N. & Sutton, P.M. (2009). What Research Shows: NARTH's Response to the APA Claims on Homosexuality. *Journal of Human Sexuality, 1,* 1–94.

[ccvii] Shidlo, A. & Schroeder, M. (2002). Changing sexual orientation: A consumers' report. *Professional Psychology: Research and Practice, 33(3),* 249–259.

[ccviii] Doyle, C. (March 18, 2013). *Transgender 'Woman' Lies About Therapy 'Torture.'* Retrieved 10/31/2013 online at: http://www.wnd.com/2013/03/transgendered-woman-lies-about-therapy-torture

[ccix] Phelan, J.E., Whitehead, N. & Sutton, P.M. (2009). What Research Shows: NARTH's Response to the APA Claims on Homosexuality. *Journal of Human Sexuality, 1,* 1–94.

[ccx] Tyler, L. (1969). An approach to public affairs: Report of the Ad Hoc Committee on Public Affairs. *American Psychologist, 24,* 1–4.

[ccxi] Fowler, R.D. (1993). Social issues stances: Why APA takes them. *APA Monitor on Psychology,* April, 2.

Endnotes

ccxii American Psychological Association. (2008). *Homosexuality and Sexual Orientation: Answers to Your Questions for a Better Understanding.* Retrieved 10/31/2013 from: http://www.apa.org/topics/sexuality/orientation.aspx?item=4

ccxiii Phelan, J.E., Whitehead, N. & Sutton, P.M. (2009). What Research Shows: NARTH's Response to the APA Claims on Homosexuality. *Journal of Human Sexuality, 1,* 1–94.

ccxiv Mock, S.E. & Eibach, R.P. (2011). Stability and Change in Sexual Orientation Identity Over a 10-Year Period in Adulthood. *Archives of Sexual Behavior.* Retrieved 10/31/2013 online at: http://midus.wisc.edu/findings/pdfs/1153.pdf

ccxv Kinnish K.K., Strassberg D.S., & Turner C.W. (2005). Sex differences in the flexibility of sexual orientation: a multidimensional retrospective assessment. *Archives of Sexual Behavior, 34,* 175–83.

ccxvi Centers for Disease Control and Prevention (2013). *HIV Surveillance in Adolescents and Young Adults.* Retrieved 10/31/2013 at: http://www.cdc.gov/hiv/pdf/statistics_surveillance_Adolescents.pdf

ccxvii U.S. Food and Drug Administration: Protecting and Promoting Your Health. (1990). *Condoms and Sexually Transmitted Diseases, Brochure.* Retrieved 10/31/2013 online at: http://www.fda.gov/ForConsumers/byAudience/ForPatientAdvocates/H IVandAIDSActivities/ucm126372.htm#strong

ccxviii http://pfox.org/Judge_Ross%27_Memorandum_Opinion.pdf

ccxix American Civil Liberties Union. (December 31, 1994). *Hate Speech on Campus.* Retrieved 11/29/2013 from: https://www.aclu.org/print/free-speech/hate-speech-campus

ccxx Sommer, S. (2/17/13). Video Touting Homophobic Gay-to-Straight Therapy Shown in, Then Dropped From, Prince George's County Classrooms. Retrieved online at: https://www.washingtoncitypaper.com/news/city-desk/blog/13066819/video-touting-homophobic-gay-to-straight-therapy-taught-in-then-dropped-from-prince-georges-county-classrooms

Endnotes

ccxxi Baye, R. (2/8/13). "Prince George's Pulls Video that Advocates Therapy for Gay Teens." *Washington Examiner*. Retrieved online at: http://washingtonexaminer.com/prince-georges-pulls-video-that-advocates-therapy-for-gay-teens/article/2520924

ccxxii Bekker, A. (4/30/13). "South African Youth Tortured and Killed in 'Gay Conversion Camp' More Activist Propaganda." Retrieved online at: https://www.voiceofthevoiceless.info/south-african-youth-tortured-and-killed-in-gay-conversion-camp-more-activist-propaganda

ccxxiii Ibid.

ccxxiv Sprigg, P. (August 27, 2014). Ex-Gay Therapy Debate: The Truth Matters. Retrieved online at: http://www. christianpost.com/news/ex-gay-therapy-debate-the-truth-matters-125479/ and: Steinmetz, K. (June 23, 2014). *The New Campaign to End Gay Conversion Therapy*. Retrieved online at: http://time.com/2907989/bornperfect-gay-conversion-reparative-therapy/

ccxxv Hunter, M. (November 14, 2014). "LGBT Activists: UN Should Classify Gay Conversion Therapy as Torture." http://www.cnsnews.com/news/article/melanie-hunter/lgbt-activists-un-should-classify-gay-conversion-therapy-torture

ccxxvi "The Mystery Surrounding "Driftwood's" Tortured Ex-Gay Survivor." (October 10, 2011). http://www.queerty.com/the-mystery-surrounding-driftwoods-tortured-ex-gay-survivor-20111010

ccxxvii Sprigg, P. (August 27, 2014). "Ex-Gay Therapy Debate: The Truth Matters." Retrieved online at: http://www.christianpost.com/news/ex-gay-therapy-debate-the-truth-matters-125479/

ccxxviii Skinner, J. (n.d.). "The United Nations appoints an LGBT 'Enforcer'." Retrieved online at: *https://www.christiantoday.com.au/news/the-united-nations-appoints-an-lgbt-enforcer.html*

ccxxix Chaudhry, S. (6/18/18). INTERVIEW-U.N. envoy wants global ban on 'barbaric' conversion therapies. Retrieved online at: https://www.reuters.com/article/un-rights-lgbt/interview-un-envoy-wants-global-ban-on-barbaric-conversion-therapies-idUSL8N1TG4NA ccxxx Langlois, J. (9/22/17). "Thousands protest ruling to overturn ban on 'conversion therapy' for gays and lesbians in Brazil." Retrieved online at: http://www.latimes.com/world/mexico-americas/la-fg-brazil-gay-conversion-therapy-20170922-story.html#

ccxxxi Moloney, A. (2/8/2018). "FEATURE-Gays in Ecuador raped and beaten in rehab clinics to "cure" them." Retrieved online at: https://af.reuters.com/article/africaTech/idAFL8N1P03QO

ccxxxii Geidner, C. (6/3/2015). "Internal Report: Major Diversity, Organizational Problems at Human Rights Campaign." Retrieved online at: https://www.buzzfeednews.com/article/chrisgeidner/internal-report-major-diversity-organizational-problems-at-h

ccxxxiii Villarreal, Y. (6/4/2014. "5 Most Disappointing Things We Learned About HRC's 'White Men's Club'." Retrieved online at: https://www.advocate.com/human-rights-campaign-hrc/2015/06/04/5-most-disappointing-things-we-learned-about-hrcs-white-mens-cl

ccxxxiv Shariatmadari, D. (6/13/2012). "Anti-gay bus ads took their cue from Stonewall's misguided campaign." Retrieved online at: https://www.theguardian.com/commentisfree/2012/apr/13/anti-gay-christian-adverstising

ccxxxv Smith, S. (10/27/18). *Ex-Gay 'X-Factor' Contestant Faces Backlash for Saying He Found Christ, Left LGBT Lifestyle.* Retrieved online at: https://www.christianpost.com/news/ex-gay-x-factor-contestant-faces-backlash-saying-he-found-christ-left-lgbt-lifestyle-228196/

ccxxxvi http://revoice.us

ccxxxvii Brown, M. (7/30/18). "The Revoice Conference and the Danger of a Big Theological Tent." Retrieved online at: https://stream.org/revoice-big-theological-tent/

ccxxxviii Galli, M. (7/25/18). "Revoice's Founder Answers the LGBT Conference's Critics." Retrieved online at: https://www.christianitytoday.com/ct/2018/july-web-only/revoices-founder-answers-lgbt-conferences-critics.html?utm_source=ctweekly-html&utm_medium=Newsletter&utm_term=26592069&utm_content=596837222&utm_campaign=email

Endnotes

ccxxxix Brown, M. (7/30/18). "The Revoice Conference and the Danger of a Big Theological Tent." Retrieved online at: https://stream.org/revoice-big-theological-tent/

ccxl Doyle, C. (2018). *The Meaning of Sex: A New Christian Ethos.* Meadville, PA: Christian Faith Publishing, 40–41.

ccxli Kellemen, B. (1/13/11). *Top Ten Trends in Biblical Counseling.* Retrieved online at: https://www.thegospelcoalition.org/article/the-top-ten-trends-in-biblical-counseling/

ccxlii Woods, M. (10/29/14). *Therapy won't turn gay people straight, says prominent Southern Baptist Russell Moore.* Retrieved online at: https://www.christiantoday.com/article/therapy-wont-turn-gay-people-straight-says-prominent-southern-baptists-russell-moore/42309.htm

ccxliii Vicari, C. (10/29/14). *Did Russell Moore Really Denounce Reparative Therapy for Same-Sex Attraction?* Retrieved online at: https://www.christianpost.com/news/did-russell-moore-really-denounce-reparative-therapy-for-same-sex-attraction-128819/

ccxliv Lopez, R.O. (6/19/18). *Sleazy Sex Games and Dirty Politics in the Southern Baptist Convention.* Retrieved online at: https://www.americanthinker.com/articles/2018/06/sleazy_sex_games_and_dirty_politics_in_the_southern_baptist_convention.html#ixzz5MHrGj4U7

ccxlv Restored Hope Network. (n.d.). "What is RHN?" Retrieved online at: https://www.restoredhopenetwork.org/what-is-rhn

ccxlvi Restored Hope Network. (n.d.). "Role of Christian Counseling for Persons with Unwanted Same-Sex Attractions." Retrieved online at: https://s3.amazonaws.com/churchplantmedia-cms/restored_hope_network/rhncounselingdocfinal.pdf

ccxlvii Merritt, J. (10/6/2015). The Downfall of the Ex-Gay Movement: What went wrong with the conversion ministry, according to Alan Chambers, who once led its largest organization. Retrieved online at: https://www.theatlantic.com/politics/archive/2015/10/the-man-who-dismantled-the-ex-gay-ministry/408970/

ccxlviii Ibid.

Endnotes

ccxlix Snow, Justin (6/20/2013). 'Ex-gay' ministry apologizes to LGBT community, shuts down. *MetroWeekly. Archived from* the original *on June 24, 2013.* Retrieved *June 20, 2013.*

ccl Black. S. (2017). *Freedom Realized: Finding Freedom from Homosexuality & Living a Life Free From Labels.* Enumclaw, WA: Redemption Press.

ccli Ibid., p. xxxvi.

cclii Ibid., p. xxxviii.

ccliii Sherwood, H. (7/82017). "Church of England Demands Ban on Conversion Therapy." Retrieved online at: https://www.theguardian.com/world/2017/jul/08/church-of-england-demands-ban-on-conversion-therapy

ccliv Gill, J. (5/20/2018). "How to make effective disciples." Sermon delivered at Blue Ridge Bible Church. Purcellville, VA.

cclv Beckstead, L. (October 28, 2017). Remarks on the Utah Reconciliation Project. Delivered at the annual meeting of the Alliance for Therapeutic Choice and Scientific Integrity. Salt Lake City, UT.

cclvi Beckstead, L. (February 2014). "What I've Learned From Meeting With My Enemies." Retrieved online at: http://conferences.circlingthewagons.org/wp-content/uploads/2014/02/CTW-2014-KEYNOTE-Beckstead.pdf

cclvii http://www.jmu.edu/safezone/area.shtml

cclviii Robinson, C.M. (no date). Ex-Gay Politics on Campus. Retrieved 11/3/2013 online from: http://www.campuspride.org/tools/ex-gay-politics-on-campus

cclix JMU—Educate Yourself! Retrieved online October 31, 2013 from: http://www.jmu.edu/safezone/wm_library/Sexual%20Orientation%20Fact%20Sheet.pdf

cclx American Psychological Association. (2008). *Homosexuality and Sexual Orientation: Answers to Your Questions for a Better Understanding.* Retrieved 10/31/2013 online from: http://www.apa.org/topics/sexuality/orientation.aspx?item=4

415

cclxi Phelan, J.E., Whitehead, N. & Sutton, P.M. (2009). What Research Shows: NARTH's Response to the APA Claims on Homosexuality. *Journal of Human Sexuality, 1,* 1–94.

cclxii Doyle, C. (March 18, 2013). *Transgender 'Woman' Lies About Therapy 'Torture.'* Retrieved 10/31/2013 online at: http://www.wnd.com/2013/03/transgendered-woman-lies-about-therapy-torture/

cclxiii National Association for Research and Therapy of Homosexuality, Task Force on Practice Guidelines for the Treatment of Unwanted Same-Sex Attractions and Behavior. (2010). Practice Guidelines for the Treatment of Unwanted Same-Sex Attractions and Behavior. *Journal of Human Sexuality, 2,* 5–65.

cclxiv Centers for Disease Control and Prevention (2013). *HIV Surveillance in Adolescents and Young Adults.* Retrieved online 10/31/2013 from: http://www.cdc.gov/hiv/pdf/statistics_surveillance_Adolescents.pdf

cclxv U.S. Food and Drug Administration: Protecting and Promoting Your Health. (1990). *Condoms and Sexually Transmitted Diseases, Brochure.* Retrieved 10/31/2013 online at: http://www.fda.gov/ForConsumers/byAudience/ForPatientAdvocates/HIVandAIDSActivities/ucm126372.htm#strong

cclxvi Phelan, J.E., Whitehead, N. & Sutton, P.M. (2009). What Research Shows: NARTH's Response to the APA Claims on Homosexuality. *Journal of Human Sexuality, 1,* 1–94.

cclxvii Mock, S.E. & Eibach, R.P. (2011). Stability and Change in Sexual Orientation Identity Over a 10-Year Period in Adulthood. *Archives of Sexual Behavior.* Retrieved 10/31/2013 online at: http://midus.wisc.edu/findings/pdfs/1153.pdf

cclxviii Kinnish K.K., Strassberg D.S., & Turner C.W. (2005). Sex differences in the flexibility of sexual orientation: a multidimensional retrospective assessment. *Archives of Sexual Behavior, 34,* 175-83.

cclxix American Psychological Association. (2008). *Homosexuality and Sexual Orientation: Answers to Your Questions For a Better*

Endnotes

Understanding. Retrieved 10/31/2013 from:
http://www.apa.org/topics/sexuality/orientation.aspx?item=4

[cclxx] Whitehead, N.E. & Whitehead, B.K. (2010). My Genes Made Me Do It! Retrieved 10/31/2013 online from:
http://www.mygenes.co.nz/download.htm